BUREAU FOR PARANORMAL • RESEARCH AND DEFENSE •

Hollow Earth & Other Stories

Created by Mike Mignola

Dark Horse Books™

SCOTT ALLIE

Collection designed by
LIA RIBACCHI & LANI SCHREIBSTEIN

Published by
MIKE RICHARDSON

NEIL HANKERSON ♦ *executive vice president*

TOM WEDDLE ♦ *vice president of finance*

RANDY STRADLEY ♦ *vice president of publishing*

CHRIS WARNER ♦ *senior books editor*

ANITA NELSON ♦ *vice president of marketing, sales & licensing*

MICHAEL MARTENS ♦ *vice president of business development*

DAVID SCROGGY ♦ *vice president of product development*

LIA RIBACCHI ♦ *art director*

DALE LAFOUNTAIN ♦ *vice president of information technology*

DARLENE VOGEL ♦ *director of purchasing*

KEN LIZZI ♦ *general counsel*

Published by Dark Horse Books
A division of Dark Horse Comics, Inc.
10956 SE Main Street
Milwaukie, OR 97222

First edition January 2003
Second edition July 2004
ISBN 978-1-59307-280-3

This book is collected from *Hellboy: Box Full of Evil, Abe Sapien: Drums of the Dead,*
B.P.R.D.: Hollow Earth, and the *Dark Horse Extra,* published by Dark Horse Comics.

9 10 8

Printed in China

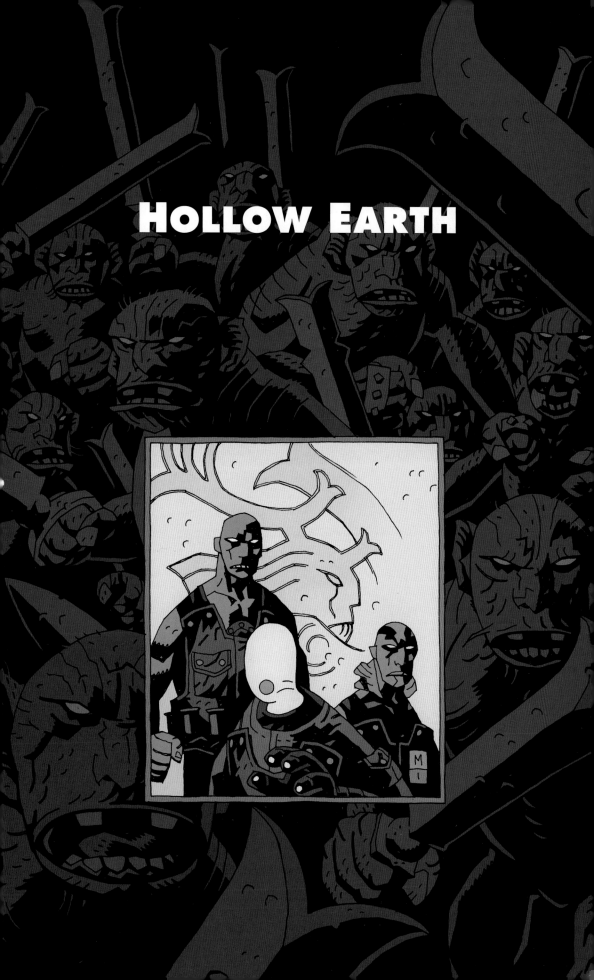

HOLLOW EARTH

HOLLOW EARTH

Story by
MIGNOLA, CHRISTOPHER GOLDEN & TOM SNIEGOSKI

Pencils by
RYAN SOOK

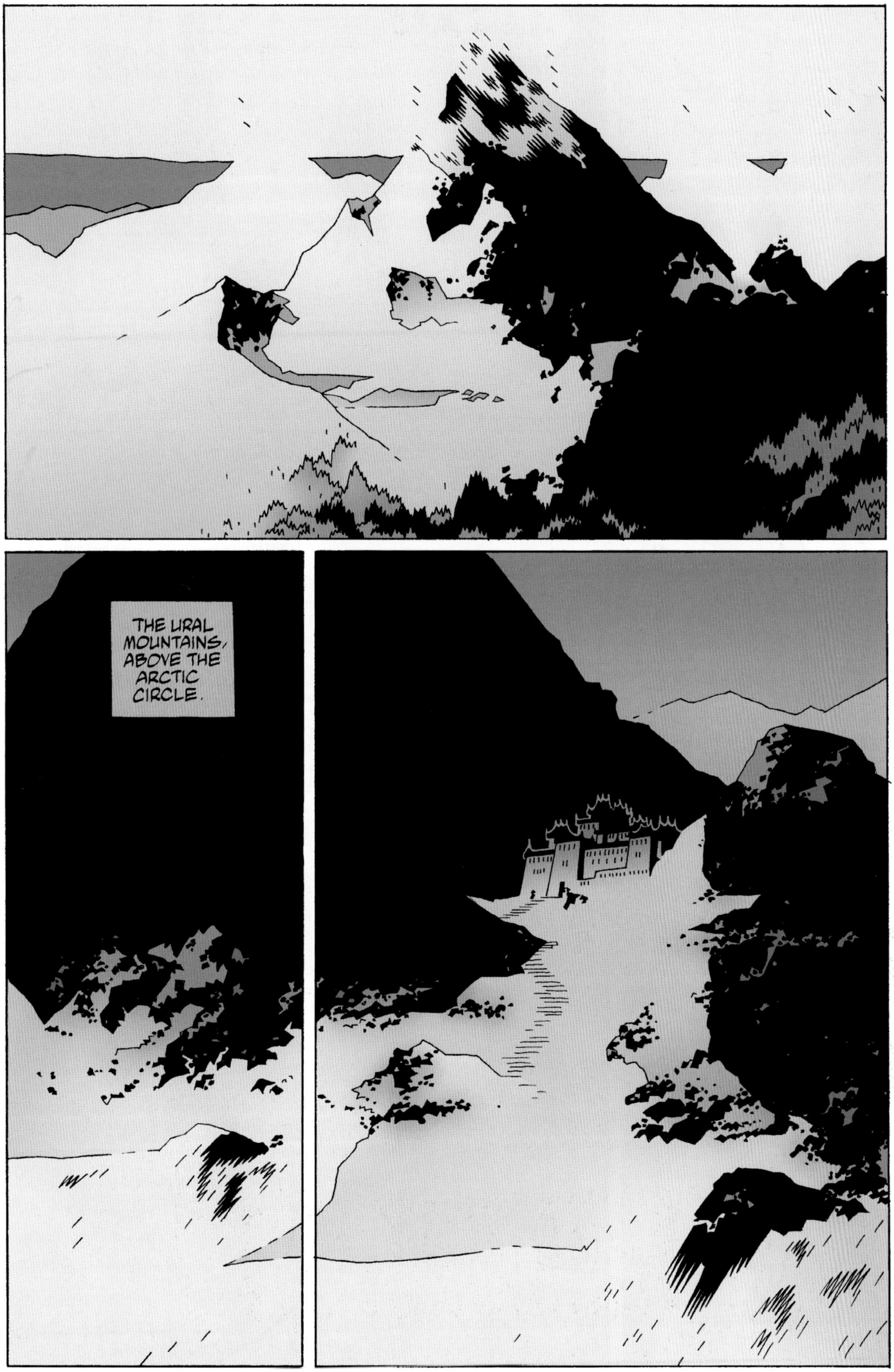
THE URAL MOUNTAINS, ABOVE THE ARCTIC CIRCLE.

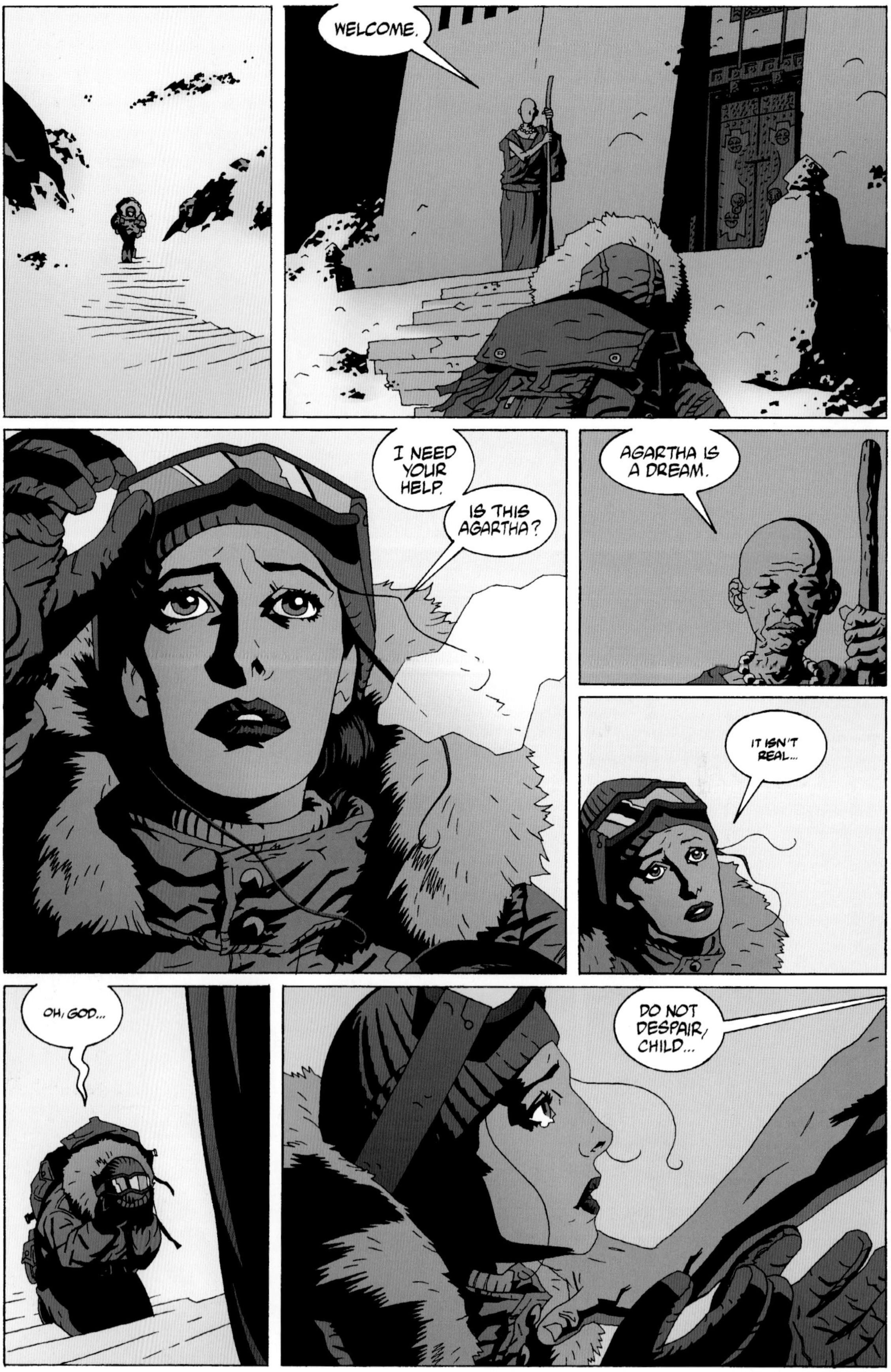
WELCOME.
I NEED YOUR HELP.
IS THIS AGARTHA?
AGARTHA IS A DREAM.
IT ISN'T REAL...
OH, GOD...
DO NOT DESPAIR, CHILD...

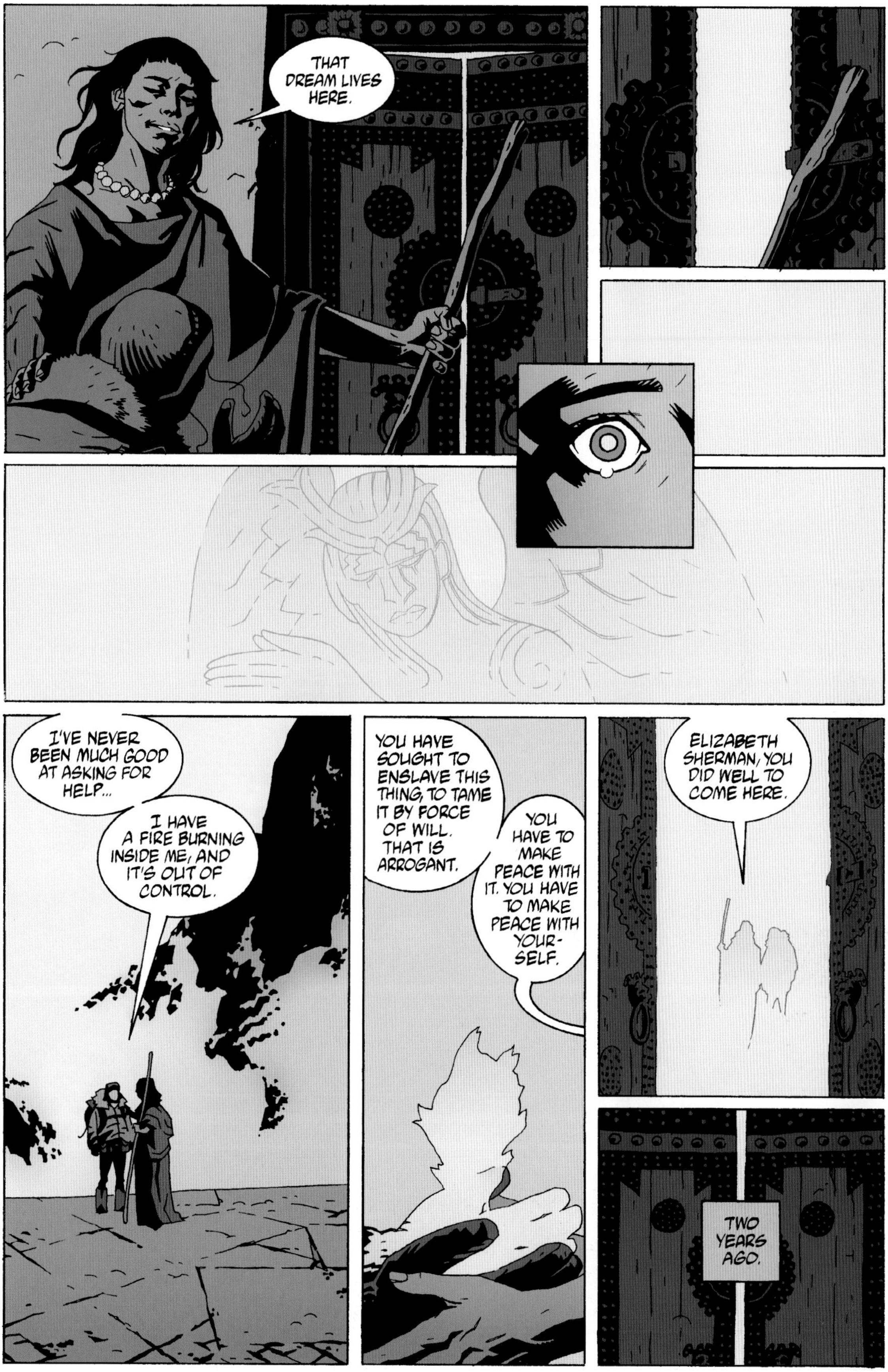
THAT DREAM LIVES HERE.
I'VE NEVER BEEN MUCH GOOD AT ASKING FOR HELP...
I HAVE A FIRE BURNING INSIDE ME, AND IT'S OUT OF CONTROL.
YOU HAVE SOUGHT TO ENSLAVE THIS THING, TO TAME IT BY FORCE OF WILL. THAT IS ARROGANT.
YOU HAVE TO MAKE PEACE WITH IT. YOU HAVE TO MAKE PEACE WITH YOUR-SELF.
ELIZABETH SHERMAN, YOU DID WELL TO COME HERE.
TWO YEARS AGO.

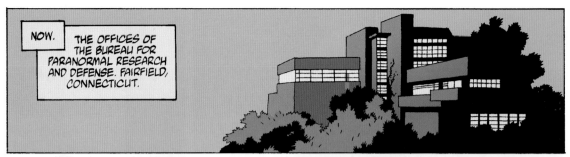

NOW. THE OFFICES OF THE BUREAU FOR PARANORMAL RESEARCH AND DEFENSE. FAIRFIELD, CONNECTICUT.

ESTABLISHED IN 1944 BY THE LATE PROFESSOR TREVOR BRUTTENHOLM AND AN INTERNATIONAL COLLECTIVE IN RESPONSE TO NAZI--AND LATER SOVIET--OCCULT EXPERIMENTS. ITS FUNCTION IN THE PRESENT IS TO MONITOR, INVESTIGATE, AND CONTAIN SUPERNATURAL EVENTS WORLDWIDE.

WE'VE GOT ANOTHER CEMETERY DESECRATION IN HAVERHILL, MASSACHUSETTS. EVIDENCE OF RITUAL.... BODIES MOVED, PIECES MISSING...

YEAH, YOU BETTER GET SOMEONE ON THAT RIGHT AWAY.

WHAT ELSE?

JUST THE USUAL.

WHAT ABOUT THE NEW MEXICO THING WITH THE CHICKENS?

NOTHING NEW. MAYBE IT WAS ONE OF THOSE FREAK, ONE-TIME-ONLY THINGS.

I HOPE SO.

NO KIDDING.

KATE, THE NEW GUY IS HERE.

MR. KRAUS? SORRY TO KEEP YOU WAITING. I'M KATE CORRIGAN.

THERE IS NO PROBLEM, MISS CORRIGAN.

AND PLEASE TO CALL ME JOHANN. IF WE ARE TO BE COLLEAGUES, THE FORMALITY IS NOT NECESSARY.

...YOU'LL FIND LIVING ON THE PREMISES HAS A LOT OF ADVANTAGES, EVEN BEYOND NOT HAVING TO GO OUT IN PUBLIC.

HEALTH FACILITIES, SWIMMING POOL, EXTENSIVE LIBRARY, AND THERE ARE HIKING TRAILS ON THE GROUNDS THAT ARE BEAUTIFUL YEAR ROUND. I THINK YOU'LL BE PLEASED WITH YOUR QUARTERS.

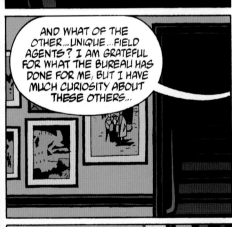

AND WHAT OF THE OTHER...UNIQUE...FIELD AGENTS? I AM GRATEFUL FOR WHAT THE BUREAU HAS DONE FOR ME, BUT I HAVE MUCH CURIOSITY ABOUT THESE OTHERS...

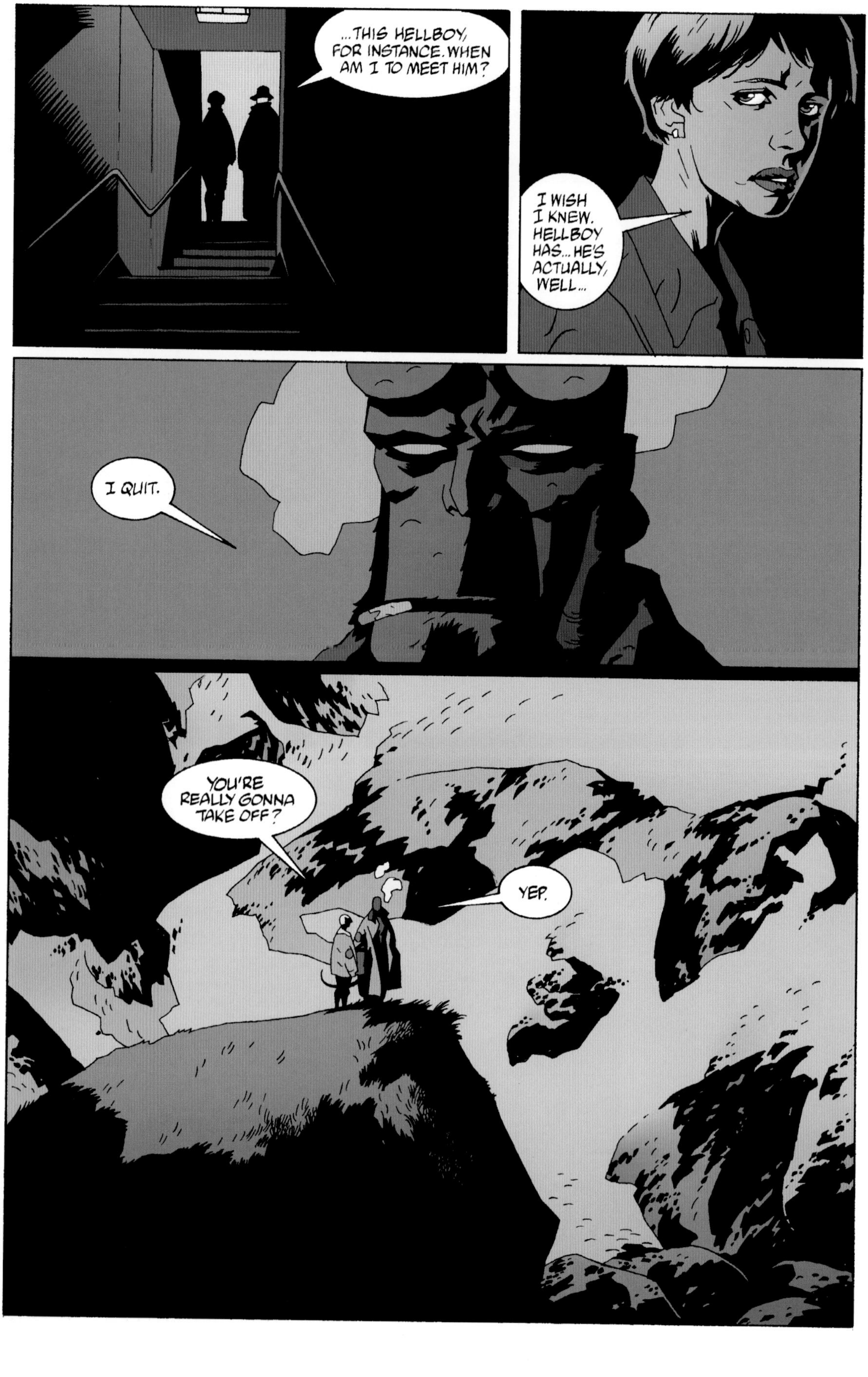
...THIS HELLBOY, FOR INSTANCE. WHEN AM I TO MEET HIM?
I WISH I KNEW. HELLBOY HAS... HE'S ACTUALLY, WELL...
I QUIT.
YOU'RE REALLY GONNA TAKE OFF?
YEP.

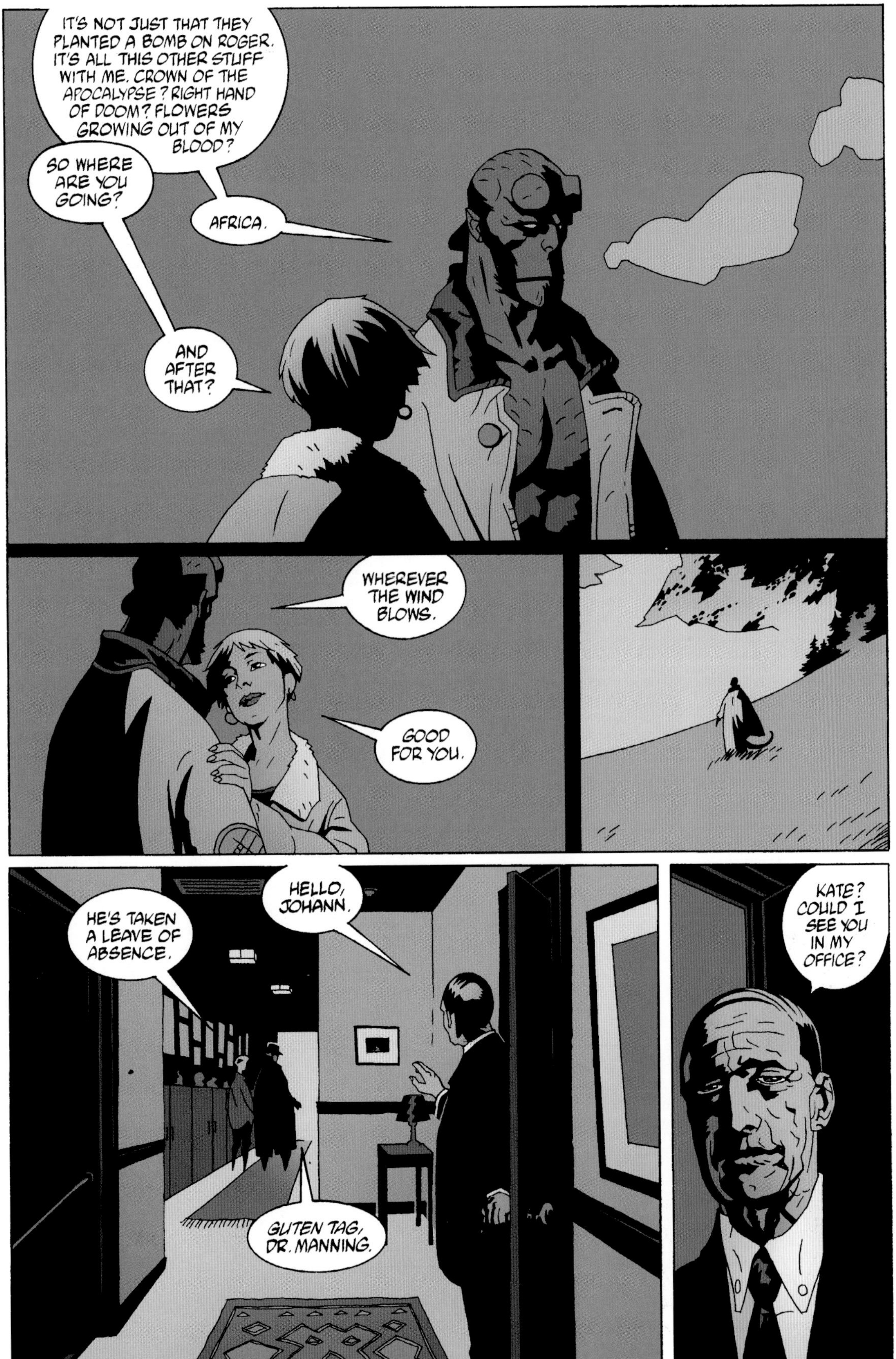
IT'S NOT JUST THAT THEY PLANTED A BOMB ON ROGER. IT'S ALL THIS OTHER STUFF WITH ME. CROWN OF THE APOCALYPSE? RIGHT HAND OF DOOM? FLOWERS GROWING OUT OF MY BLOOD?
SO WHERE ARE YOU GOING?
AFRICA.
AND AFTER THAT?
WHEREVER THE WIND BLOWS.
GOOD FOR YOU.
HE'S TAKEN A LEAVE OF ABSENCE.
HELLO, JOHANN.
GUTEN TAG, DR. MANNING.
KATE? COULD I SEE YOU IN MY OFFICE?

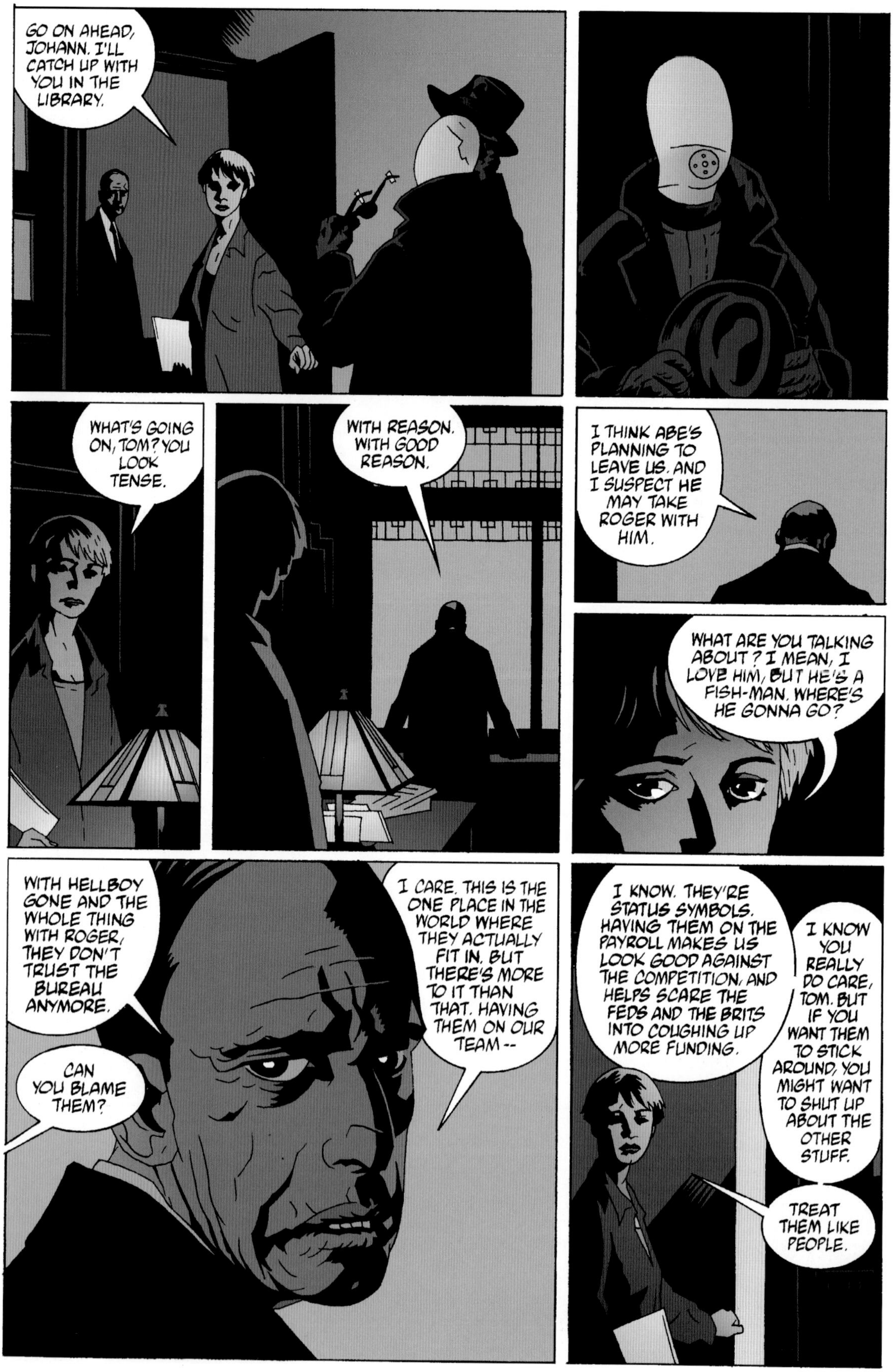
GO ON AHEAD, JOHANN. I'LL CATCH UP WITH YOU IN THE LIBRARY.
WHAT'S GOING ON, TOM? YOU LOOK TENSE.
WITH REASON. WITH GOOD REASON.
I THINK ABE'S PLANNING TO LEAVE US. AND I SUSPECT HE MAY TAKE ROGER WITH HIM.
WHAT ARE YOU TALKING ABOUT? I MEAN, I LOVE HIM, BUT HE'S A FISH-MAN. WHERE'S HE GONNA GO?
WITH HELLBOY GONE AND THE WHOLE THING WITH ROGER, THEY DON'T TRUST THE BUREAU ANYMORE.
CAN YOU BLAME THEM?
I CARE. THIS IS THE ONE PLACE IN THE WORLD WHERE THEY ACTUALLY FIT IN. BUT THERE'S MORE TO IT THAN THAT. HAVING THEM ON OUR TEAM --
I KNOW. THEY'RE STATUS SYMBOLS. HAVING THEM ON THE PAYROLL MAKES US LOOK GOOD AGAINST THE COMPETITION, AND HELPS SCARE THE FEDS AND THE BRITS INTO COUGHING UP MORE FUNDING.
I KNOW YOU REALLY DO CARE, TOM. BUT IF YOU WANT THEM TO STICK AROUND, YOU MIGHT WANT TO SHUT UP ABOUT THE OTHER STUFF.
TREAT THEM LIKE PEOPLE.

"...NOT PETS."

K-JINK JINK JINK

RRRR

RRRRMMMMBBBLLL

LRRMBE

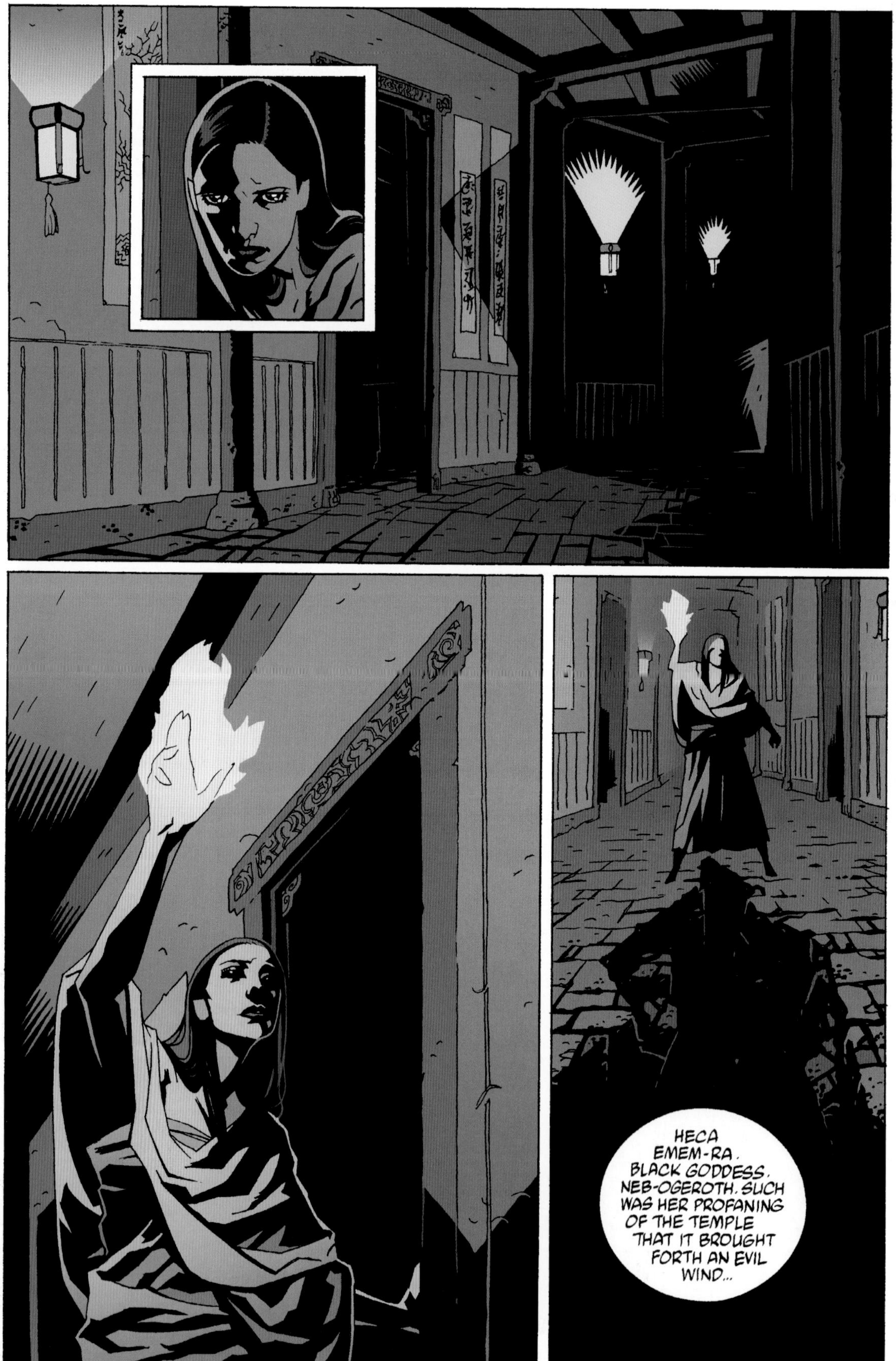
HECA EMEM-RA. BLACK GODDESS. NEB-OGEROTH. SUCH WAS HER PROFANING OF THE TEMPLE THAT IT BROUGHT FORTH AN EVIL WIND...

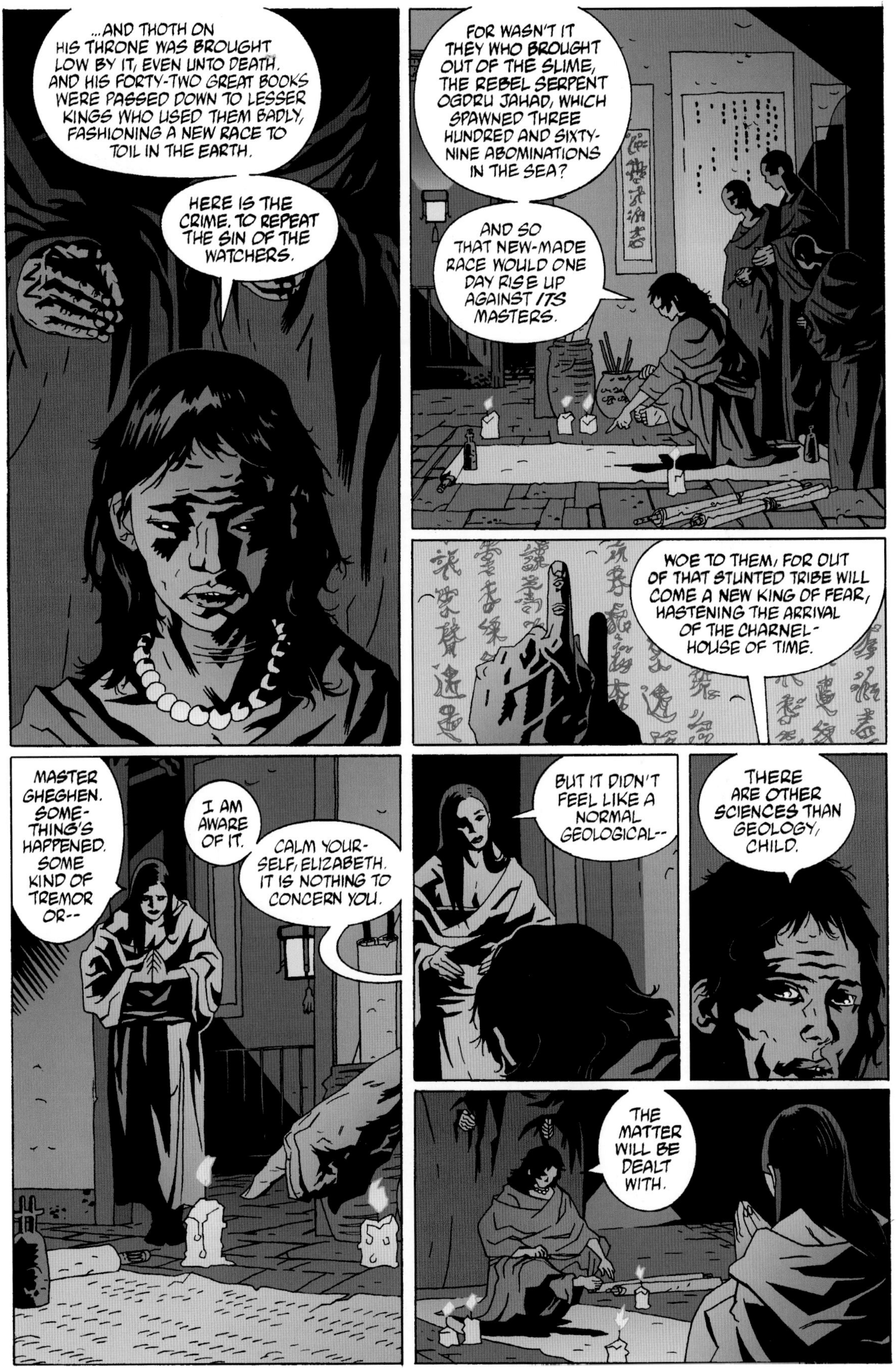
...AND THOTH ON HIS THRONE WAS BROUGHT LOW BY IT, EVEN UNTO DEATH. AND HIS FORTY-TWO GREAT BOOKS WERE PASSED DOWN TO LESSER KINGS WHO USED THEM BADLY, FASHIONING A NEW RACE TO TOIL IN THE EARTH.
HERE IS THE CRIME. TO REPEAT THE SIN OF THE WATCHERS.
FOR WASN'T IT THEY WHO BROUGHT OUT OF THE SLIME, THE REBEL SERPENT OGDRU JAHAD, WHICH SPAWNED THREE HUNDRED AND SIXTY-NINE ABOMINATIONS IN THE SEA?
AND SO THAT NEW-MADE RACE WOULD ONE DAY RISE UP AGAINST *ITS* MASTERS.
WOE TO THEM, FOR OUT OF THAT STUNTED TRIBE WILL COME A NEW KING OF FEAR, HASTENING THE ARRIVAL OF THE CHARNEL-HOUSE OF TIME.
MASTER GHEGHEN. SOME-THING'S HAPPENED. SOME KIND OF TREMOR OR--
I AM AWARE OF IT.
CALM YOUR-SELF, ELIZABETH. IT IS NOTHING TO CONCERN YOU.
BUT IT DIDN'T FEEL LIKE A NORMAL GEOLOGICAL--
THERE ARE OTHER SCIENCES THAN GEOLOGY, CHILD.
THE MATTER WILL BE DEALT WITH.

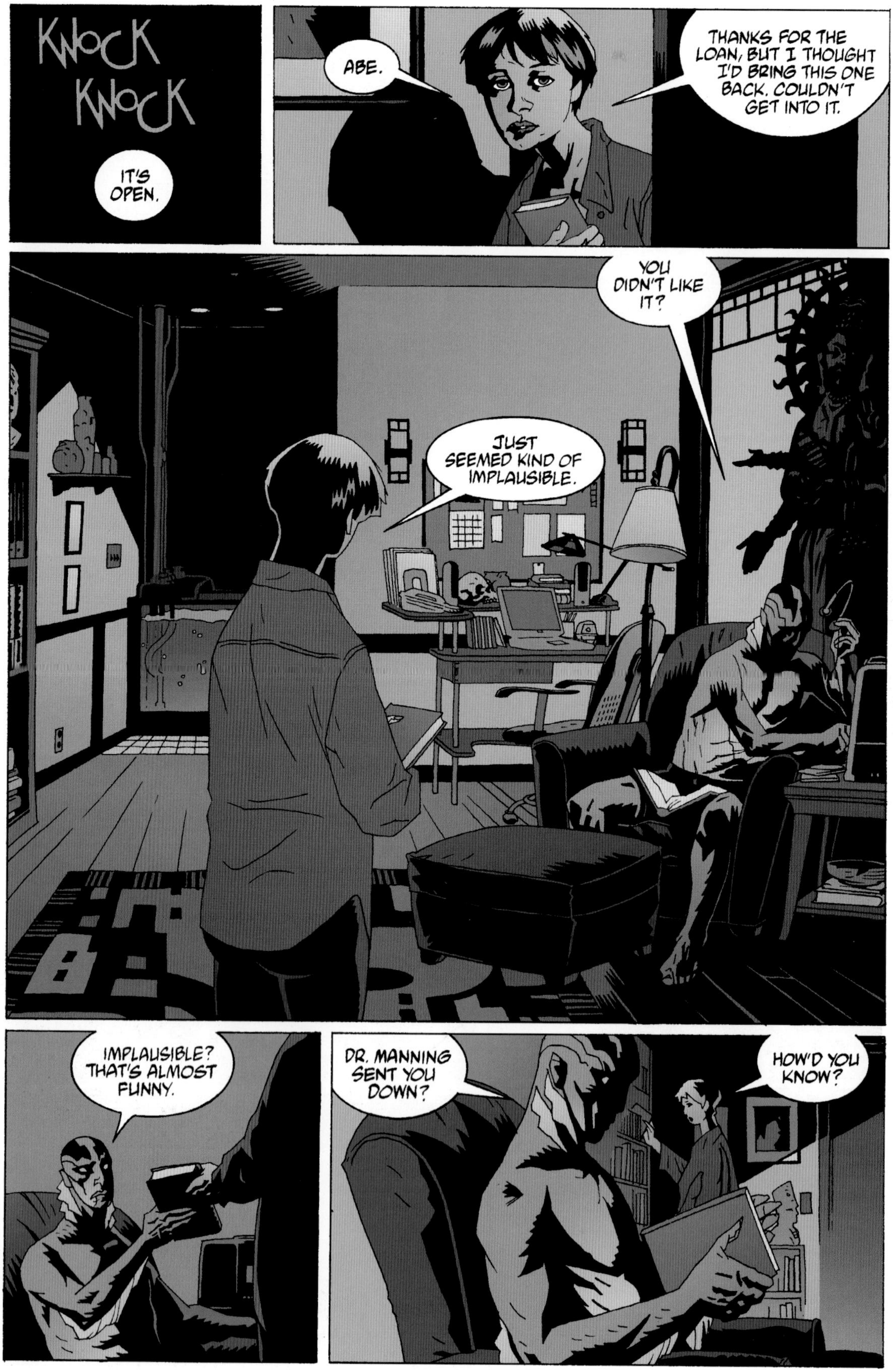
KNOCK KNOCK
IT'S OPEN.
ABE.
THANKS FOR THE LOAN, BUT I THOUGHT I'D BRING THIS ONE BACK. COULDN'T GET INTO IT.
YOU DIDN'T LIKE IT?
JUST SEEMED KIND OF IMPLAUSIBLE.
IMPLAUSIBLE? THAT'S ALMOST FUNNY.
DR. MANNING SENT YOU DOWN?
HOW'D YOU KNOW?

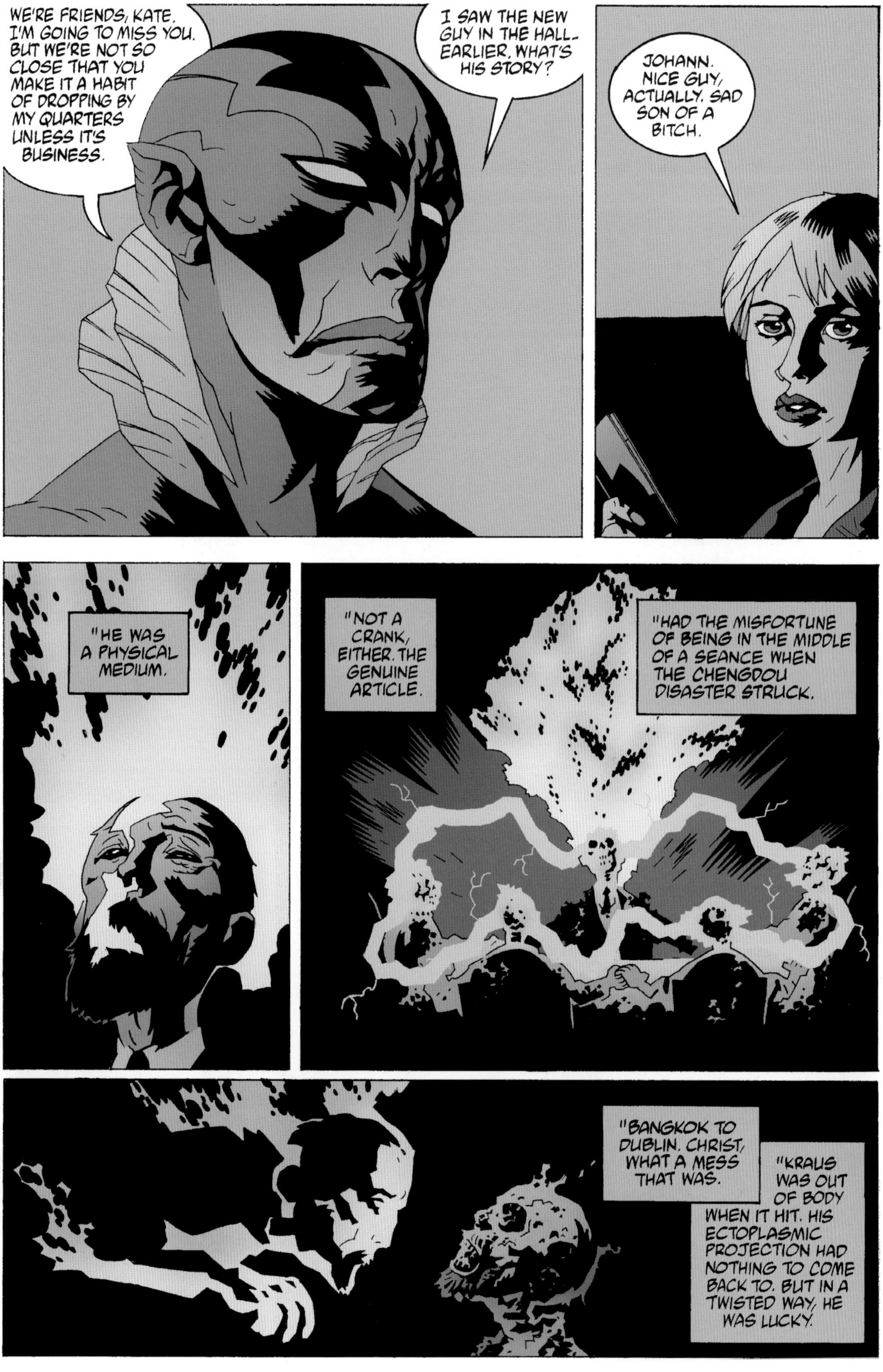
WE'RE FRIENDS, KATE. I'M GOING TO MISS YOU. BUT WE'RE NOT SO CLOSE THAT YOU MAKE IT A HABIT OF DROPPING BY MY QUARTERS UNLESS IT'S BUSINESS.
I SAW THE NEW GUY IN THE HALL- EARLIER. WHAT'S HIS STORY?
JOHANN. NICE GUY, ACTUALLY. SAD SON OF A BITCH.
"HE WAS A PHYSICAL MEDIUM.
"NOT A CRANK, EITHER. THE GENUINE ARTICLE.
"HAD THE MISFORTUNE OF BEING IN THE MIDDLE OF A SEANCE WHEN THE CHENGDOU DISASTER STRUCK.
"BANGKOK TO DUBLIN. CHRIST, WHAT A MESS THAT WAS.
"KRAUS WAS OUT OF BODY WHEN IT HIT. HIS ECTOPLASMIC PROJECTION HAD NOTHING TO COME BACK TO. BUT IN A TWISTED WAY, HE WAS LUCKY.

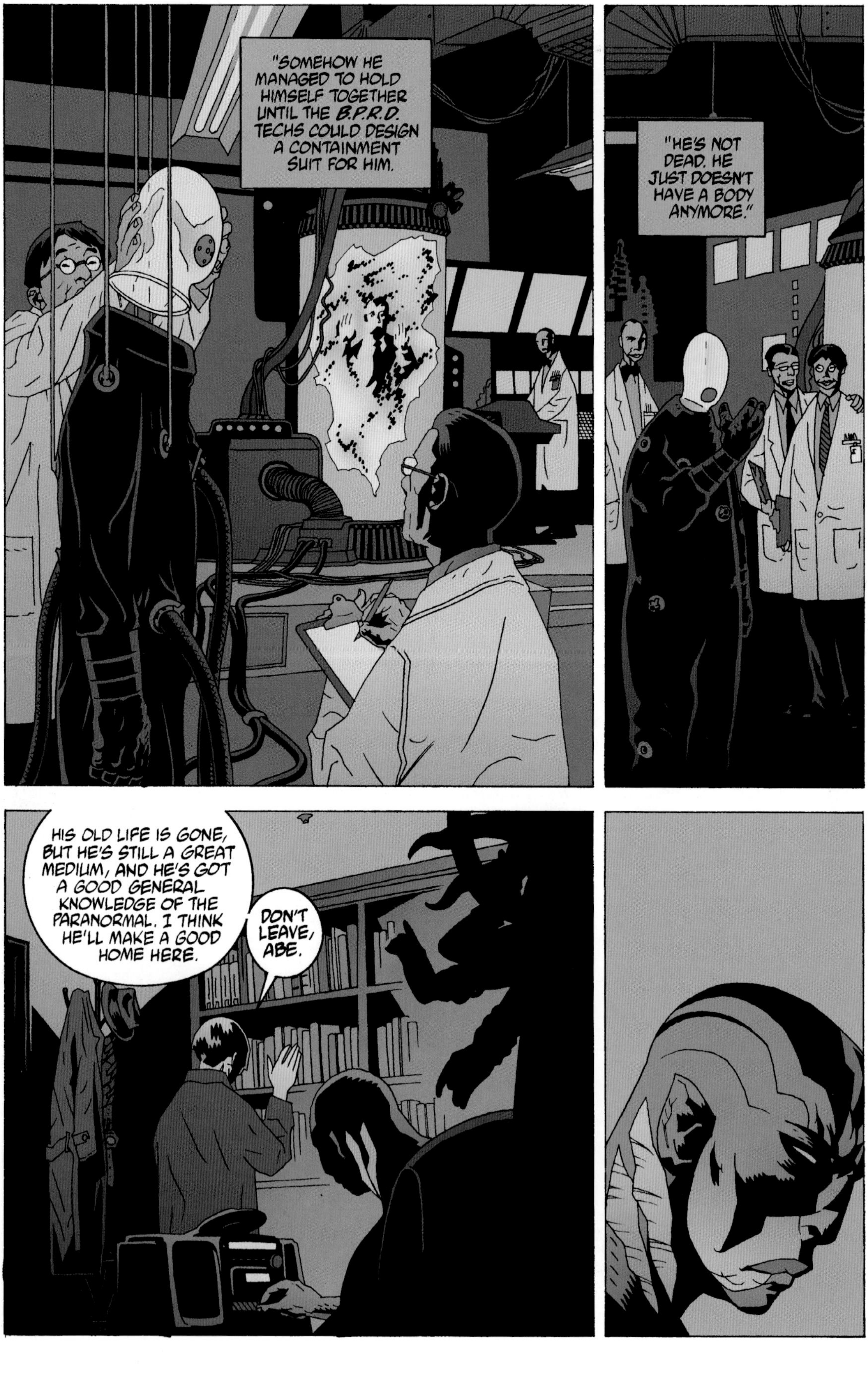
"SOMEHOW HE MANAGED TO HOLD HIMSELF TOGETHER UNTIL THE B.P.R.D. TECHS COULD DESIGN A CONTAINMENT SUIT FOR HIM.
"HE'S NOT DEAD. HE JUST DOESN'T HAVE A BODY ANYMORE."
HIS OLD LIFE IS GONE, BUT HE'S STILL A GREAT MEDIUM, AND HE'S GOT A GOOD GENERAL KNOWLEDGE OF THE PARANORMAL. I THINK HE'LL MAKE A GOOD HOME HERE.
DON'T LEAVE, ABE.

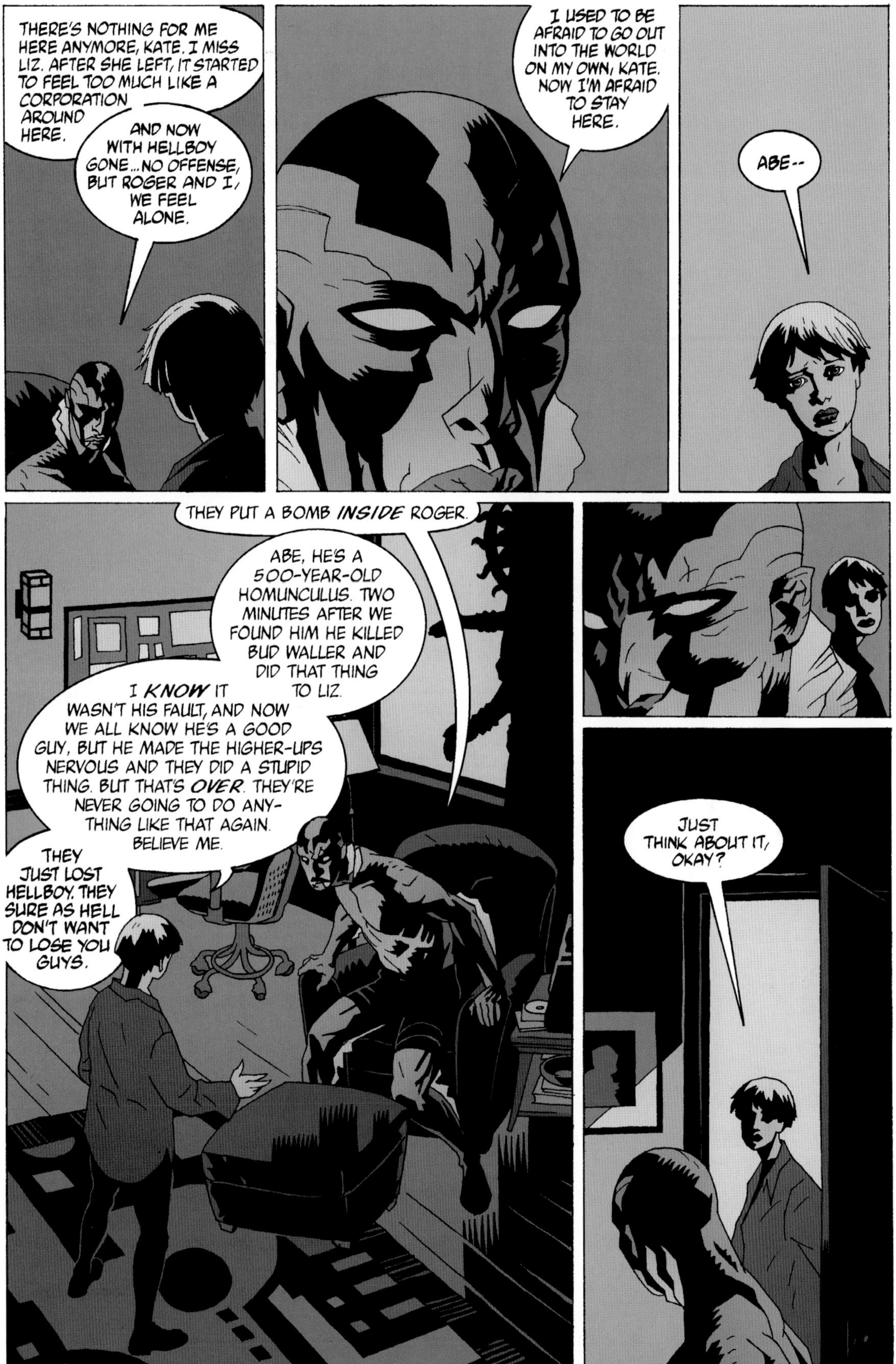
THERE'S NOTHING FOR ME HERE ANYMORE, KATE. I MISS LIZ. AFTER SHE LEFT, IT STARTED TO FEEL TOO MUCH LIKE A CORPORATION AROUND HERE.
AND NOW WITH HELLBOY GONE... NO OFFENSE, BUT ROGER AND I, WE FEEL ALONE.
I USED TO BE AFRAID TO GO OUT INTO THE WORLD ON MY OWN, KATE. NOW I'M AFRAID TO STAY HERE.
ABE--
THEY PUT A BOMB INSIDE ROGER.
ABE, HE'S A 500-YEAR-OLD HOMUNCULUS. TWO MINUTES AFTER WE FOUND HIM HE KILLED BUD WALLER AND DID THAT THING TO LIZ.
I KNOW IT WASN'T HIS FAULT, AND NOW WE ALL KNOW HE'S A GOOD GUY, BUT HE MADE THE HIGHER-UPS NERVOUS AND THEY DID A STUPID THING. BUT THAT'S OVER. THEY'RE NEVER GOING TO DO ANYTHING LIKE THAT AGAIN. BELIEVE ME.
THEY JUST LOST HELLBOY. THEY SURE AS HELL DON'T WANT TO LOSE YOU GUYS.
JUST THINK ABOUT IT, OKAY?

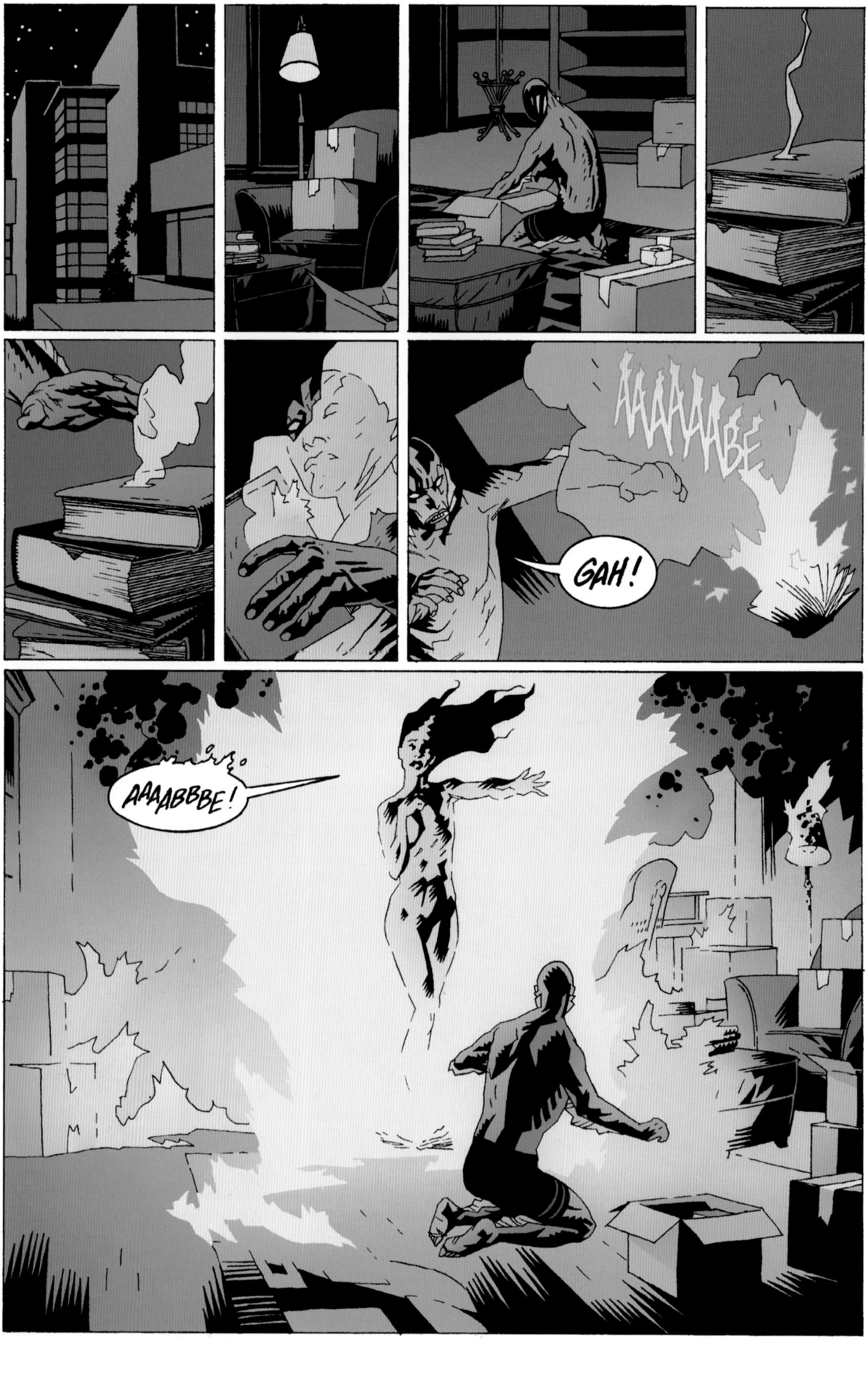
AAAAAABE
GAH!
AAAABBBE!

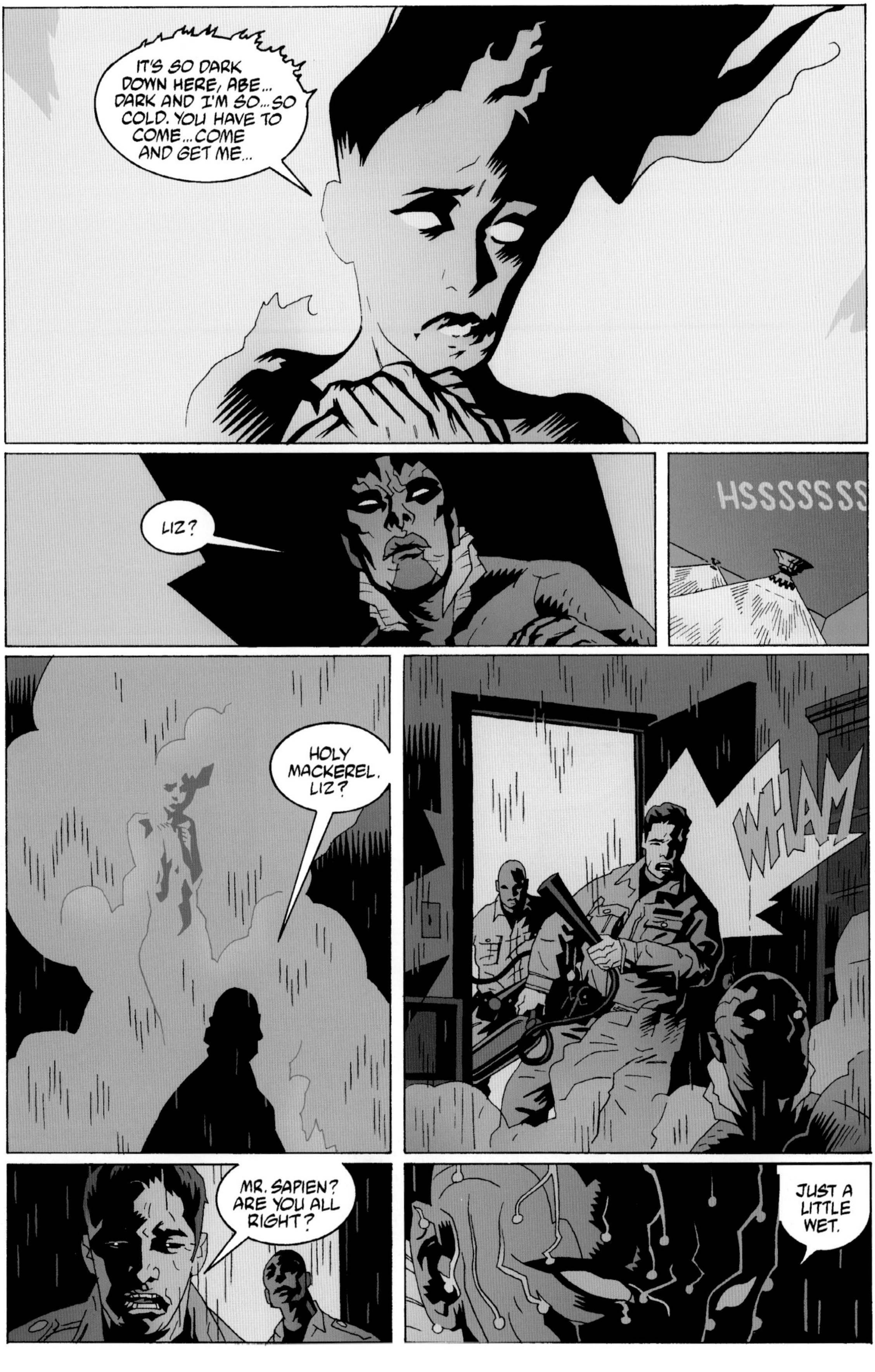
IT'S SO DARK DOWN HERE, ABE... DARK AND I'M SO...SO COLD. YOU HAVE TO COME...COME AND GET ME...
LIZ?
HSSSSSSS
HOLY MACKEREL. LIZ?
WHAM
MR. SAPIEN? ARE YOU ALL RIGHT?
JUST A LITTLE WET.

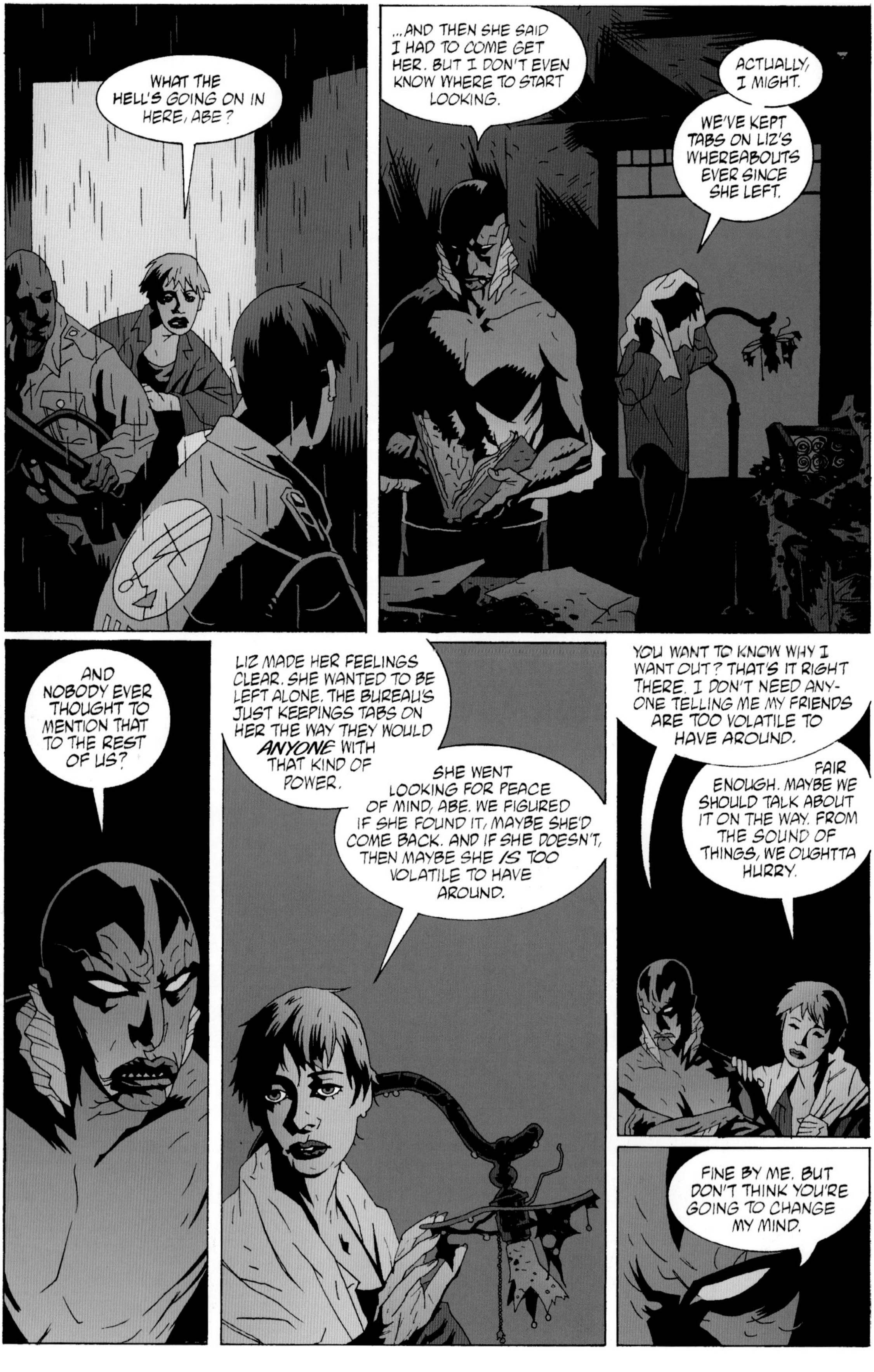
WHAT THE HELL'S GOING ON IN HERE, ABE?
...AND THEN SHE SAID I HAD TO COME GET HER. BUT I DON'T EVEN KNOW WHERE TO START LOOKING.
ACTUALLY, I MIGHT.
WE'VE KEPT TABS ON LIZ'S WHEREABOUTS EVER SINCE SHE LEFT.
AND NOBODY EVER THOUGHT TO MENTION THAT TO THE REST OF US?
LIZ MADE HER FEELINGS CLEAR. SHE WANTED TO BE LEFT ALONE. THE BUREAU'S JUST KEEPINGS TABS ON HER THE WAY THEY WOULD ANYONE WITH THAT KIND OF POWER.
SHE WENT LOOKING FOR PEACE OF MIND, ABE. WE FIGURED IF SHE FOUND IT, MAYBE SHE'D COME BACK. AND IF SHE DOESN'T, THEN MAYBE SHE IS TOO VOLATILE TO HAVE AROUND.
YOU WANT TO KNOW WHY I WANT OUT? THAT'S IT RIGHT THERE. I DON'T NEED ANY-ONE TELLING ME MY FRIENDS ARE TOO VOLATILE TO HAVE AROUND.
FAIR ENOUGH. MAYBE WE SHOULD TALK ABOUT IT ON THE WAY. FROM THE SOUND OF THINGS, WE OUGHTTA HURRY.
FINE BY ME. BUT DON'T THINK YOU'RE GOING TO CHANGE MY MIND.

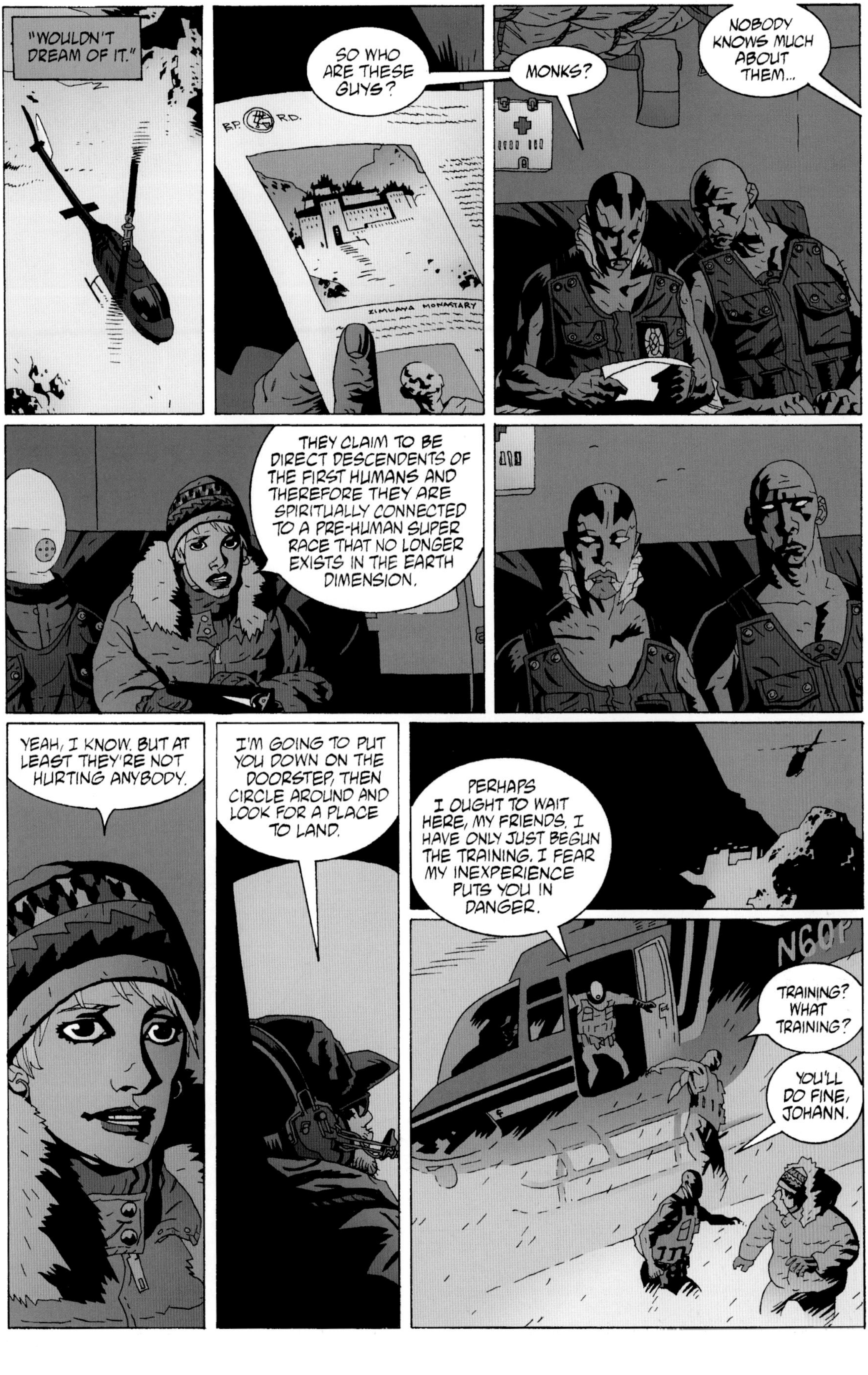
"WOULDN'T DREAM OF IT."
B.P.R.D.
ZIMLAYA MONASTARY
SO WHO ARE THESE GUYS?
MONKS?
NOBODY KNOWS MUCH ABOUT THEM...
THEY CLAIM TO BE DIRECT DESCENDENTS OF THE FIRST HUMANS AND THEREFORE THEY ARE SPIRITUALLY CONNECTED TO A PRE-HUMAN SUPER RACE THAT NO LONGER EXISTS IN THE EARTH DIMENSION.
YEAH, I KNOW. BUT AT LEAST THEY'RE NOT HURTING ANYBODY.
I'M GOING TO PUT YOU DOWN ON THE DOORSTEP, THEN CIRCLE AROUND AND LOOK FOR A PLACE TO LAND.
PERHAPS I OUGHT TO WAIT HERE, MY FRIENDS. I HAVE ONLY JUST BEGUN THE TRAINING. I FEAR MY INEXPERIENCE PUTS YOU IN DANGER.
N60
TRAINING? WHAT TRAINING?
YOU'LL DO FINE, JOHANN.

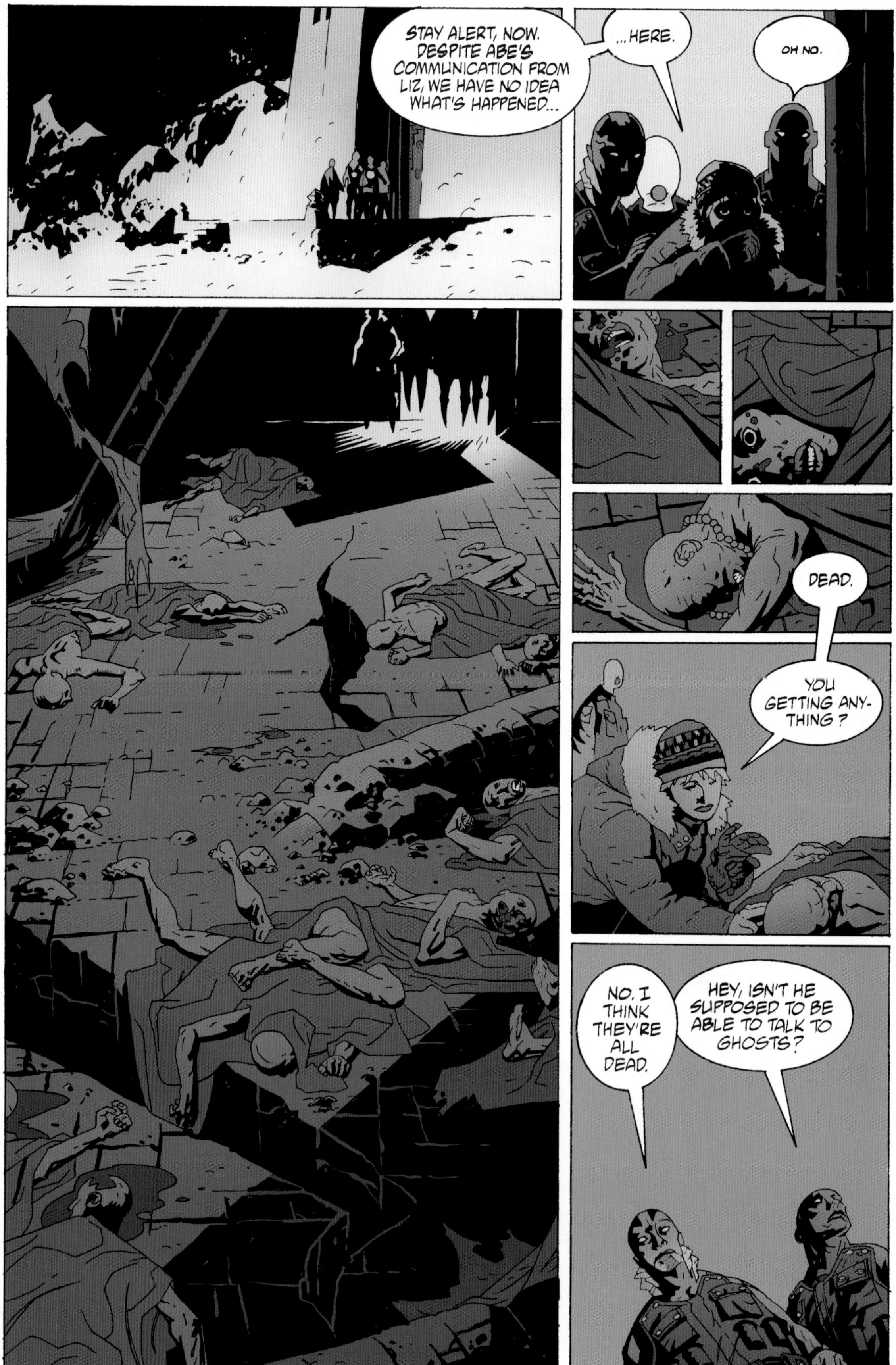
STAY ALERT, NOW. DESPITE ABE'S COMMUNICATION FROM LIZ, WE HAVE NO IDEA WHAT'S HAPPENED...
...HERE.
OH NO.
DEAD.
YOU GETTING ANY-THING ?
NO. I THINK THEY'RE ALL DEAD.
HEY, ISN'T HE SUPPOSED TO BE ABLE TO TALK TO GHOSTS?

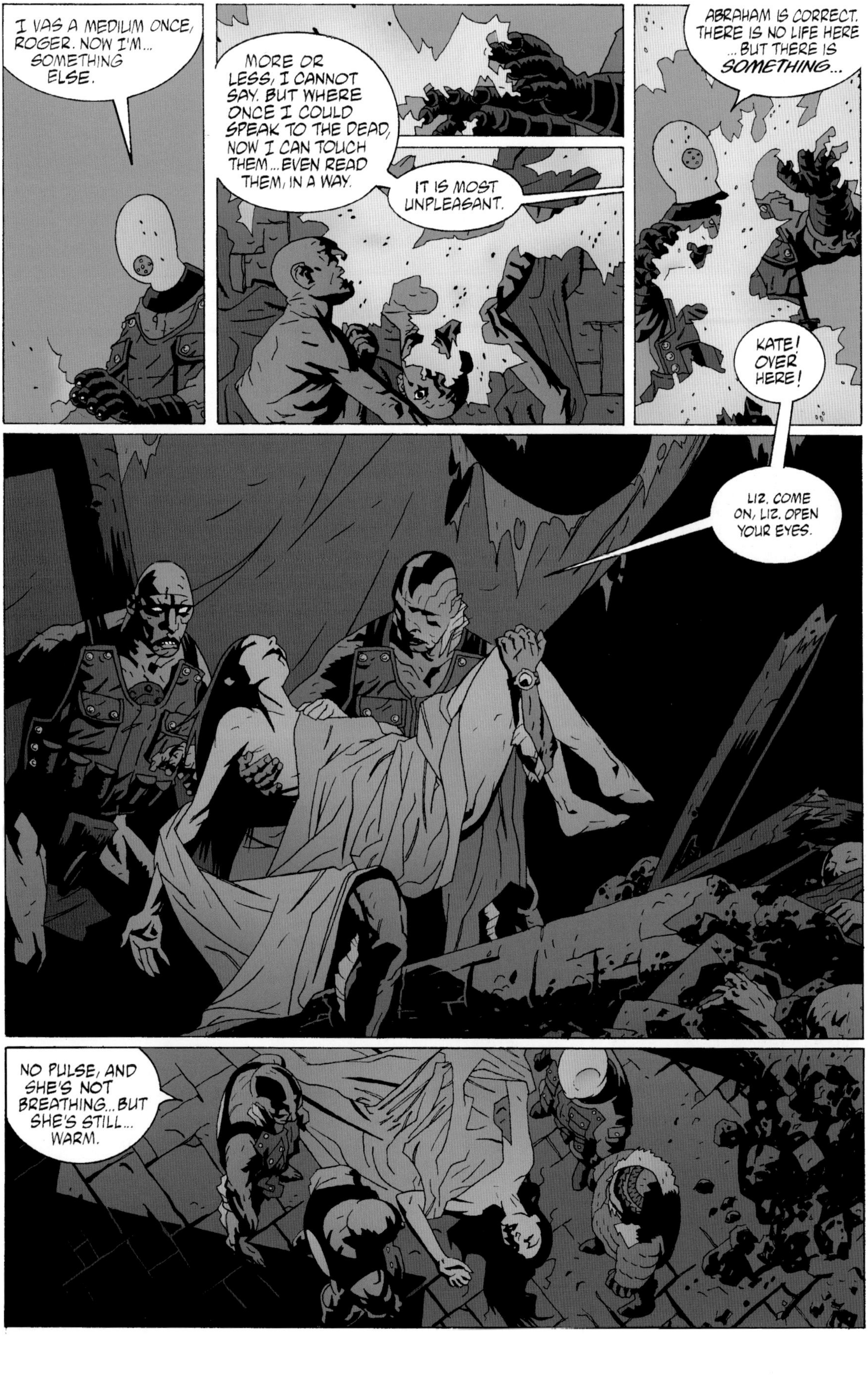
I VAS A MEDIUM ONCE, ROGER. NOW I'M... SOMETHING ELSE.
MORE OR LESS, I CANNOT SAY. BUT WHERE ONCE I COULD SPEAK TO THE DEAD, NOW I CAN TOUCH THEM...EVEN READ THEM, IN A WAY.
IT IS MOST UNPLEASANT.
ABRAHAM IS CORRECT. THERE IS NO LIFE HERE ...BUT THERE IS SOMETHING...
KATE! OVER HERE!
LIZ. COME ON, LIZ. OPEN YOUR EYES.
NO PULSE, AND SHE'S NOT BREATHING...BUT SHE'S STILL... WARM.

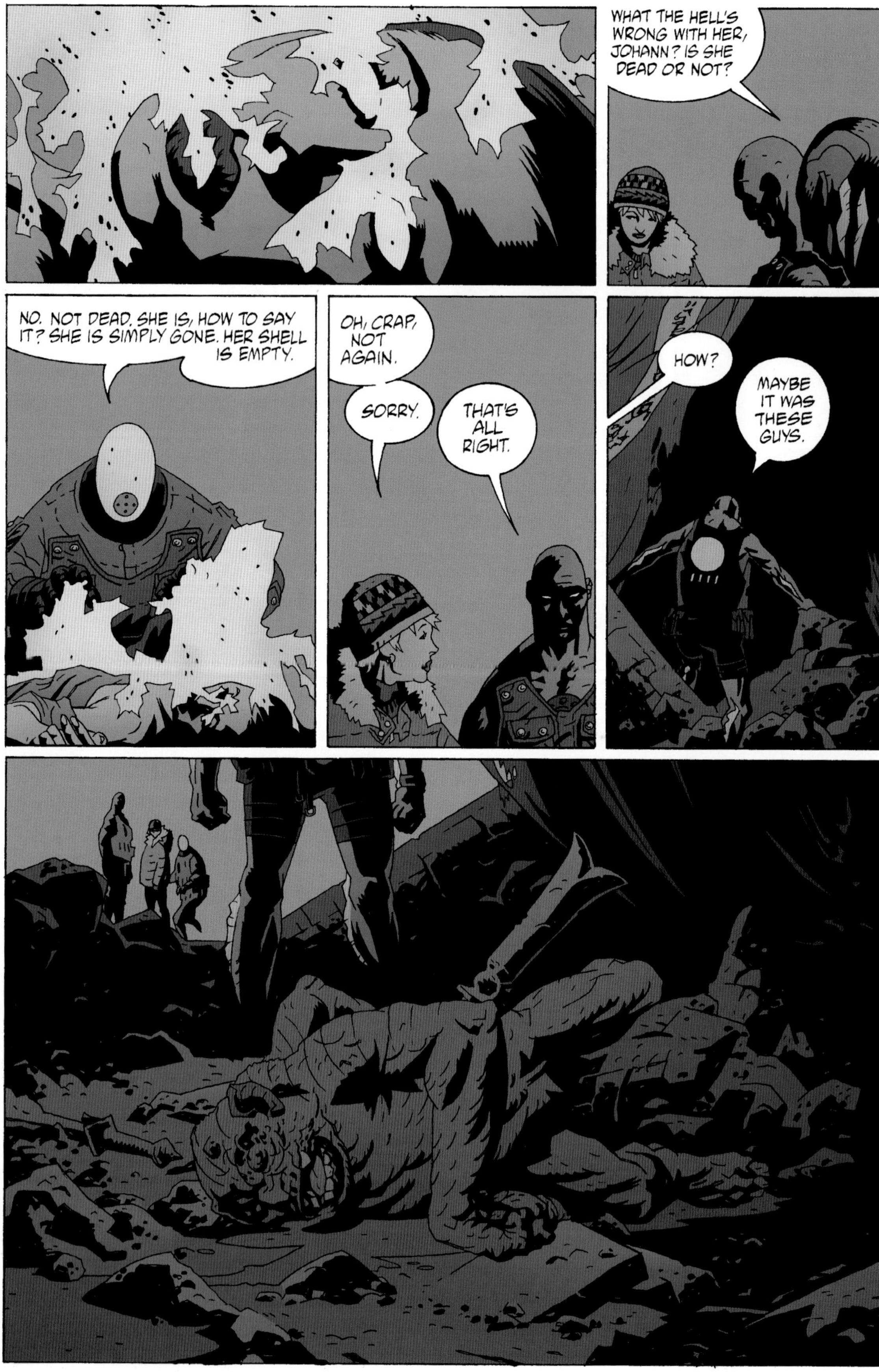

WHAT THE HELL'S WRONG WITH HER, JOHANN? IS SHE DEAD OR NOT?
NO. NOT DEAD. SHE IS, HOW TO SAY IT? SHE IS SIMPLY GONE. HER SHELL IS EMPTY.
OH, CRAP, NOT AGAIN.
SORRY.
THAT'S ALL RIGHT.
HOW?
MAYBE IT WAS THESE GUYS.

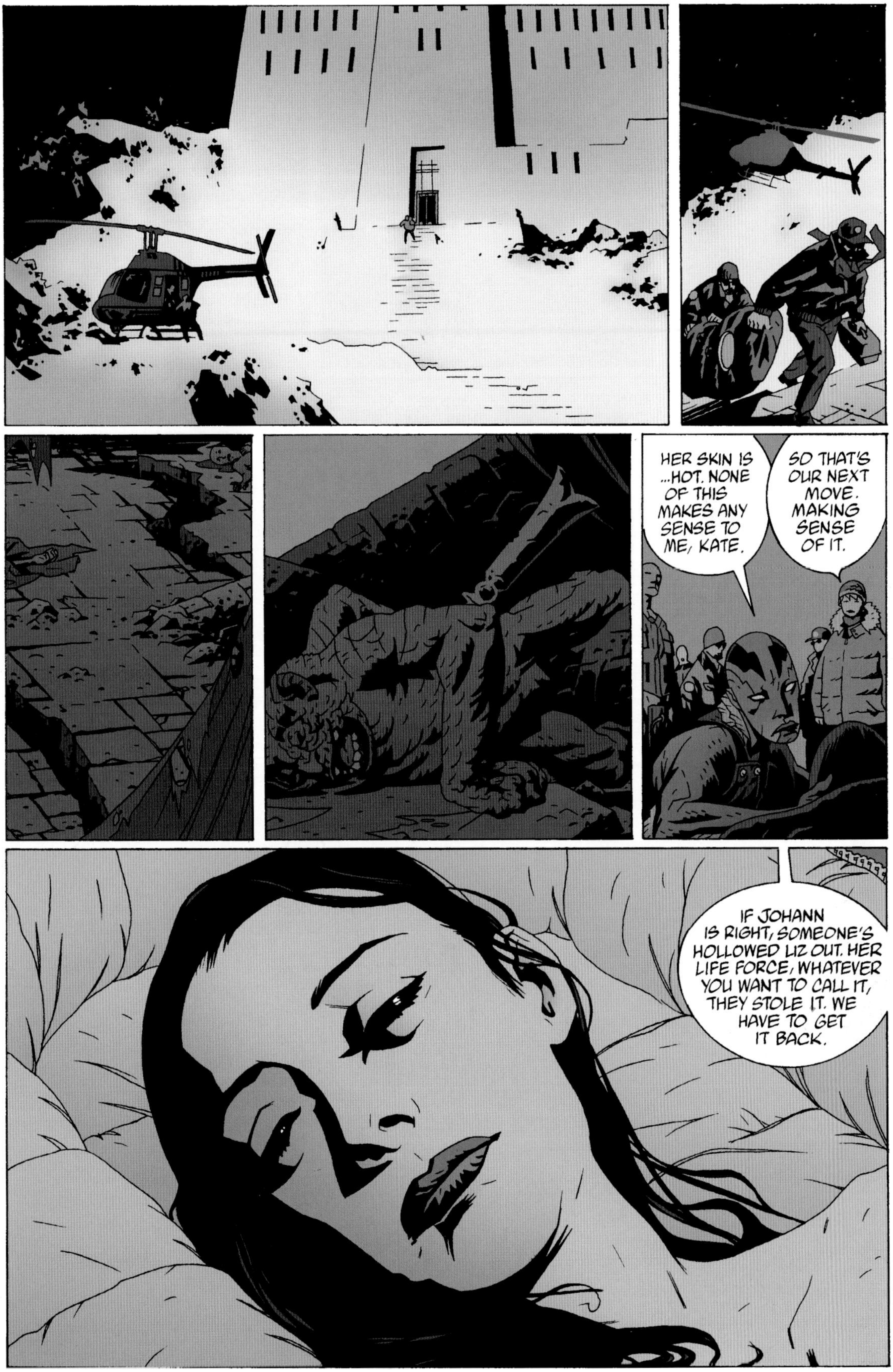
HER SKIN IS ...HOT. NONE OF THIS MAKES ANY SENSE TO ME, KATE.
SO THAT'S OUR NEXT MOVE. MAKING SENSE OF IT.
IF JOHANN IS RIGHT, SOMEONE'S HOLLOWED LIZ OUT. HER LIFE FORCE, WHATEVER YOU WANT TO CALL IT, THEY STOLE IT. WE HAVE TO GET IT BACK.

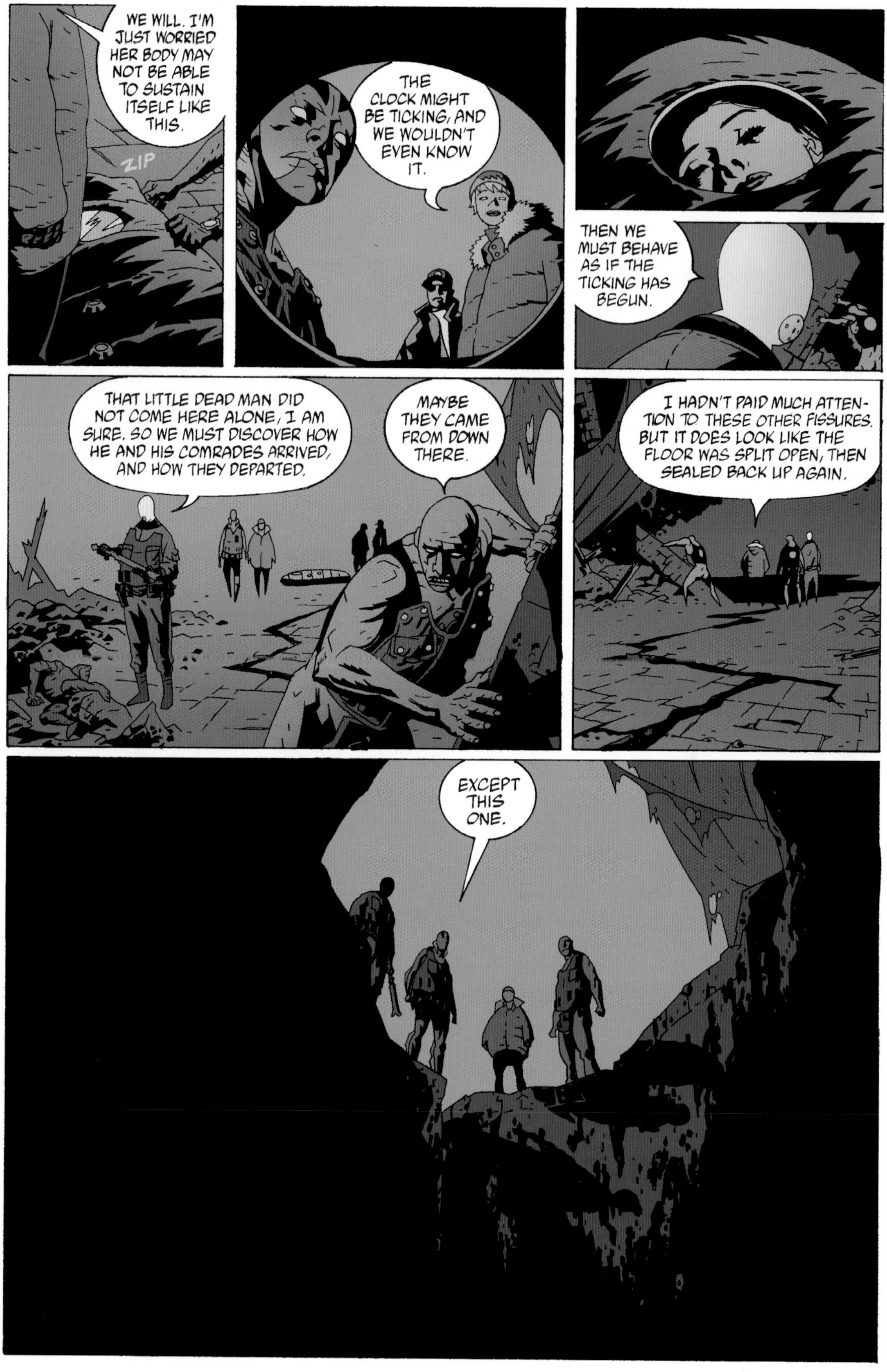
WE WILL. I'M JUST WORRIED HER BODY MAY NOT BE ABLE TO SUSTAIN ITSELF LIKE THIS.
ZIP
THE CLOCK MIGHT BE TICKING, AND WE WOULDN'T EVEN KNOW IT.
THEN WE MUST BEHAVE AS IF THE TICKING HAS BEGUN.
THAT LITTLE DEAD MAN DID NOT COME HERE ALONE, I AM SURE. SO WE MUST DISCOVER HOW HE AND HIS COMRADES ARRIVED, AND HOW THEY DEPARTED.
MAYBE THEY CAME FROM DOWN THERE.
I HADN'T PAID MUCH ATTENTION TO THESE OTHER FISSURES. BUT IT DOES LOOK LIKE THE FLOOR WAS SPLIT OPEN, THEN SEALED BACK UP AGAIN.
EXCEPT THIS ONE.

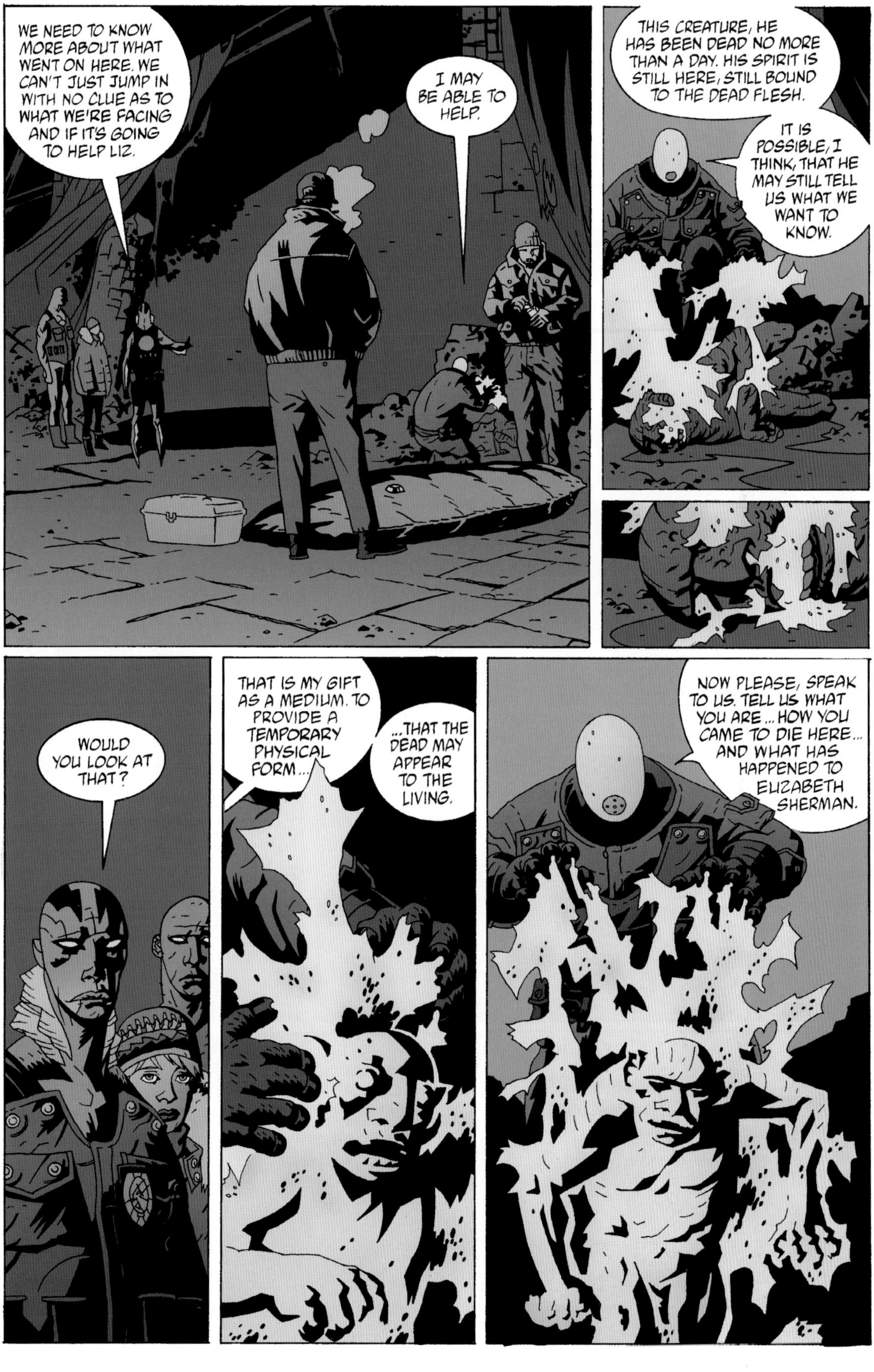
WE NEED TO KNOW MORE ABOUT WHAT WENT ON HERE. WE CAN'T JUST JUMP IN WITH NO CLUE AS TO WHAT WE'RE FACING AND IF IT'S GOING TO HELP LIZ.
I MAY BE ABLE TO HELP.
THIS CREATURE, HE HAS BEEN DEAD NO MORE THAN A DAY. HIS SPIRIT IS STILL HERE, STILL BOUND TO THE DEAD FLESH.
IT IS POSSIBLE, I THINK, THAT HE MAY STILL TELL US WHAT WE WANT TO KNOW.
WOULD YOU LOOK AT THAT?
THAT IS MY GIFT AS A MEDIUM. TO PROVIDE A TEMPORARY PHYSICAL FORM...
...THAT THE DEAD MAY APPEAR TO THE LIVING.
NOW PLEASE, SPEAK TO US. TELL US WHAT YOU ARE... HOW YOU CAME TO DIE HERE... AND WHAT HAS HAPPENED TO ELIZABETH SHERMAN.

WE ARE CREATURES OF THE LEFT HAND. NOT CHILDREN, BUT *THINGS*. NOT MEN...

THE RIGHT HAND, THE KEEPERS OF SECRETS, THEY ABANDONED US IN THE EARTH. THEY LEFT US TO THE LEFT HAND AND *THAT* HAND IS A CRUEL AND EVIL MASTER...

SO WHEN *HE* CAME, HE LED US TO THROW DOWN THAT HAND.

NOW, FINALLY, *HE* HAS FOUND THE SPARK AND *HE* WILL MAKE OF IT A BURNING TORCH TO SCORCH THIS WORLD...

I GUESS THAT EXPLAINS EVERYTHING.

YOU UNDERSTOOD THAT?

NO. I WAS BEING SARCASTIC.

OH.

THE SPARK. THAT COULD BE LIZ.

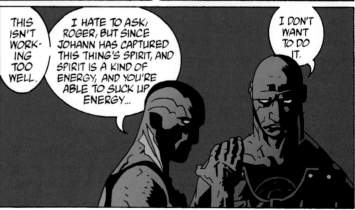

THIS ISN'T WORKING TOO WELL.

I HATE TO ASK, ROGER, BUT SINCE JOHANN HAS CAPTURED THIS THING'S SPIRIT, AND SPIRIT IS A KIND OF ENERGY, AND YOU'RE ABLE TO SUCK UP ENERGY...

I DON'T WANT TO DO IT.

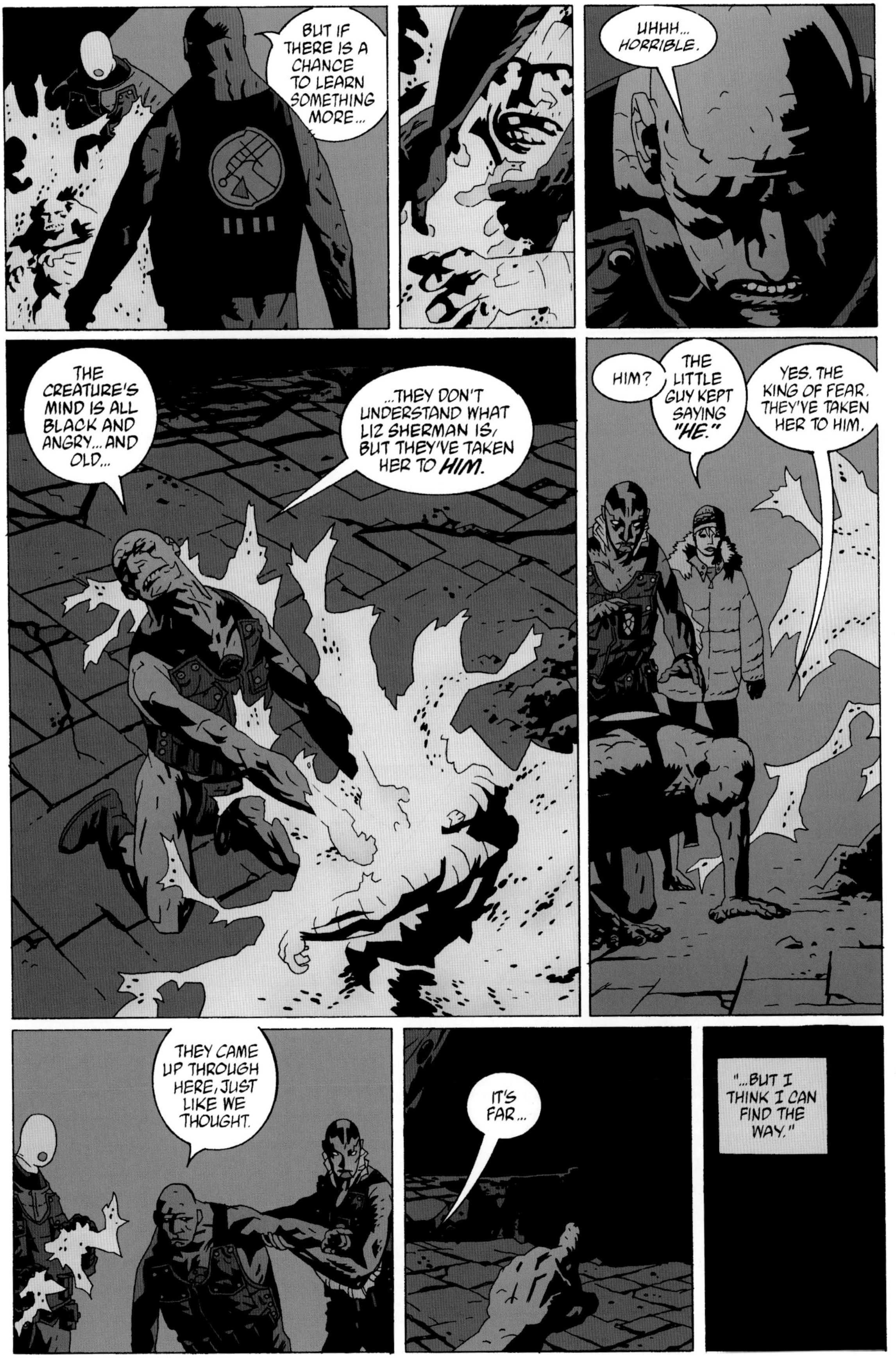

BUT IF THERE IS A CHANCE TO LEARN SOMETHING MORE...
UHHH... HORRIBLE.
THE CREATURE'S MIND IS ALL BLACK AND ANGRY... AND OLD...
...THEY DON'T UNDERSTAND WHAT LIZ SHERMAN IS, BUT THEY'VE TAKEN HER TO HIM.
HIM?
THE LITTLE GUY KEPT SAYING "HE."
YES. THE KING OF FEAR. THEY'VE TAKEN HER TO HIM.
THEY CAME UP THROUGH HERE, JUST LIKE WE THOUGHT.
IT'S FAR...
"...BUT I THINK I CAN FIND THE WAY."

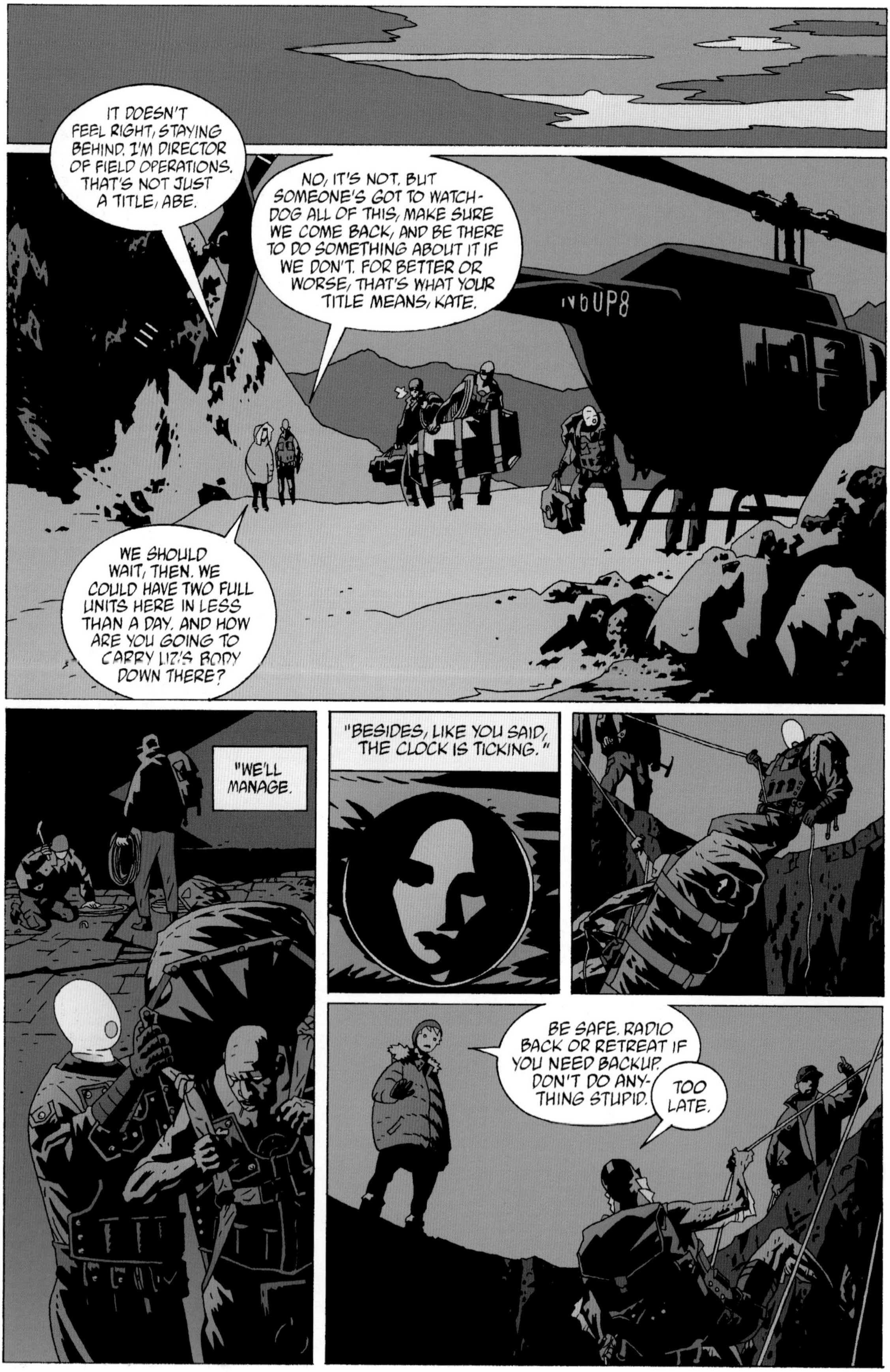
IT DOESN'T FEEL RIGHT, STAYING BEHIND. I'M DIRECTOR OF FIELD OPERATIONS. THAT'S NOT JUST A TITLE, ABE.
NO, IT'S NOT, BUT SOMEONE'S GOT TO WATCH-DOG ALL OF THIS, MAKE SURE WE COME BACK, AND BE THERE TO DO SOMETHING ABOUT IT IF WE DON'T. FOR BETTER OR WORSE, THAT'S WHAT YOUR TITLE MEANS, KATE.
WE SHOULD WAIT, THEN. WE COULD HAVE TWO FULL UNITS HERE IN LESS THAN A DAY. AND HOW ARE YOU GOING TO CARRY LIZ'S BODY DOWN THERE?
"WE'LL MANAGE.
"BESIDES, LIKE YOU SAID, THE CLOCK IS TICKING."
BE SAFE. RADIO BACK OR RETREAT IF YOU NEED BACKUP. DON'T DO ANY-THING STUPID.
TOO LATE.

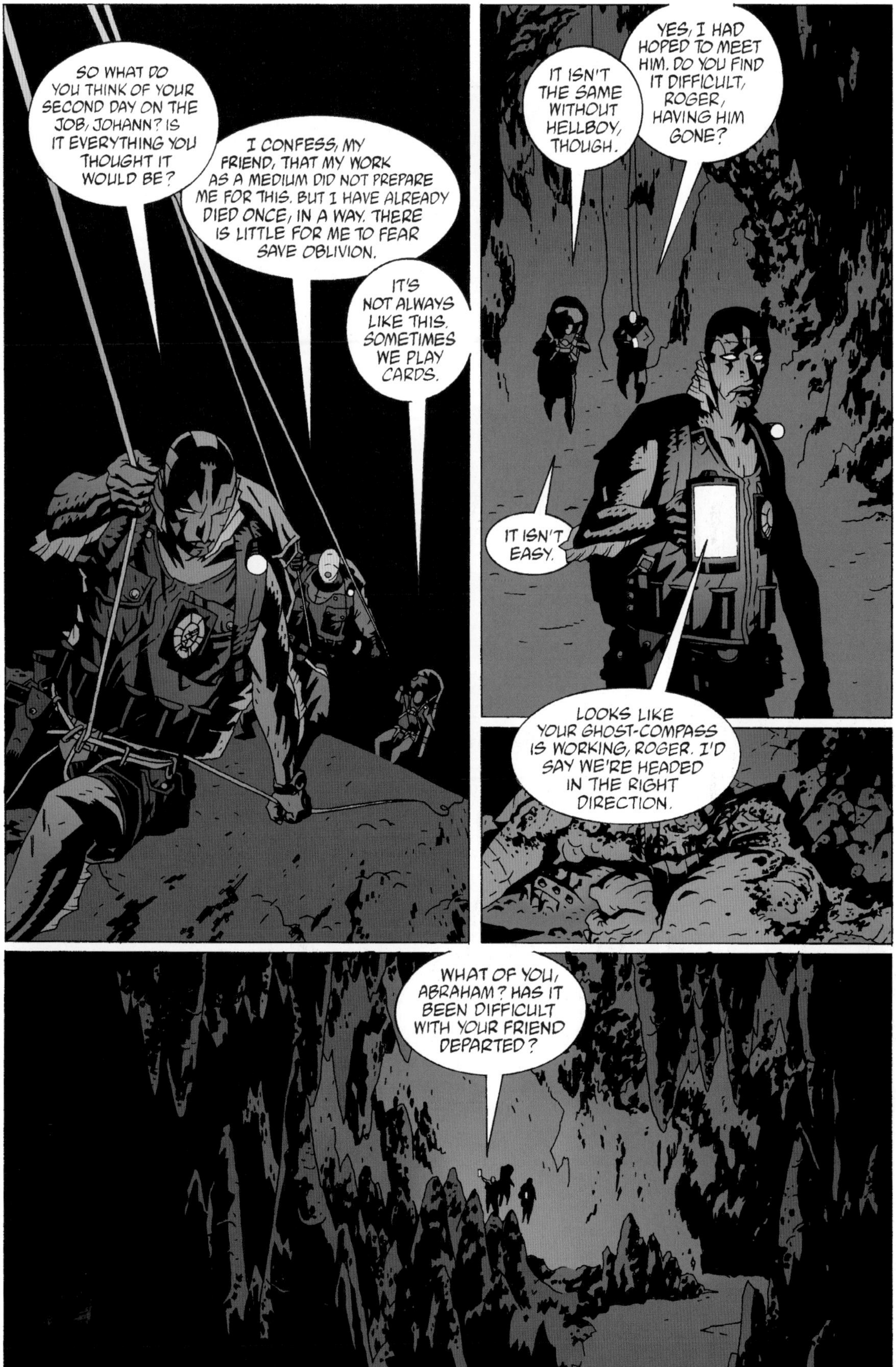
SO WHAT DO YOU THINK OF YOUR SECOND DAY ON THE JOB, JOHANN? IS IT EVERYTHING YOU THOUGHT IT WOULD BE?
I CONFESS, MY FRIEND, THAT MY WORK AS A MEDIUM DID NOT PREPARE ME FOR THIS. BUT I HAVE ALREADY DIED ONCE, IN A WAY. THERE IS LITTLE FOR ME TO FEAR SAVE OBLIVION.
IT'S NOT ALWAYS LIKE THIS. SOMETIMES WE PLAY CARDS.
IT ISN'T THE SAME WITHOUT HELLBOY, THOUGH.
YES, I HAD HOPED TO MEET HIM. DO YOU FIND IT DIFFICULT, ROGER, HAVING HIM GONE?
IT ISN'T EASY.
LOOKS LIKE YOUR GHOST-COMPASS IS WORKING, ROGER. I'D SAY WE'RE HEADED IN THE RIGHT DIRECTION.
WHAT OF YOU, ABRAHAM? HAS IT BEEN DIFFICULT WITH YOUR FRIEND DEPARTED?

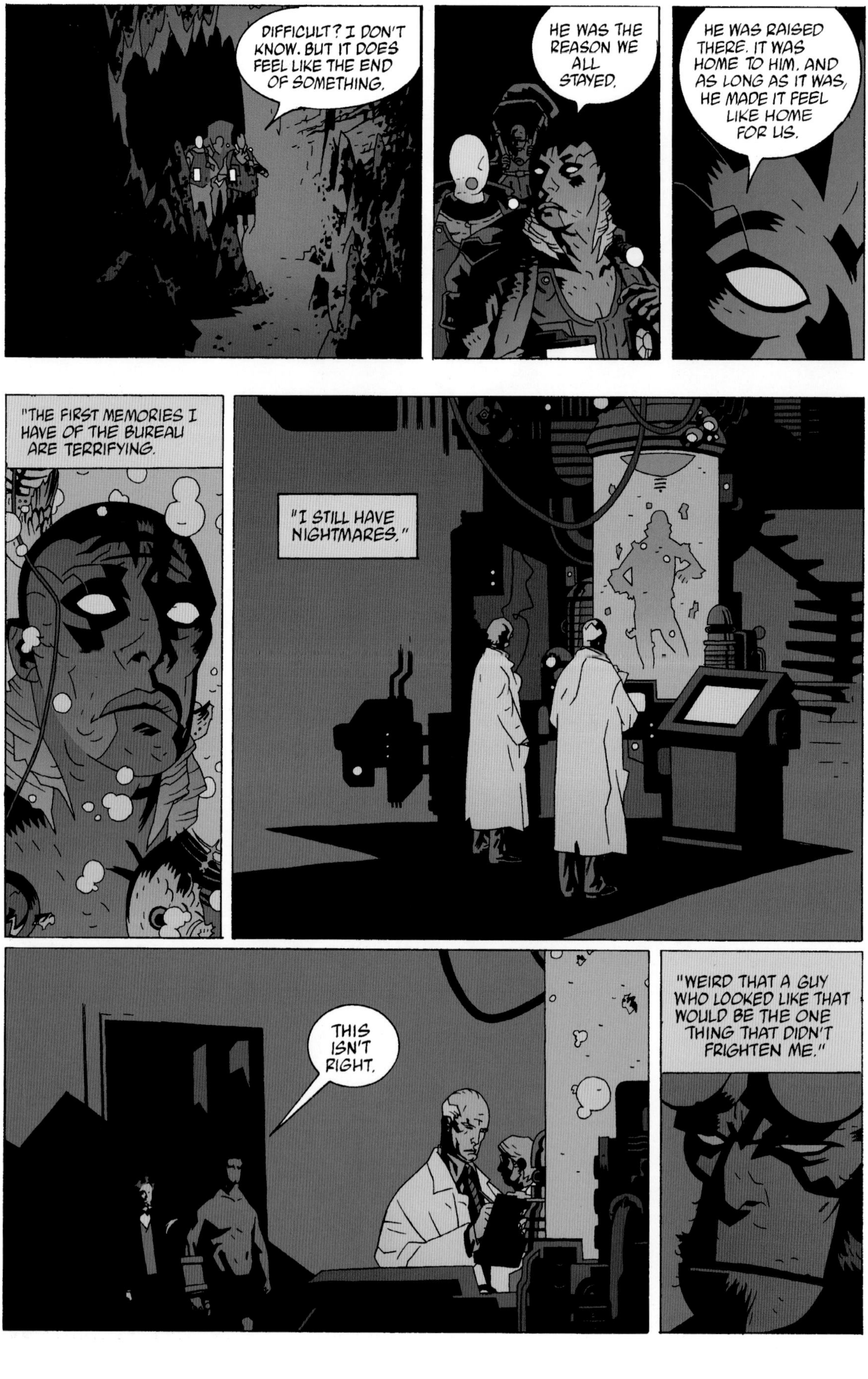
DIFFICULT? I DON'T KNOW. BUT IT DOES FEEL LIKE THE END OF SOMETHING.
HE WAS THE REASON WE ALL STAYED.
HE WAS RAISED THERE. IT WAS HOME TO HIM. AND AS LONG AS IT WAS, HE MADE IT FEEL LIKE HOME FOR US.
"THE FIRST MEMORIES I HAVE OF THE BUREAU ARE TERRIFYING.
"I STILL HAVE NIGHTMARES."
THIS ISN'T RIGHT.
"WEIRD THAT A GUY WHO LOOKED LIKE THAT WOULD BE THE ONE THING THAT DIDN'T FRIGHTEN ME."

COME AWAY, MY BOY. LEAVE THEM TO THEIR WORK. THESE TESTS MUST BE PERFORMED IF WE ARE TO FULLY UNDERSTAND THE NATURE OF THIS CREATURE.

YEAH, BUT HE'S BEEN IN THERE FOR DAYS.

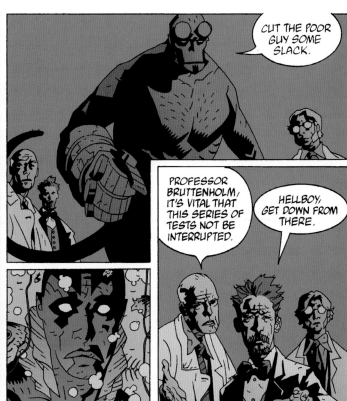

CUT THE POOR GUY SOME SLACK.

PROFESSOR BRUTTENHOLM, IT'S VITAL THAT THIS SERIES OF TESTS NOT BE INTERRUPTED.

HELLBOY, GET DOWN FROM THERE.

I DON'T THINK SO. I GREW UP WITH THE BUREAU'S "TESTS," REMEMBER?

YOU GUYS'LL JUST KEEP GOING UNTIL SOMEONE SAYS, "THAT'S ENOUGH."

WELL GUESS WHAT?

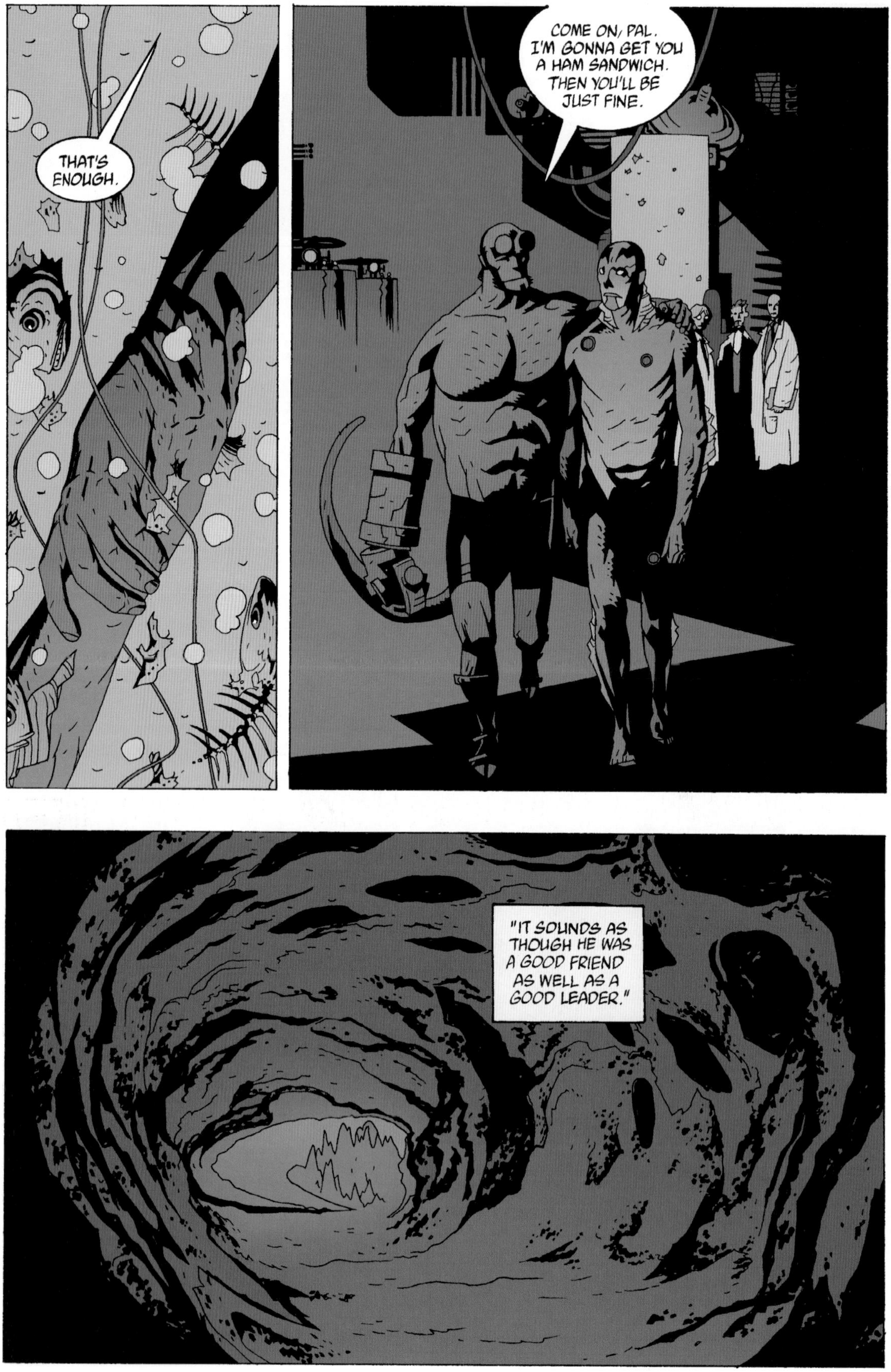
THAT'S ENOUGH.
COME ON, PAL. I'M GONNA GET YOU A HAM SANDWICH. THEN YOU'LL BE JUST FINE.
"IT SOUNDS AS THOUGH HE WAS A GOOD FRIEND AS WELL AS A GOOD LEADER."

AND NOW THAT HE IS GONE, YOU ARE THE LEADER OF THE UNIT.
I AM? WHERE'D YOU GET THAT IDEA?
WELL, IT ISN'T ME.
IT ISN'T ME. THEY WERE GOING TO BLOW ME UP.
HAVE A REST, ROGER. WE'LL TAKE A TURN WITH HER NOW.
SEE. LEADER.
TIC
TIC
OW!
HUH?

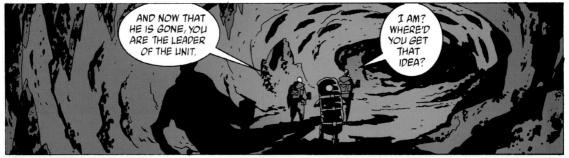

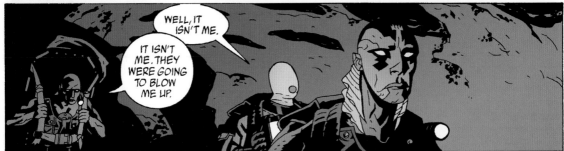

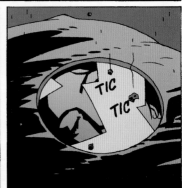

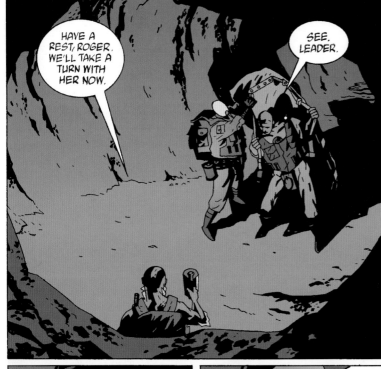

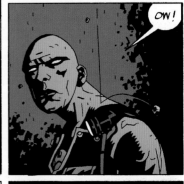

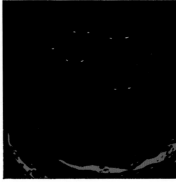

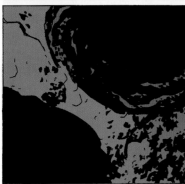

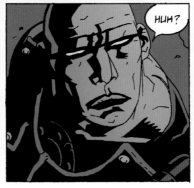

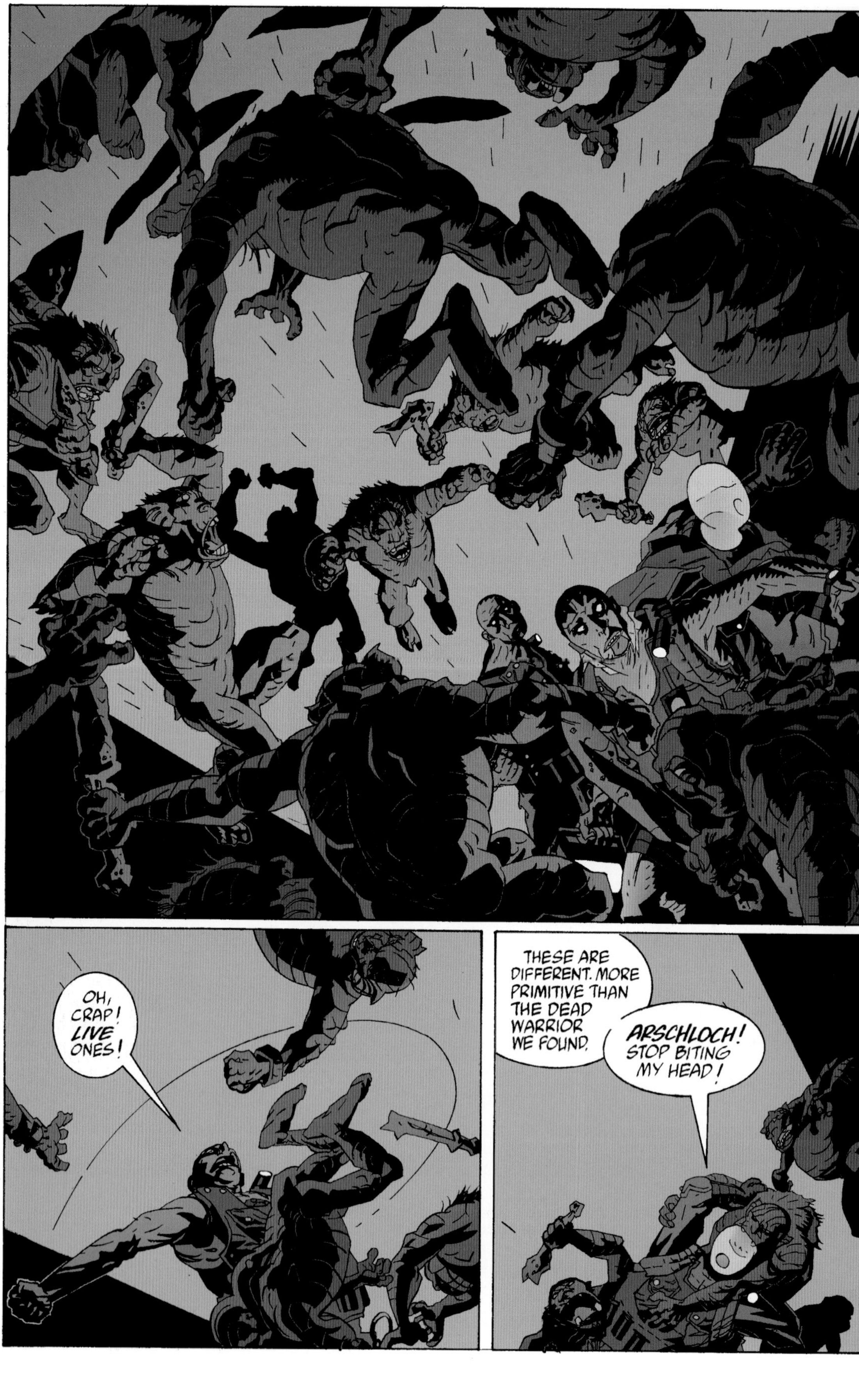
OH, CRAP! **LIVE** ONES!
THESE ARE DIFFERENT. MORE PRIMITIVE THAN THE DEAD WARRIOR WE FOUND.
ARSCHLOCH! STOP BITING MY HEAD!

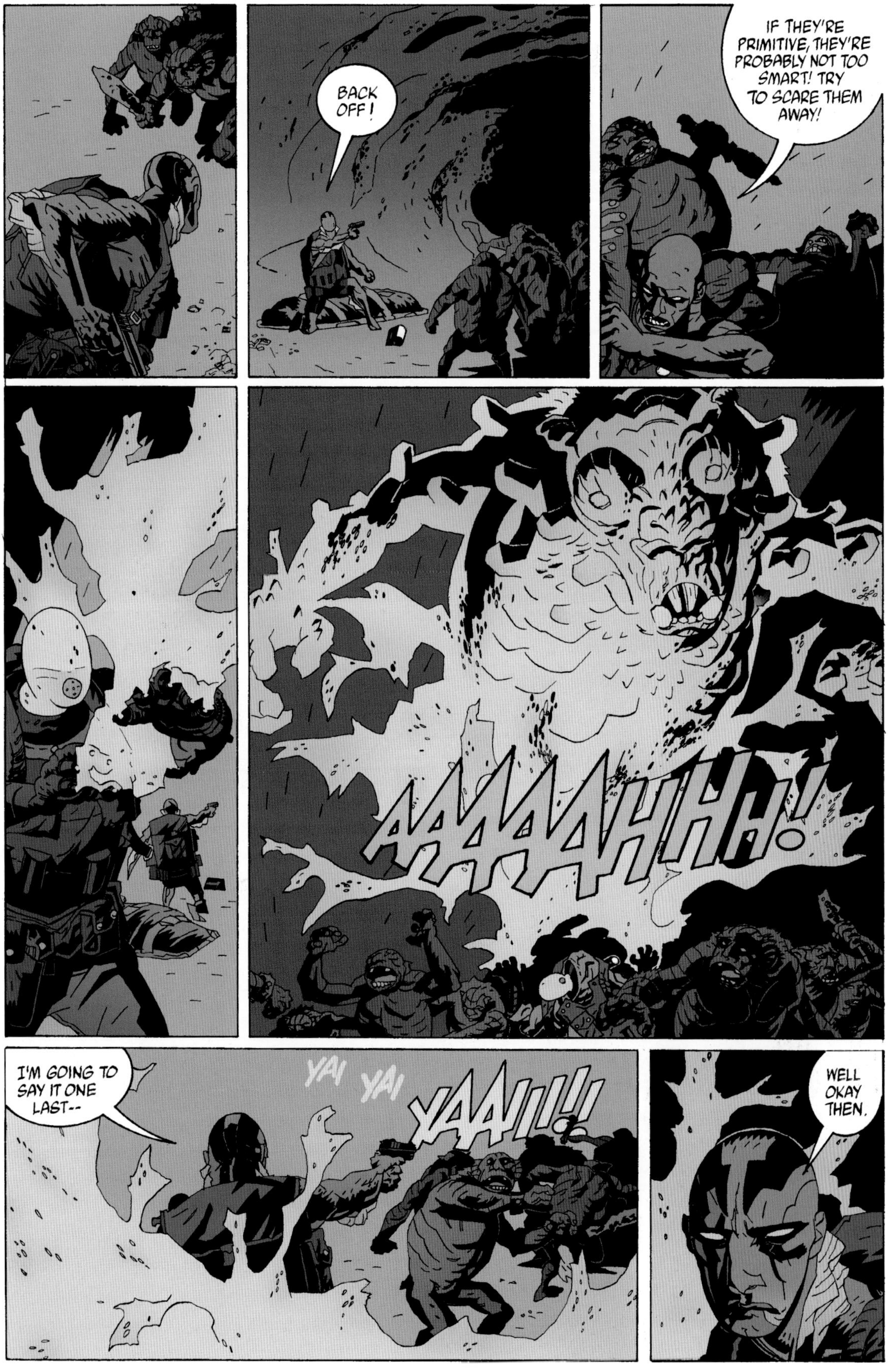
BACK OFF!
IF THEY'RE PRIMITIVE, THEY'RE PROBABLY NOT TOO SMART! TRY TO SCARE THEM AWAY!
AAAAHHH!
I'M GOING TO SAY IT ONE LAST--
YAI YAI YAAIII!!
WELL OKAY THEN.

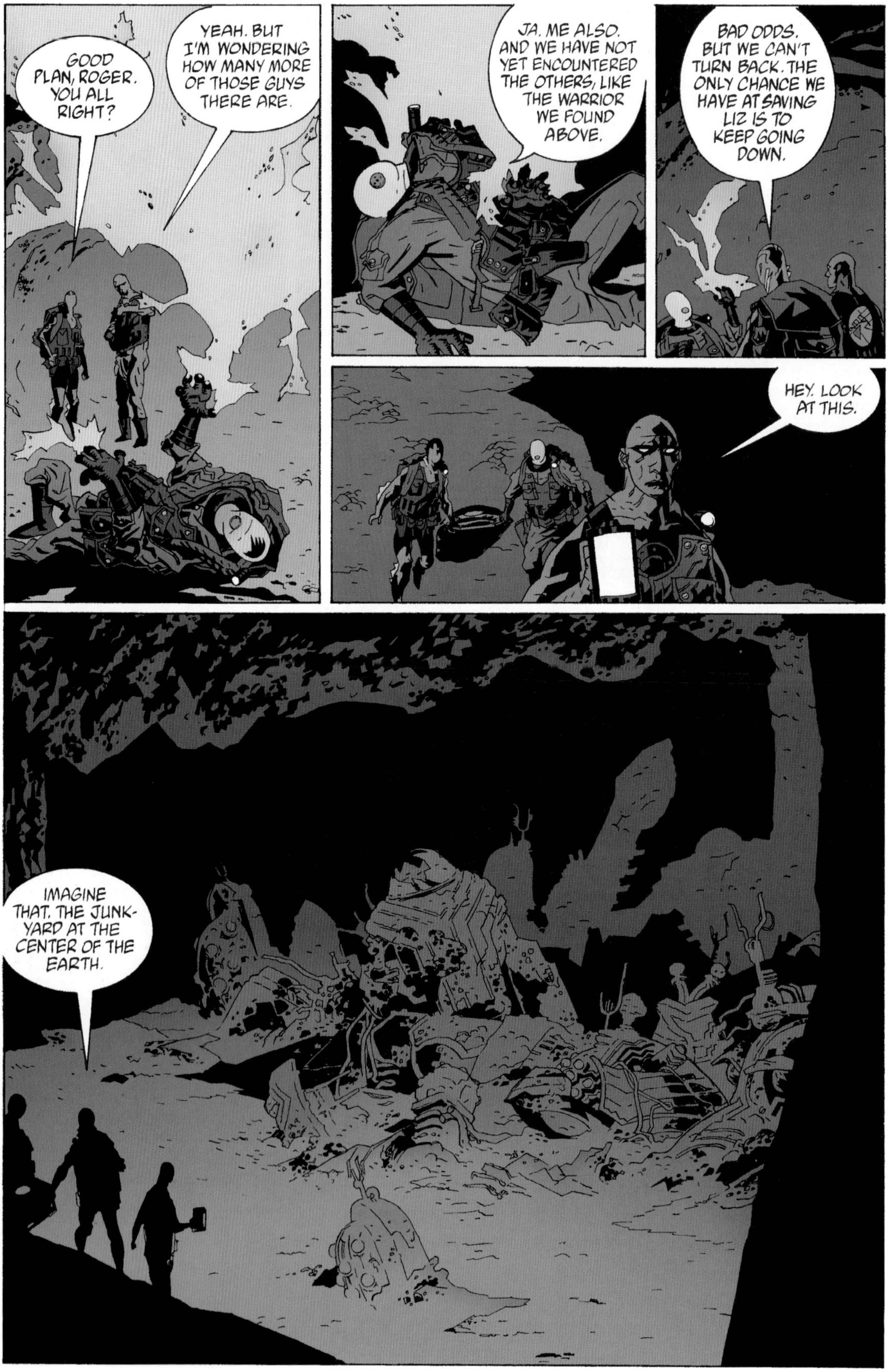
GOOD PLAN, ROGER. YOU ALL RIGHT?
YEAH. BUT I'M WONDERING HOW MANY MORE OF THOSE GUYS THERE ARE.
JA. ME ALSO. AND WE HAVE NOT YET ENCOUNTERED THE OTHERS, LIKE THE WARRIOR WE FOUND ABOVE.
BAD ODDS. BUT WE CAN'T TURN BACK. THE ONLY CHANCE WE HAVE AT SAVING LIZ IS TO KEEP GOING DOWN.
HEY. LOOK AT THIS.
IMAGINE THAT. THE JUNK-YARD AT THE CENTER OF THE EARTH.

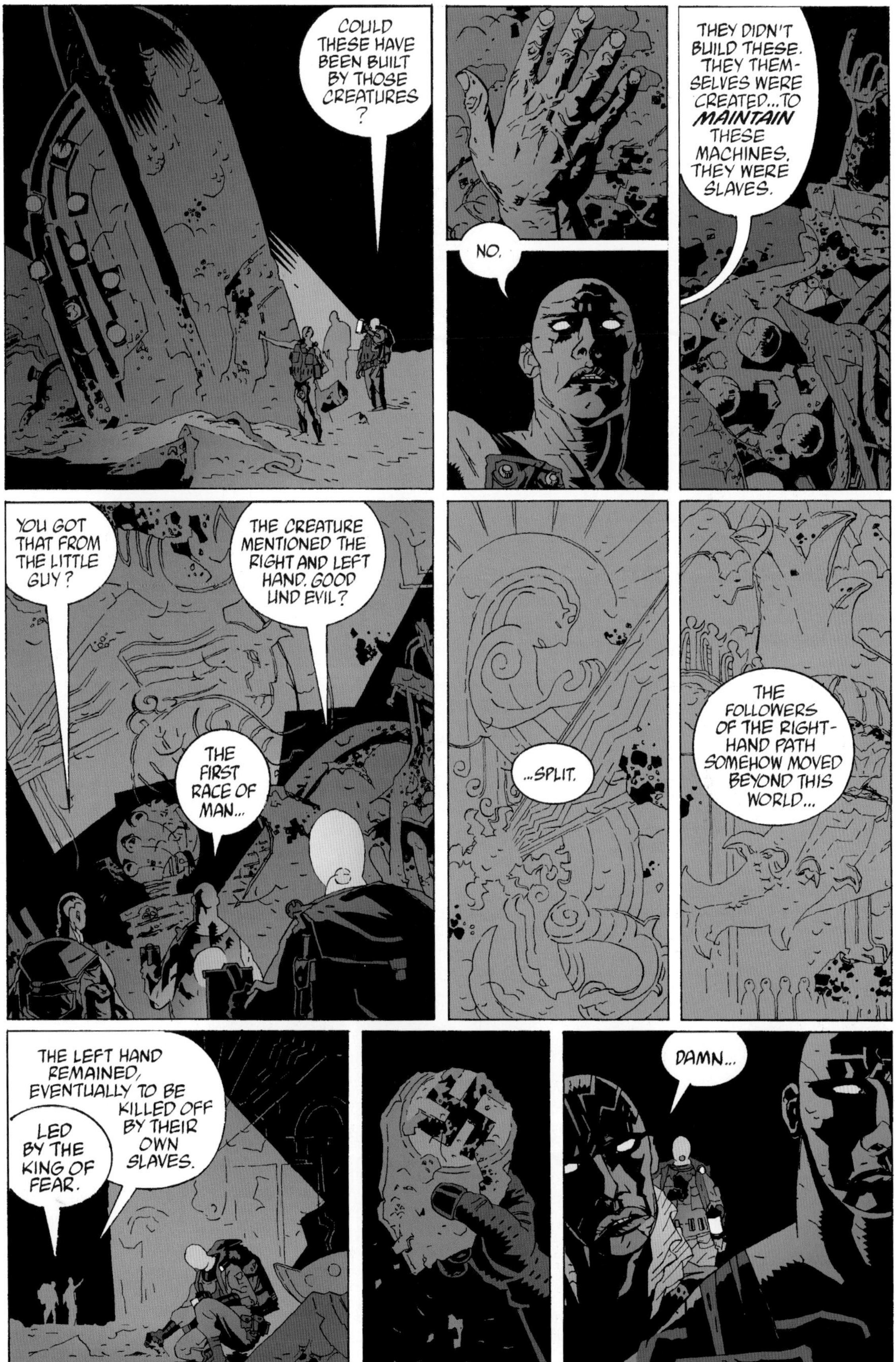
COULD THESE HAVE BEEN BUILT BY THOSE CREATURES ?
NO.
THEY DIDN'T BUILD THESE. THEY THEM-SELVES WERE CREATED...TO MAINTAIN THESE MACHINES. THEY WERE SLAVES.
YOU GOT THAT FROM THE LITTLE GUY ?
THE CREATURE MENTIONED THE RIGHT AND LEFT HAND. GOOD UND EVIL?
THE FIRST RACE OF MAN...
...SPLIT.
THE FOLLOWERS OF THE RIGHT-HAND PATH SOMEHOW MOVED BEYOND THIS WORLD...
THE LEFT HAND REMAINED, EVENTUALLY TO BE KILLED OFF BY THEIR OWN SLAVES.
LED BY THE KING OF FEAR.
DAMN...

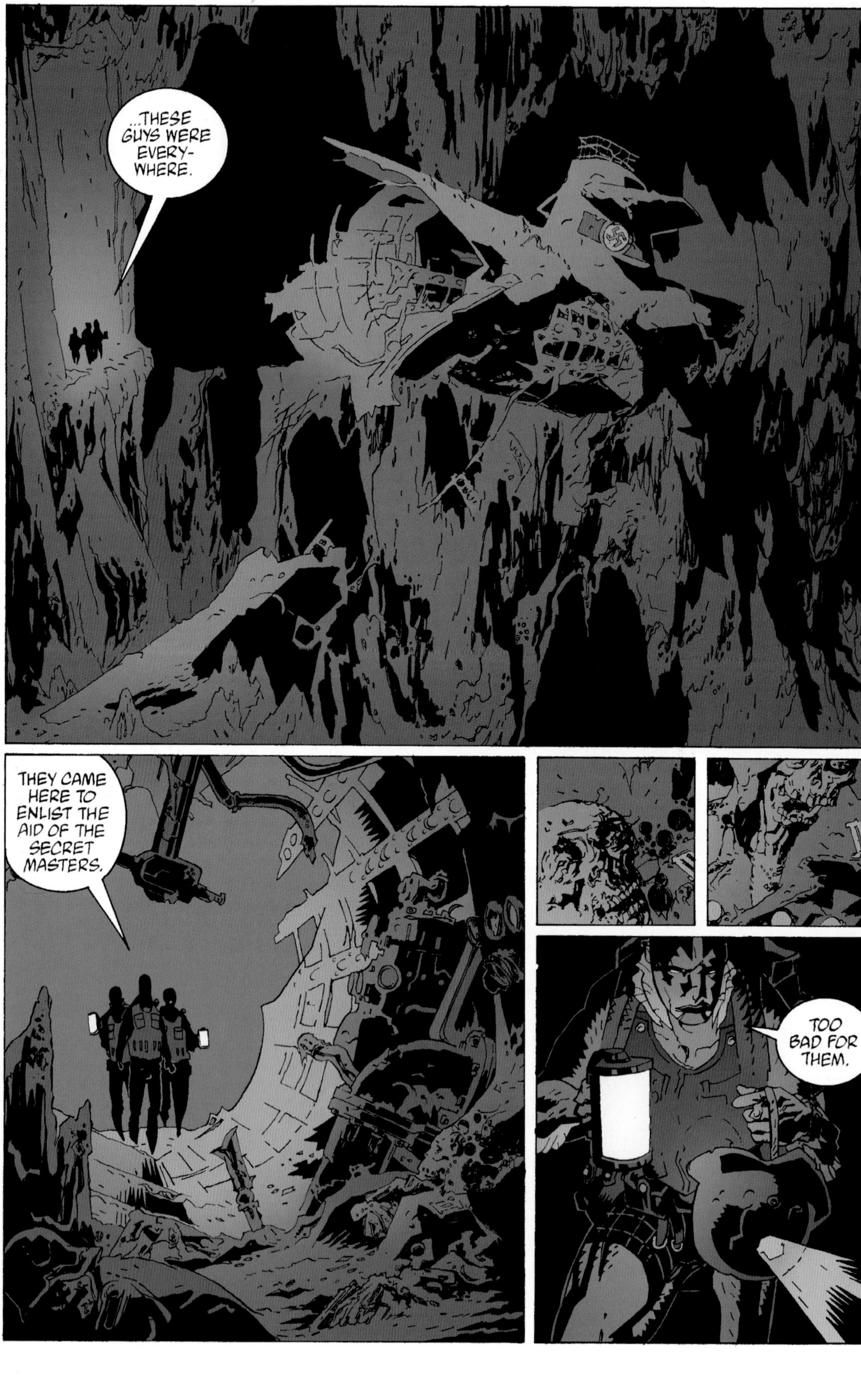
...THESE GUYS WERE EVERY-WHERE.
THEY CAME HERE TO ENLIST THE AID OF THE SECRET MASTERS.
TOO BAD FOR THEM.

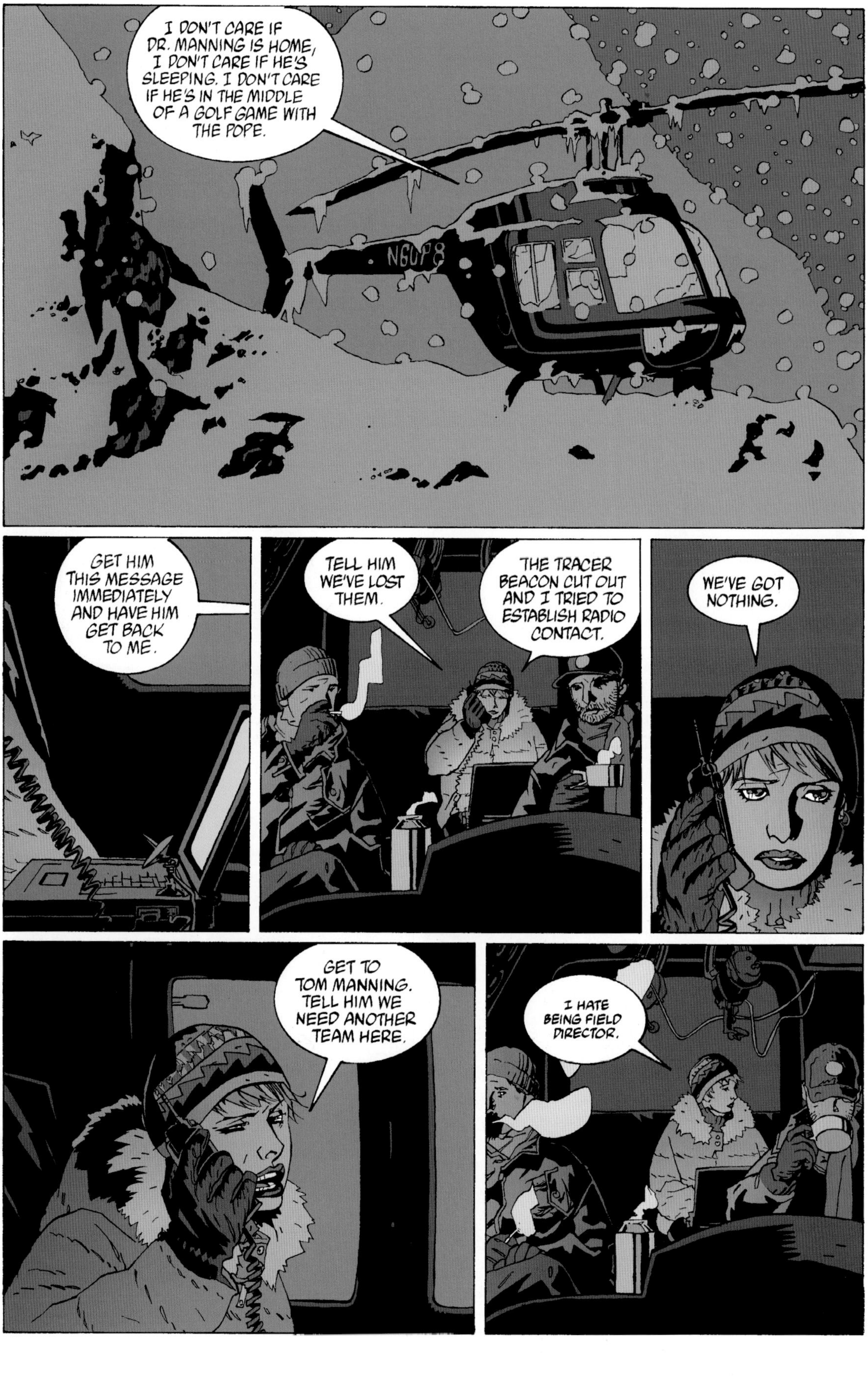
I DON'T CARE IF DR. MANNING IS HOME, I DON'T CARE IF HE'S SLEEPING. I DON'T CARE IF HE'S IN THE MIDDLE OF A GOLF GAME WITH THE POPE.
N6UP8
GET HIM THIS MESSAGE IMMEDIATELY AND HAVE HIM GET BACK TO ME.
TELL HIM WE'VE LOST THEM.
THE TRACER BEACON CUT OUT AND I TRIED TO ESTABLISH RADIO CONTACT.
WE'VE GOT NOTHING.
GET TO TOM MANNING. TELL HIM WE NEED ANOTHER TEAM HERE.
I HATE BEING FIELD DIRECTOR.

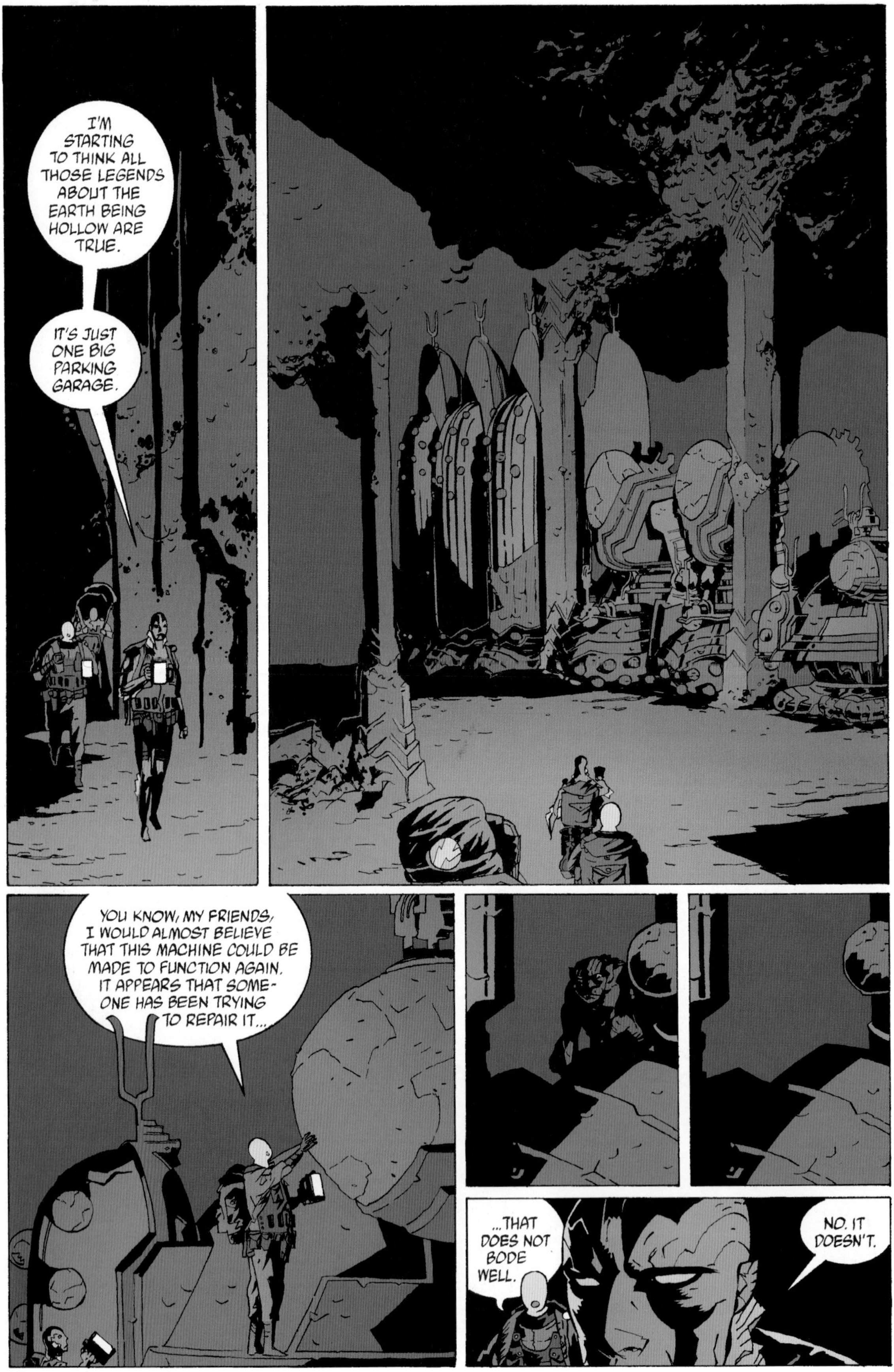
I'M STARTING TO THINK ALL THOSE LEGENDS ABOUT THE EARTH BEING HOLLOW ARE TRUE.
IT'S JUST ONE BIG PARKING GARAGE.
YOU KNOW, MY FRIENDS, I WOULD ALMOST BELIEVE THAT THIS MACHINE COULD BE MADE TO FUNCTION AGAIN. IT APPEARS THAT SOME-ONE HAS BEEN TRYING TO REPAIR IT...
...THAT DOES NOT BODE WELL.
NO. IT DOESN'T.

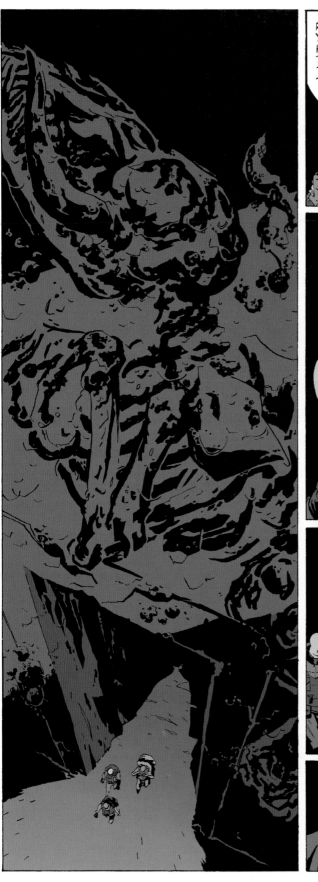

ROGER, SOMETHING YOU SAID EARLIER HAS LEFT ME UNSETTLED. YOU MENTIONED THE BUREAU WANTING TO... HOW DID YOU SAY IT? TO BLOW YOU UP.

OH. YES. HELLBOY TOLD THEM THEY COULD TRUST ME, BUT THEY DIDN'T BELIEVE HIM.

HE IS A *GOOD* FRIEND.

THE BEST.

SSSH. DO YOU HEAR THAT?

RRRMMB

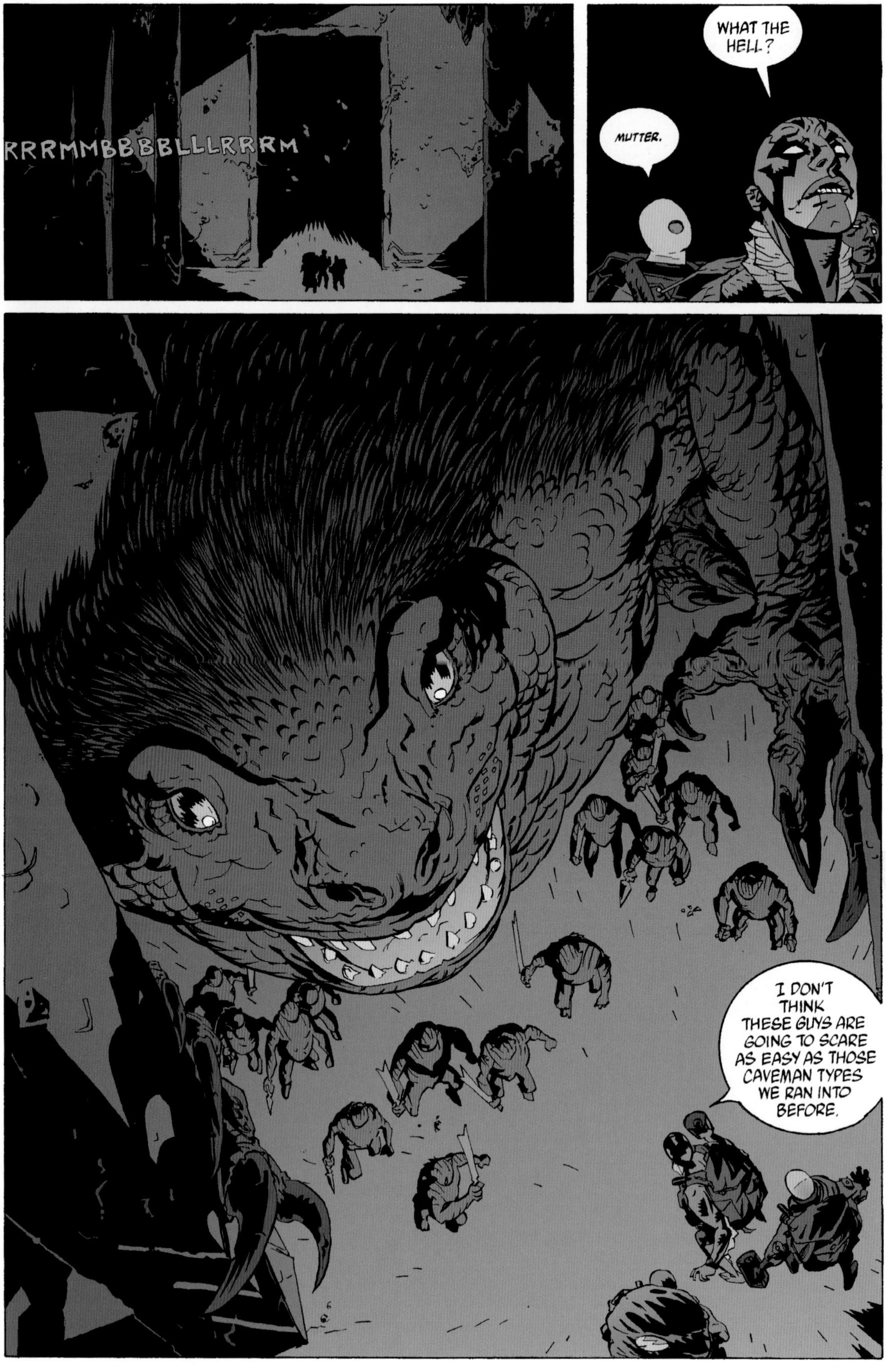
RRRMMBBBBLLLRRRM
WHAT THE HELL?
MUTTER.
I DON'T THINK THESE GUYS ARE GOING TO SCARE AS EASY AS THOSE CAVEMAN TYPES WE RAN INTO BEFORE.

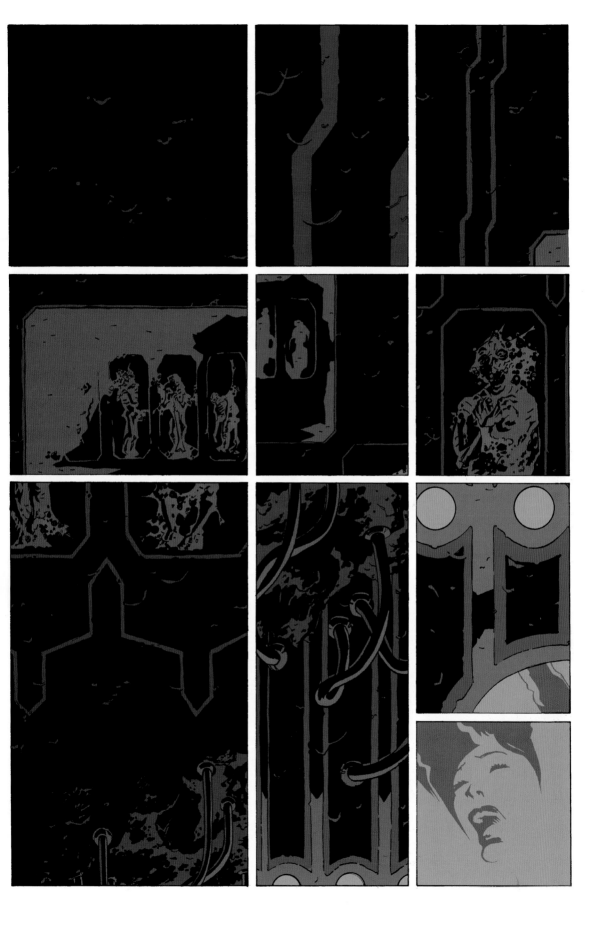

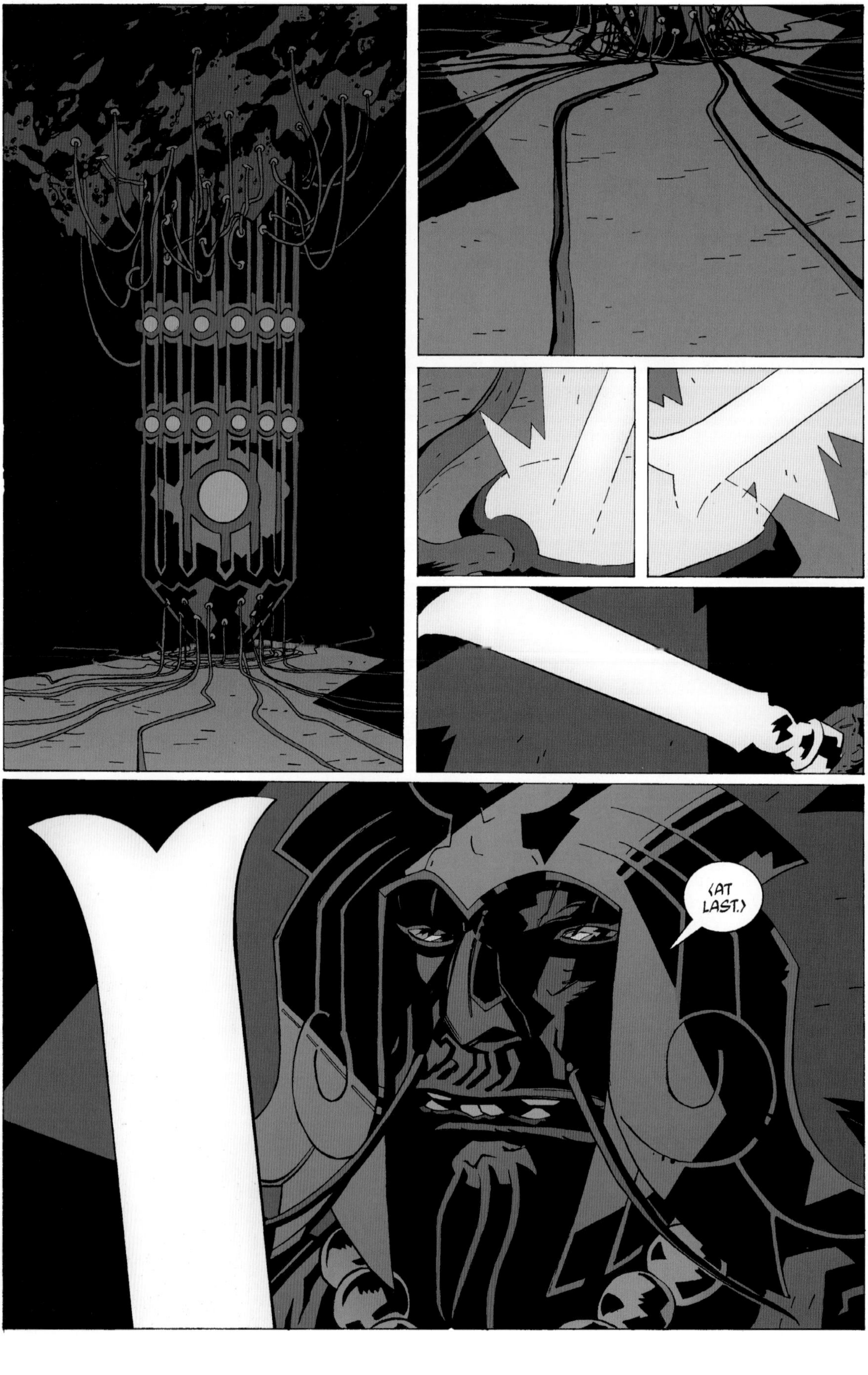
<AT LAST.>

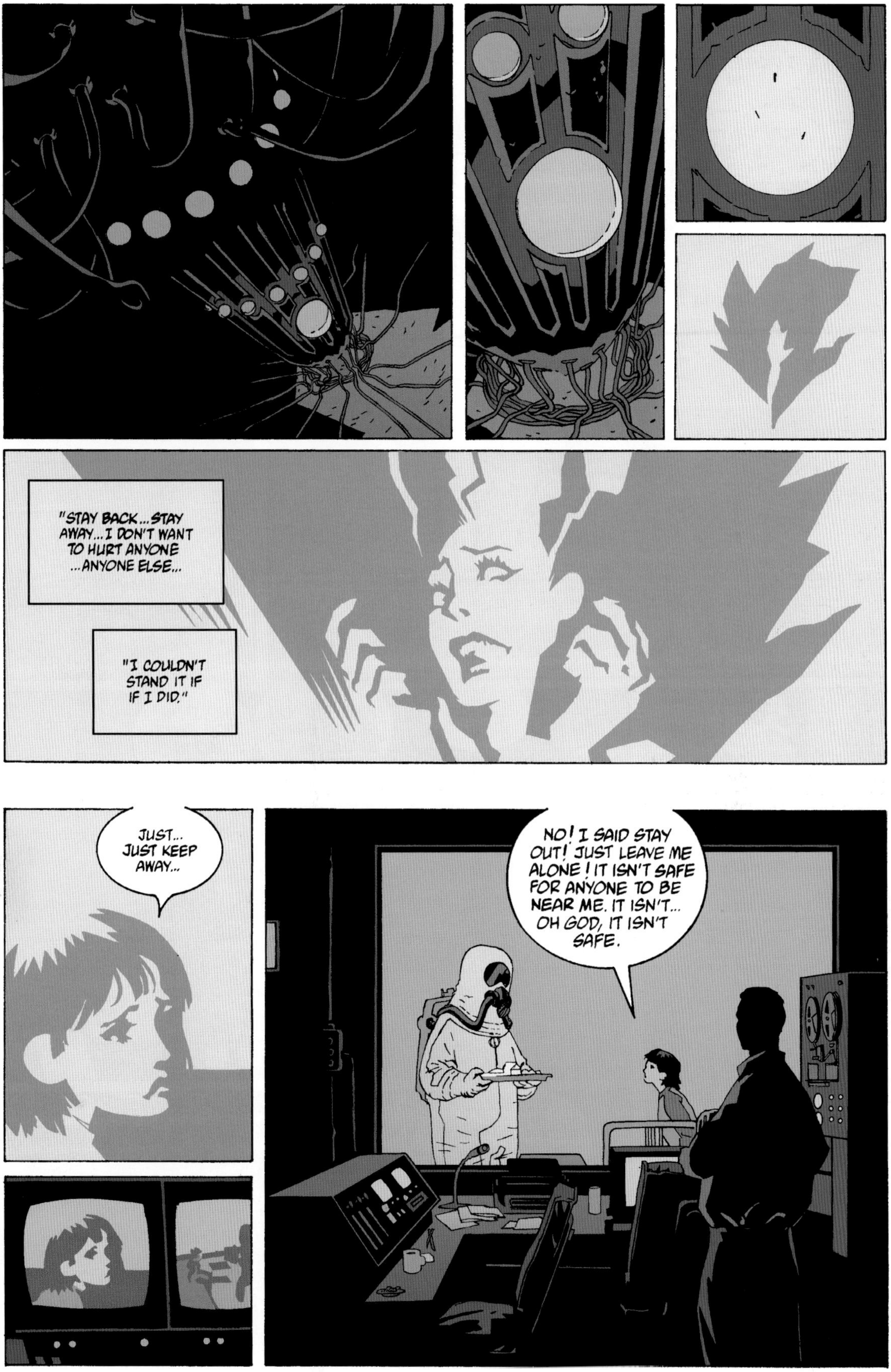
"STAY BACK...STAY AWAY...I DON'T WANT TO HURT ANYONE ...ANYONE ELSE...
"I COULDN'T STAND IT IF IF I DID."
JUST... JUST KEEP AWAY...
NO! I SAID STAY OUT! JUST LEAVE ME ALONE! IT ISN'T SAFE FOR ANYONE TO BE NEAR ME. IT ISN'T... OH GOD, IT ISN'T SAFE.

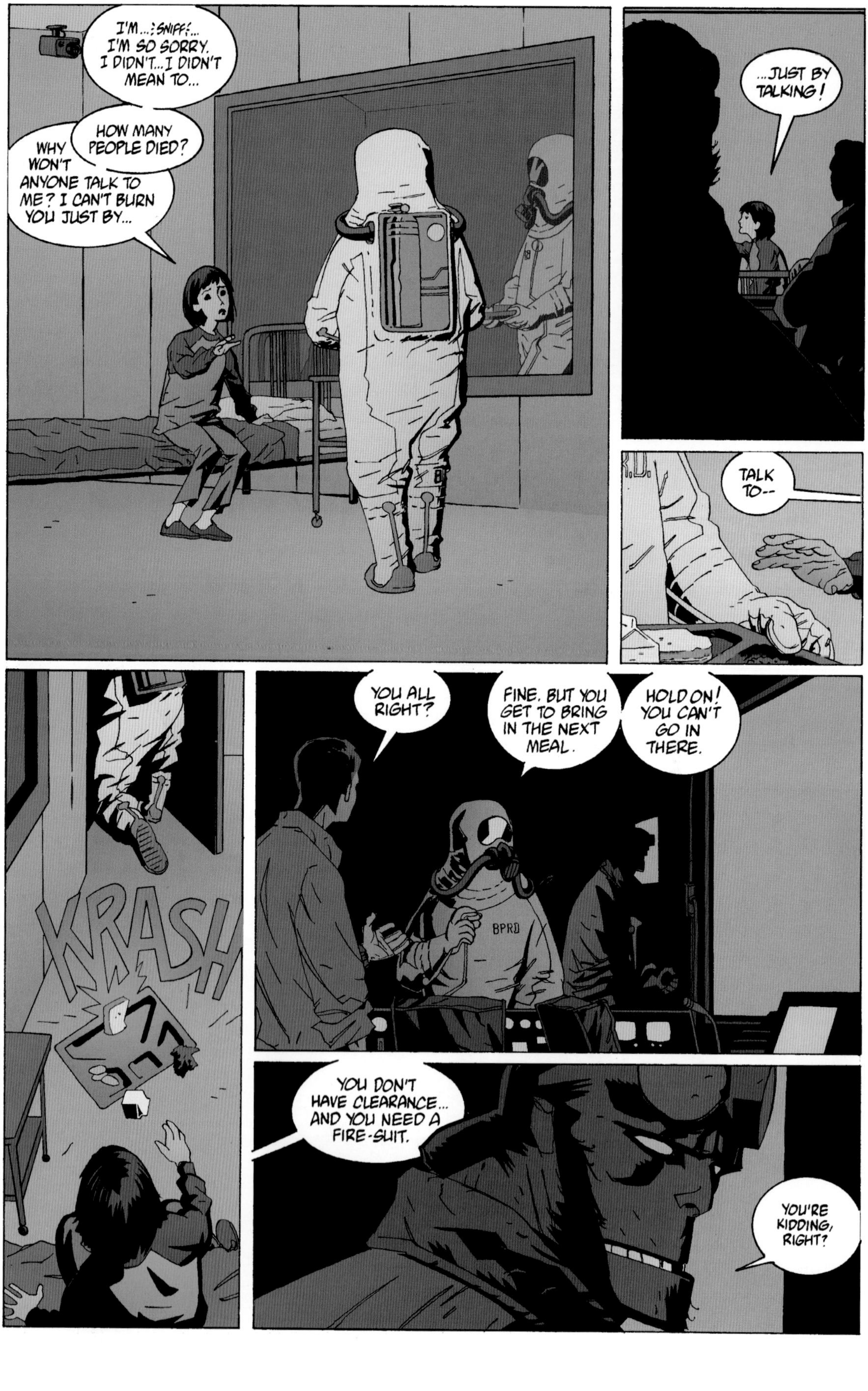
I'M ...SNIFF... I'M SO SORRY. I DIDN'T...I DIDN'T MEAN TO...
HOW MANY PEOPLE DIED?
WHY WON'T ANYONE TALK TO ME? I CAN'T BURN YOU JUST BY...
...JUST BY TALKING!
TALK TO--
KRASH
YOU ALL RIGHT?
FINE. BUT YOU GET TO BRING IN THE NEXT MEAL.
HOLD ON! YOU CAN'T GO IN THERE.
BPRD
YOU DON'T HAVE CLEARANCE... AND YOU NEED A FIRE-SUIT.
YOU'RE KIDDING, RIGHT?

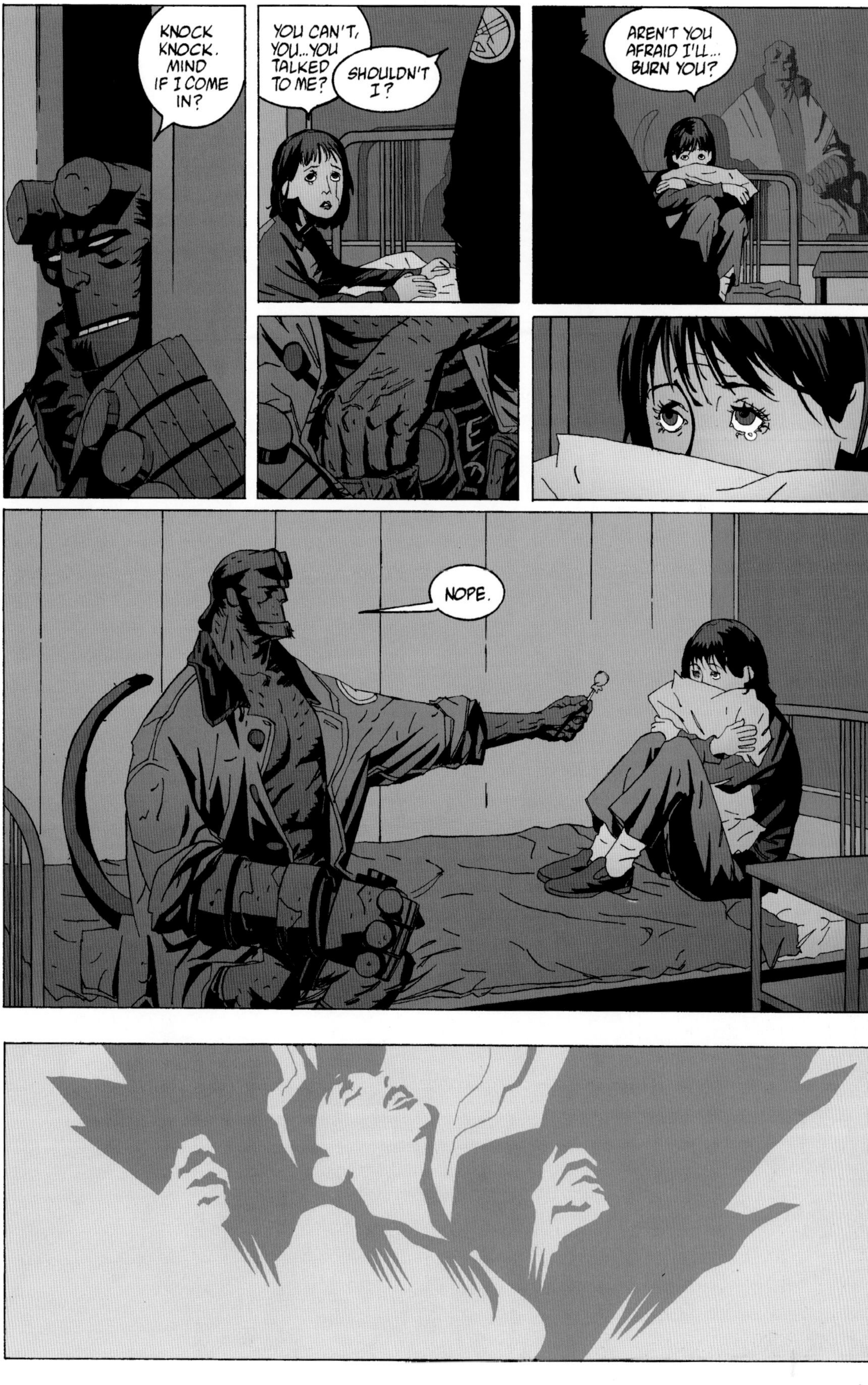
KNOCK KNOCK. MIND IF I COME IN?
YOU CAN'T, YOU...YOU TALKED TO ME?
SHOULDN'T I?
AREN'T YOU AFRAID I'LL... BURN YOU?
NOPE.

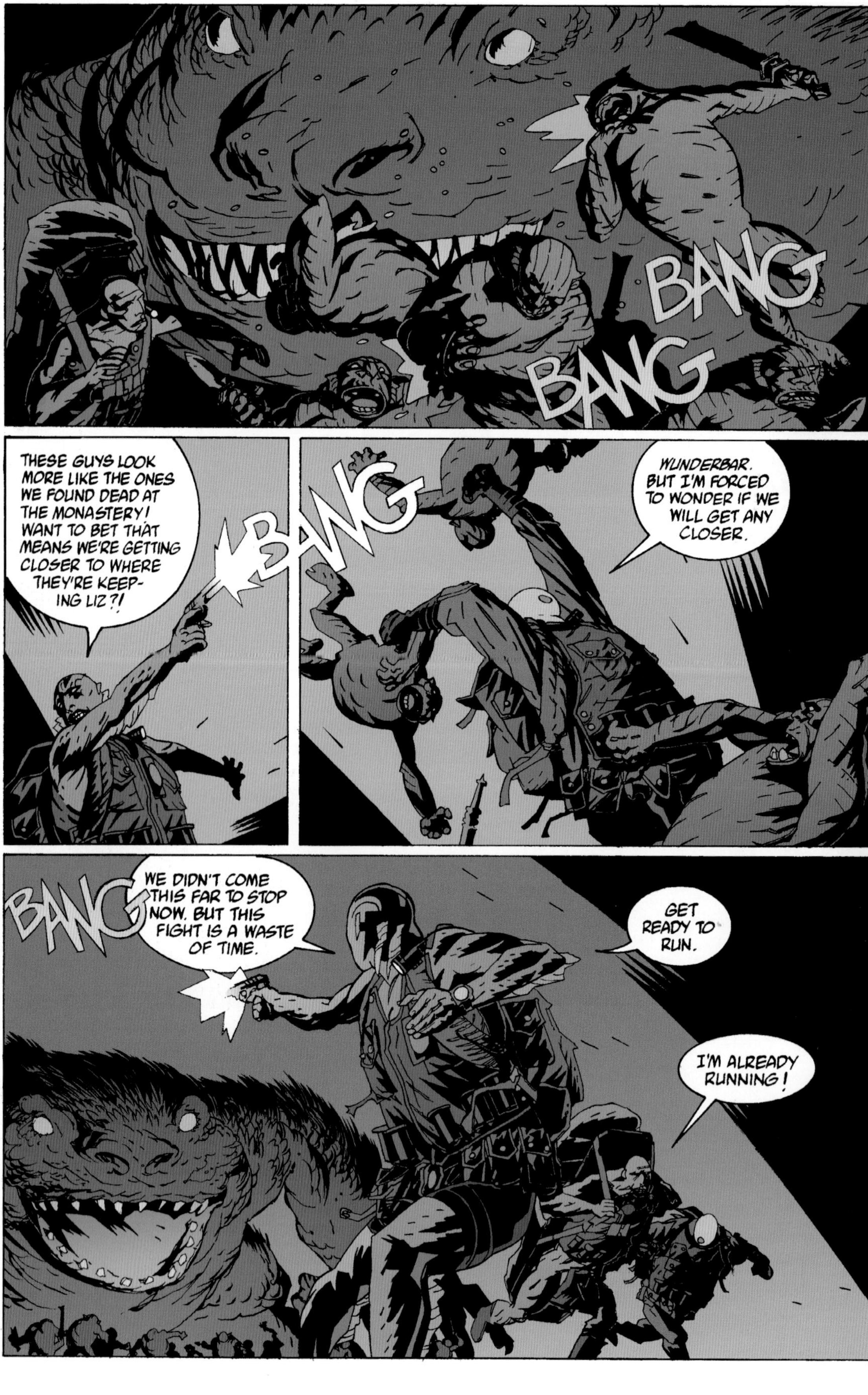
BANG
BANG
THESE GUYS LOOK MORE LIKE THE ONES WE FOUND DEAD AT THE MONASTERY! WANT TO BET THAT MEANS WE'RE GETTING CLOSER TO WHERE THEY'RE KEEP-ING LIZ?!
BANG
WUNDERBAR. BUT I'M FORCED TO WONDER IF WE WILL GET ANY CLOSER.
BANG
WE DIDN'T COME THIS FAR TO STOP NOW. BUT THIS FIGHT IS A WASTE OF TIME.
GET READY TO RUN.
I'M ALREADY RUNNING!

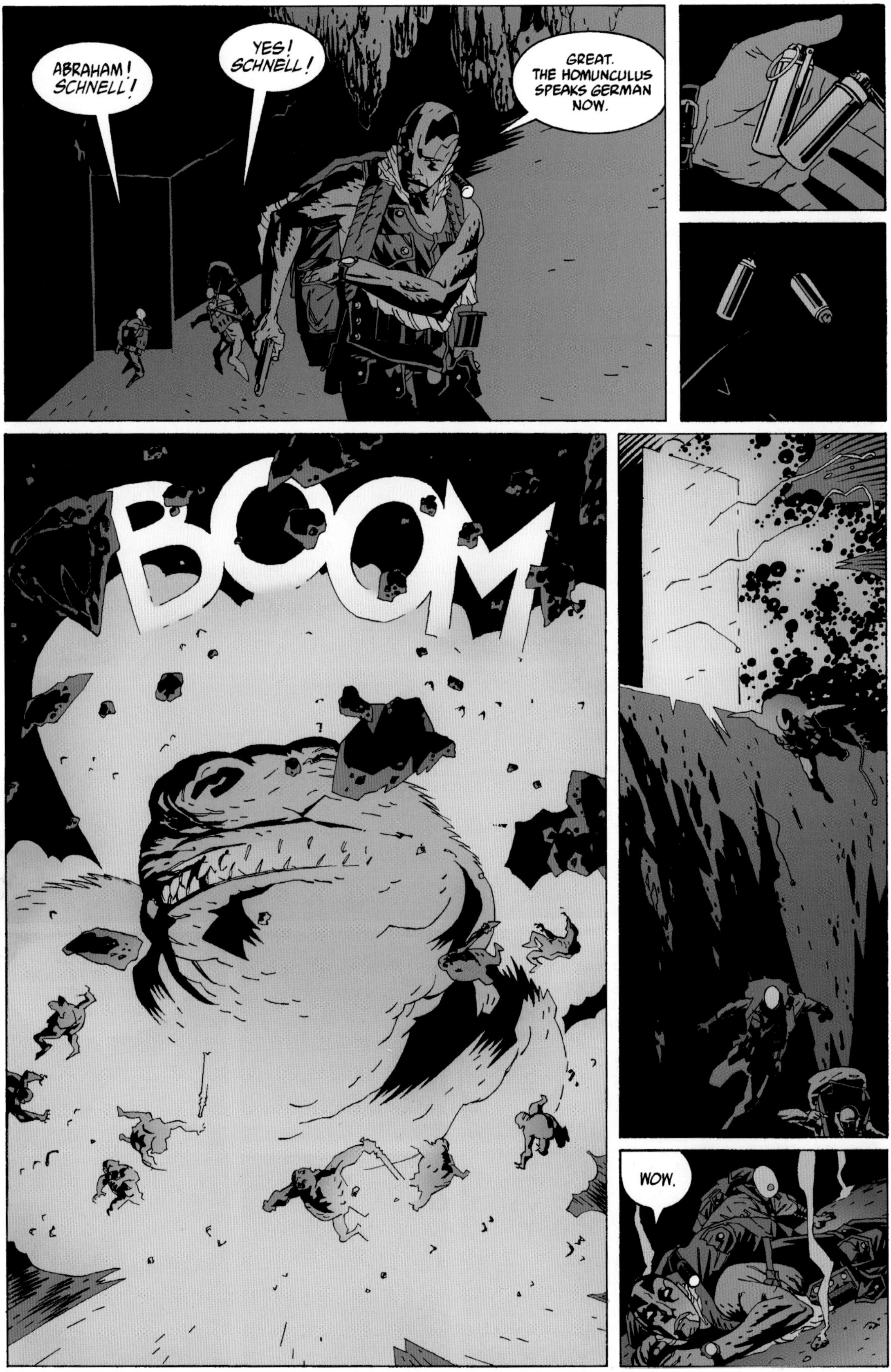
ABRAHAM! SCHNELL!
YES! SCHNELL!
GREAT. THE HOMUNCULUS SPEAKS GERMAN NOW.
BOOM
WOW.

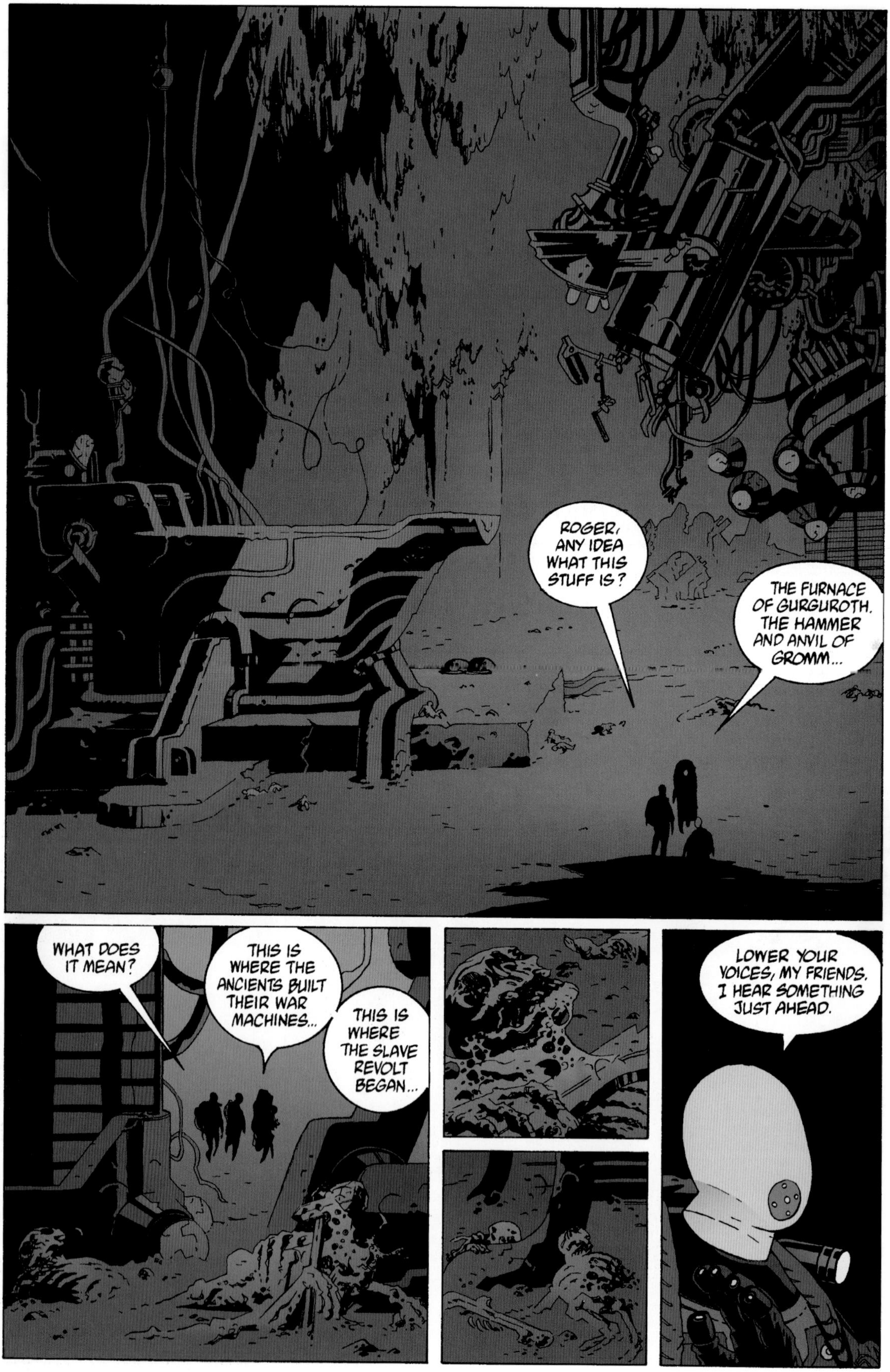
ROGER, ANY IDEA WHAT THIS STUFF IS?
THE FURNACE OF GURGUROTH. THE HAMMER AND ANVIL OF GROMM...
WHAT DOES IT MEAN?
THIS IS WHERE THE ANCIENTS BUILT THEIR WAR MACHINES...
THIS IS WHERE THE SLAVE REVOLT BEGAN...
LOWER YOUR VOICES, MY FRIENDS. I HEAR SOMETHING JUST AHEAD.

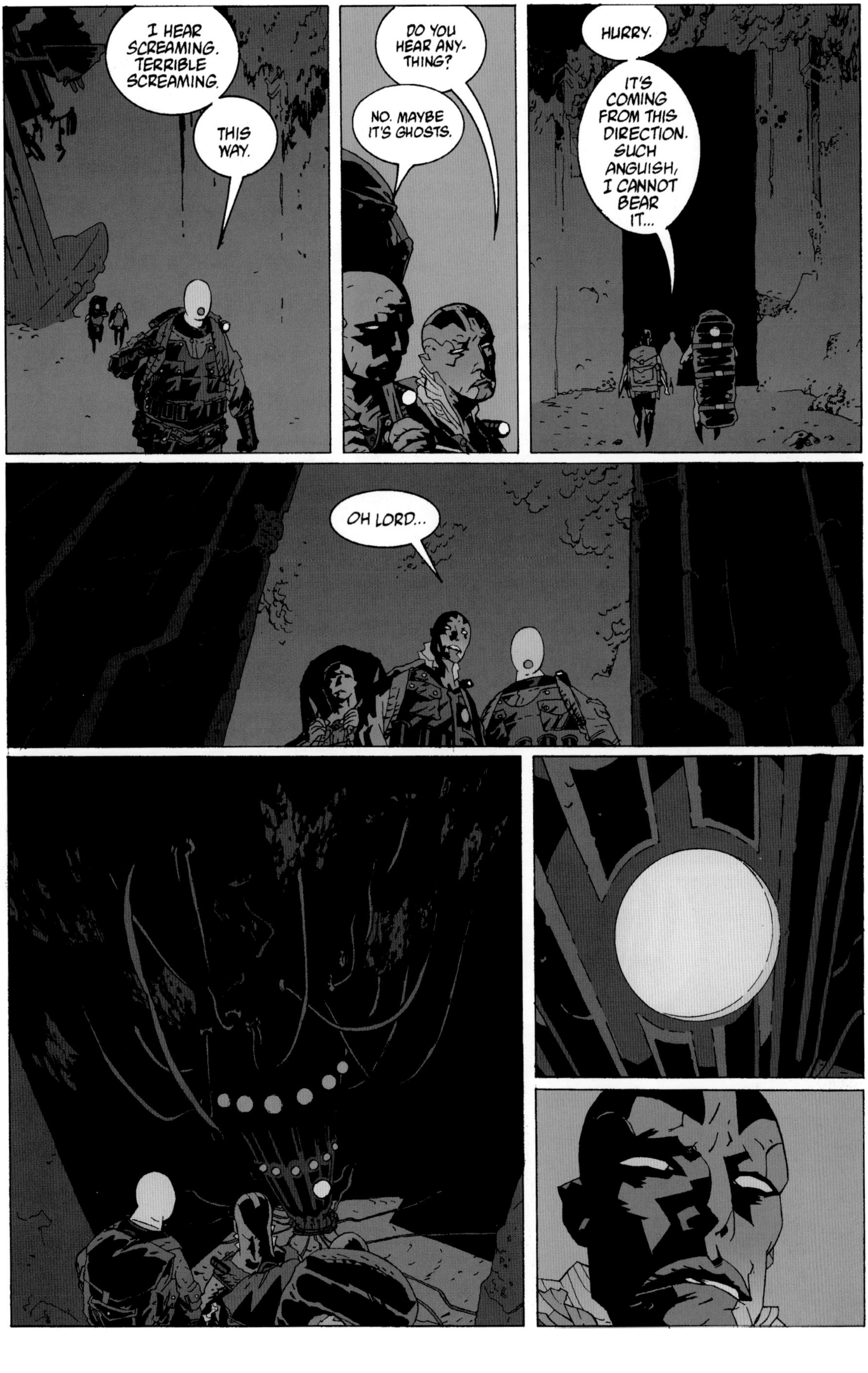
I HEAR SCREAMING. TERRIBLE SCREAMING.
THIS WAY.
DO YOU HEAR ANY-THING?
NO. MAYBE IT'S GHOSTS.
HURRY.
IT'S COMING FROM THIS DIRECTION. SUCH ANGUISH, I CANNOT BEAR IT...
OH LORD...

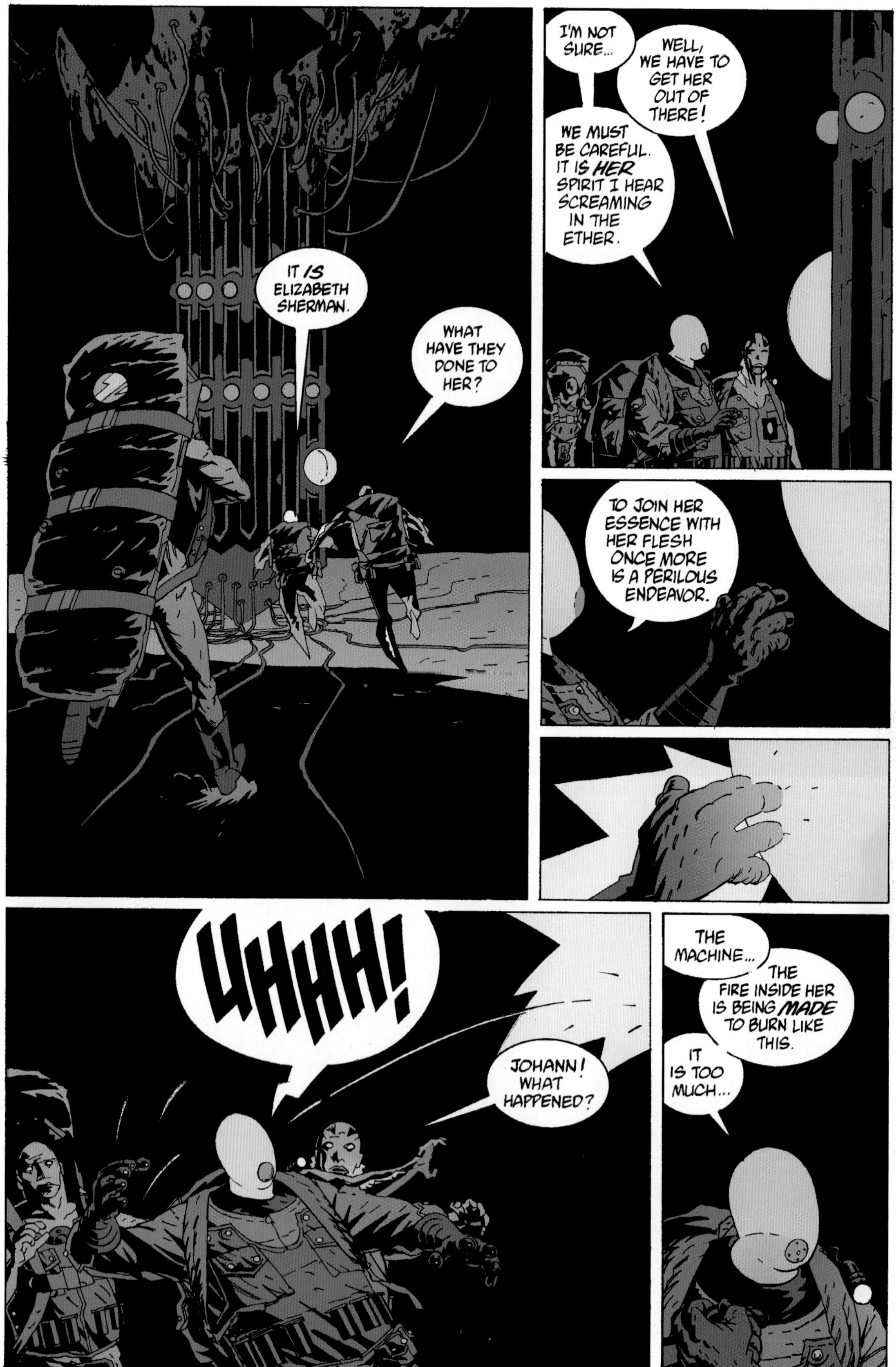
IT IS ELIZABETH SHERMAN.
WHAT HAVE THEY DONE TO HER?
I'M NOT SURE...
WE MUST BE CAREFUL. IT IS HER SPIRIT I HEAR SCREAMING IN THE ETHER.
WELL, WE HAVE TO GET HER OUT OF THERE!
TO JOIN HER ESSENCE WITH HER FLESH ONCE MORE IS A PERILOUS ENDEAVOR.
UHHH!
JOHANN! WHAT HAPPENED?
THE MACHINE...
THE FIRE INSIDE HER IS BEING MADE TO BURN LIKE THIS.
IT IS TOO MUCH...

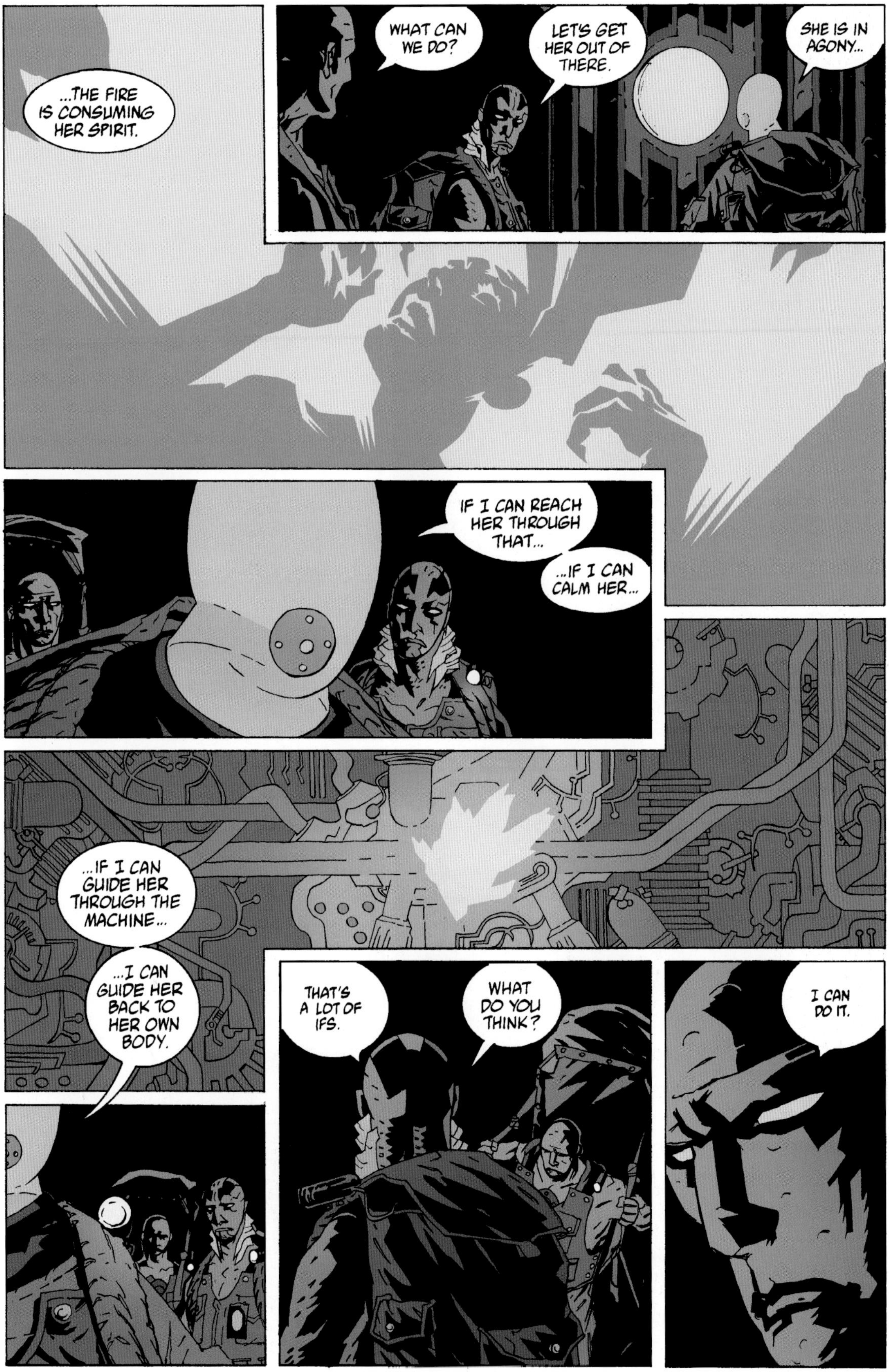
...THE FIRE IS CONSUMING HER SPIRIT.
WHAT CAN WE DO?
LET'S GET HER OUT OF THERE.
SHE IS IN AGONY...
IF I CAN REACH HER THROUGH THAT...
...IF I CAN CALM HER...
...IF I CAN GUIDE HER THROUGH THE MACHINE...
...I CAN GUIDE HER BACK TO HER OWN BODY.
THAT'S A LOT OF IFS.
WHAT DO YOU THINK?
I CAN DO IT.

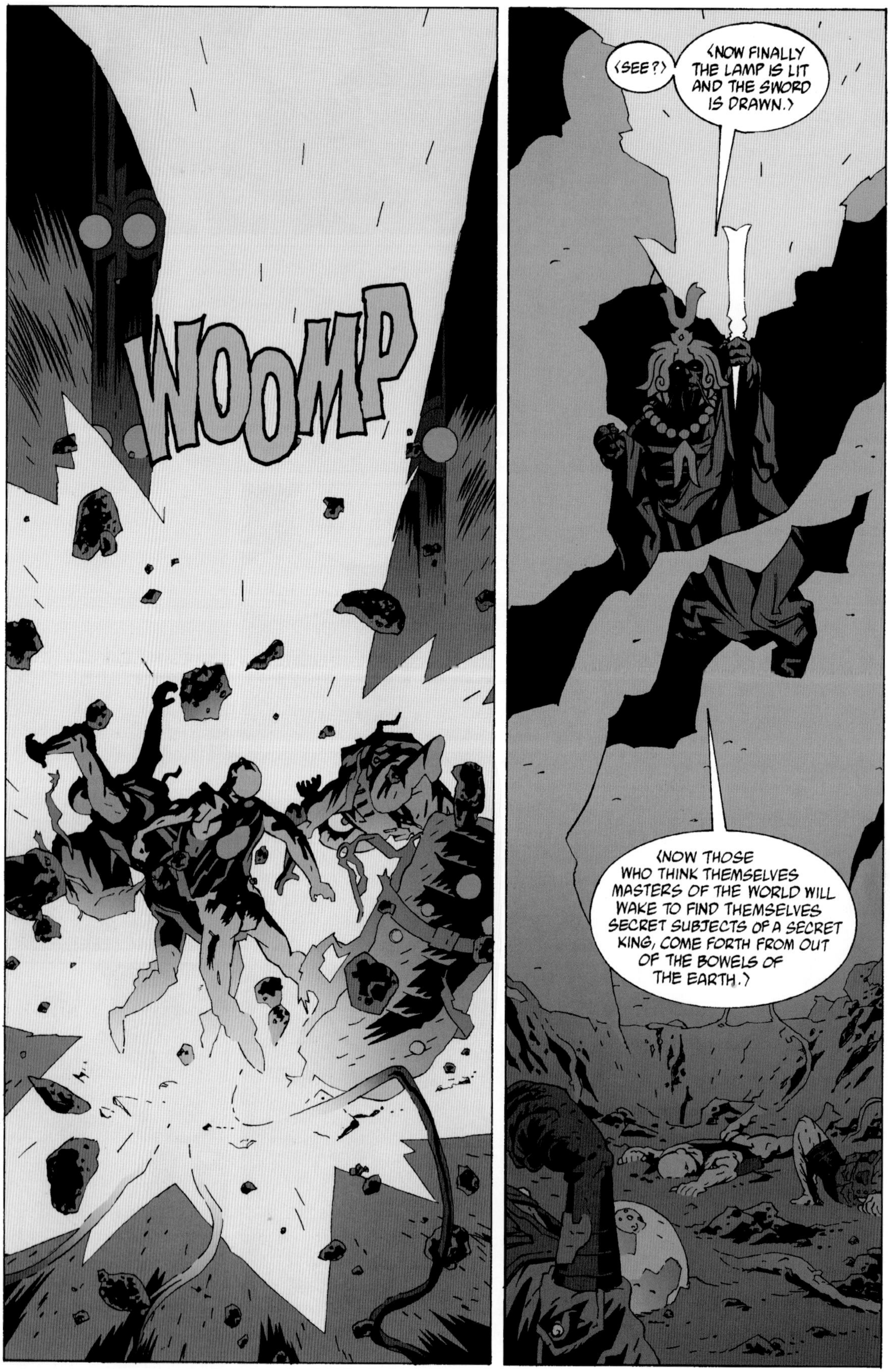
WOOMP
‹SEE?›
‹NOW FINALLY THE LAMP IS LIT AND THE SWORD IS DRAWN.›
‹NOW THOSE WHO THINK THEMSELVES MASTERS OF THE WORLD WILL WAKE TO FIND THEMSELVES SECRET SUBJECTS OF A SECRET KING, COME FORTH FROM OUT OF THE BOWELS OF THE EARTH.›

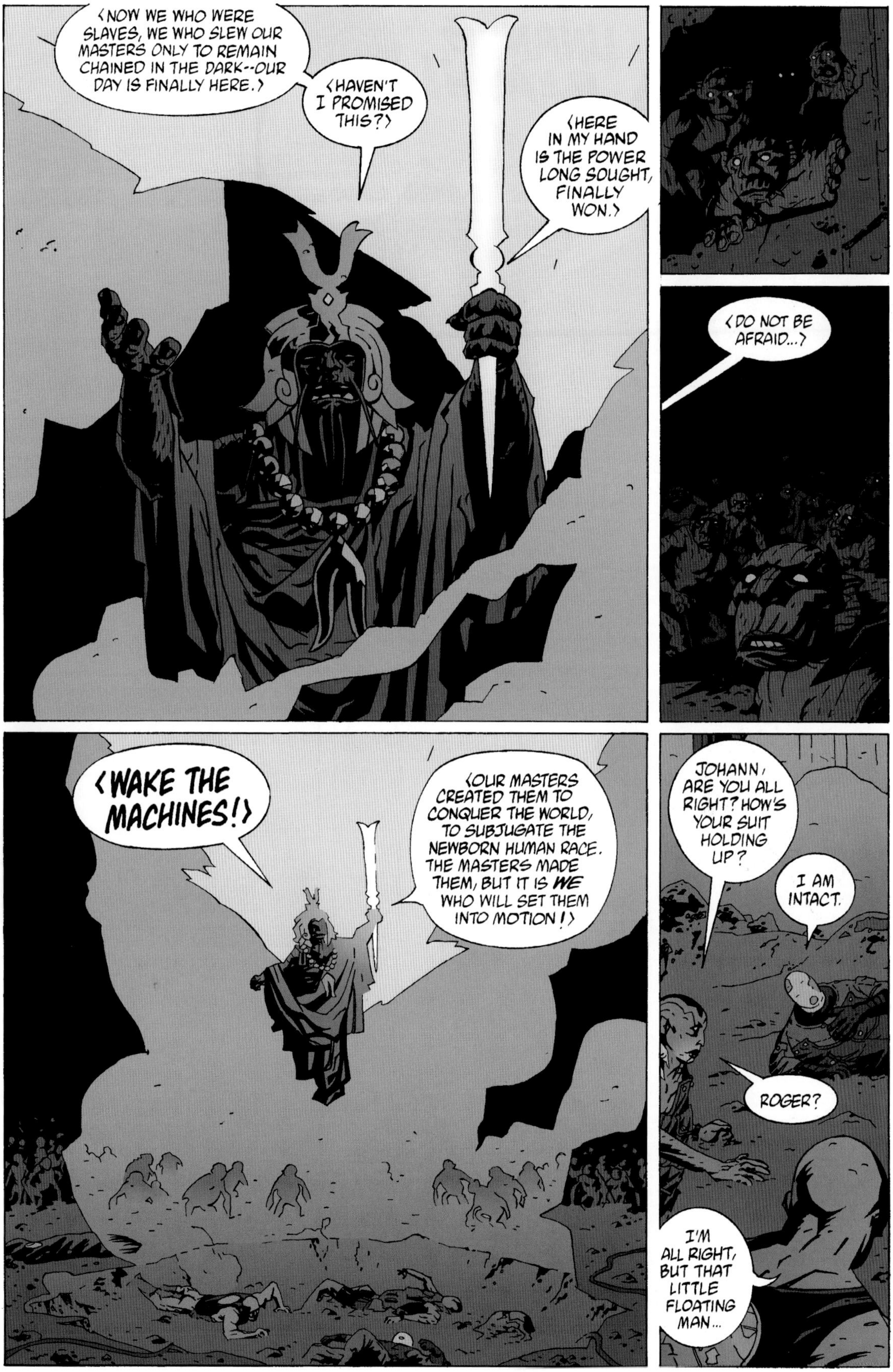
‹NOW WE WHO WERE SLAVES, WE WHO SLEW OUR MASTERS ONLY TO REMAIN CHAINED IN THE DARK--OUR DAY IS FINALLY HERE.›
‹HAVEN'T I PROMISED THIS?›
‹HERE IN MY HAND IS THE POWER LONG SOUGHT, FINALLY WON.›
‹DO NOT BE AFRAID...›
‹WAKE THE MACHINES!›
‹OUR MASTERS CREATED THEM TO CONQUER THE WORLD, TO SUBJUGATE THE NEWBORN HUMAN RACE. THE MASTERS MADE THEM, BUT IT IS WE WHO WILL SET THEM INTO MOTION!›
JOHANN, ARE YOU ALL RIGHT? HOW'S YOUR SUIT HOLDING UP?
I AM INTACT.
ROGER?
I'M ALL RIGHT, BUT THAT LITTLE FLOATING MAN...

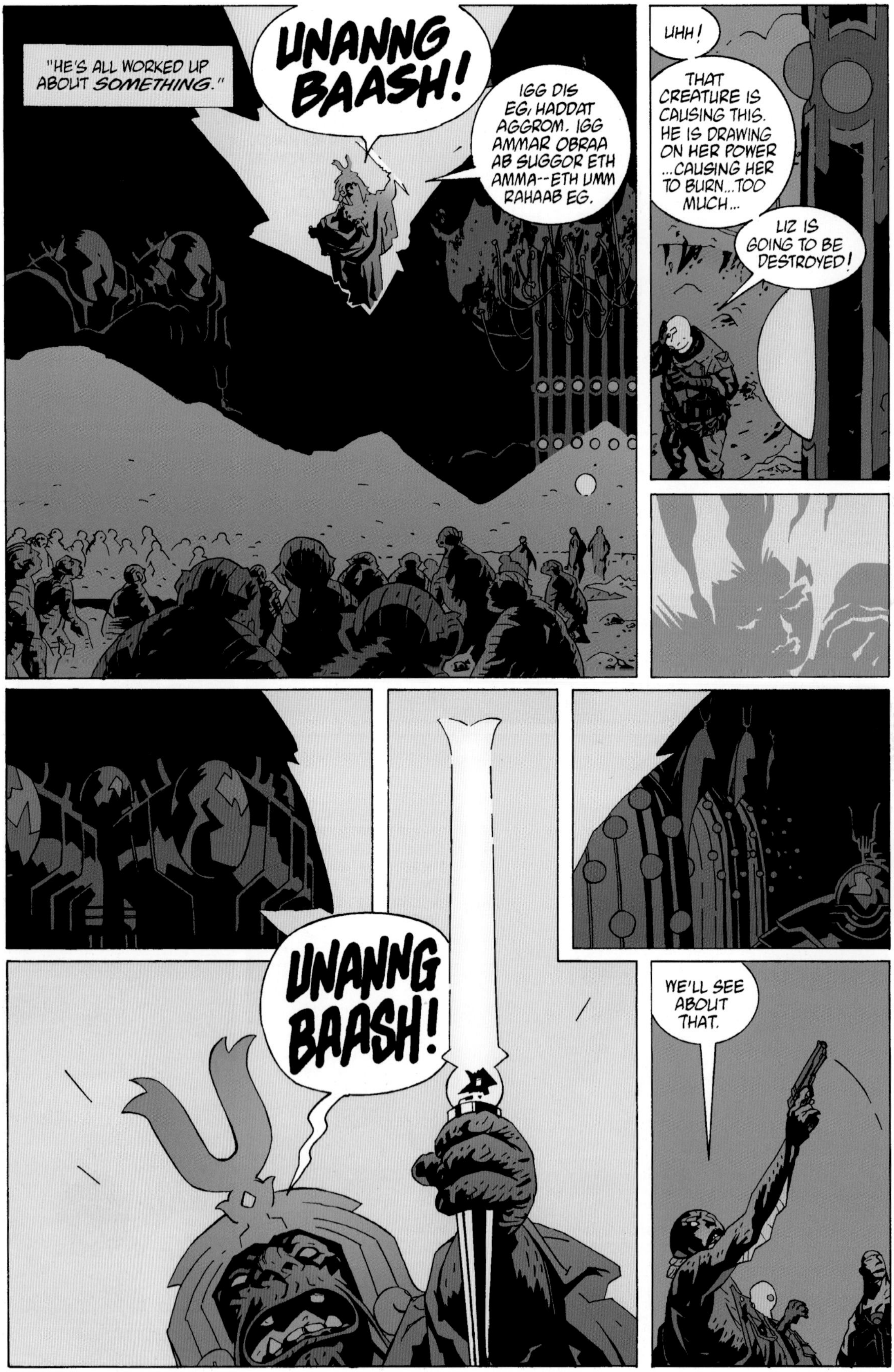
"HE'S ALL WORKED UP ABOUT *SOMETHING*."
UNANNG BAASH!
IGG DIS EG, HADDAT AGGROM. IGG AMMAR OBRAA AB SUGGOR ETH AMMA--ETH UMM RAHAAB EG.
UHH!
THAT CREATURE IS CAUSING THIS. HE IS DRAWING ON HER POWER ...CAUSING HER TO BURN...TOO MUCH...
LIZ IS GOING TO BE DESTROYED!
UNANNG BAASH!
WE'LL SEE ABOUT THAT.

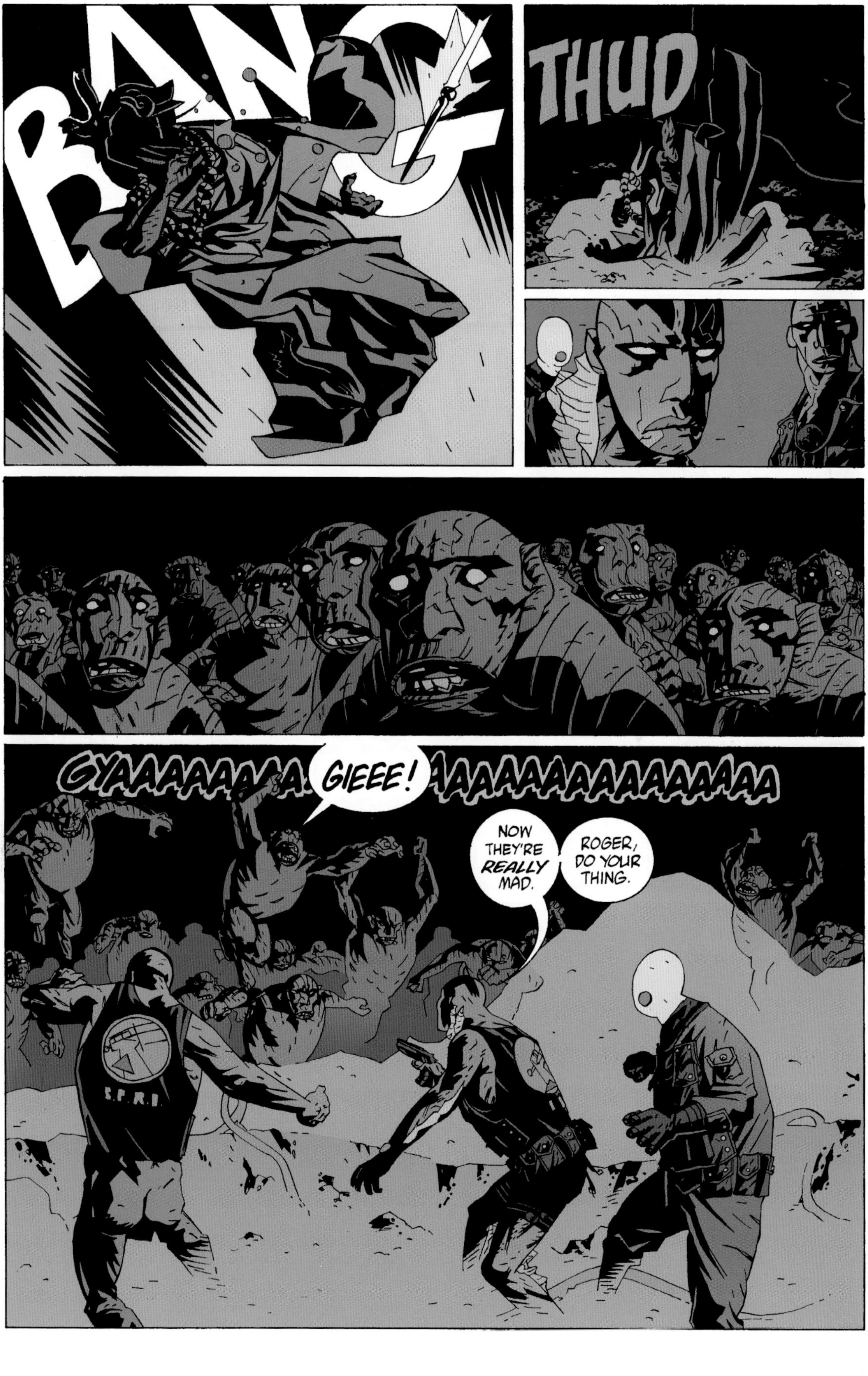
BANG
THUD
GYAAAAAAAAAAAAAAAAAAAAAAAAAA
GIEEE!
NOW THEY'RE *REALLY* MAD.
ROGER, DO YOUR THING.

AAAAAAAAAAAAA

AAHHHHH

YAI
YAI YAI

SPOOSH!

ROGER--

I KNOW.

GYAA

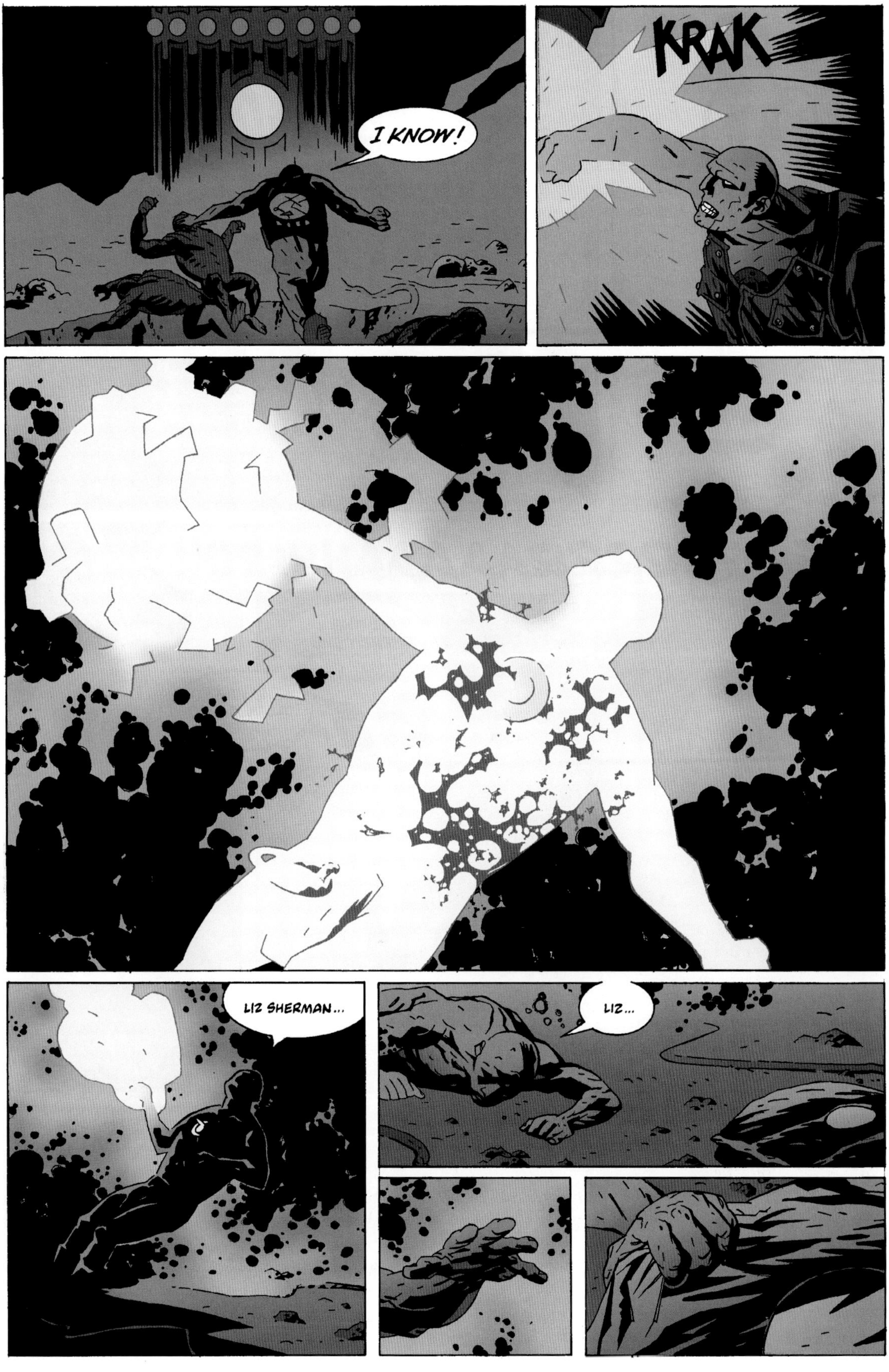
I KNOW!
KRAK
LIZ SHERMAN...
LIZ...

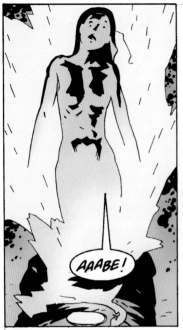

AAABE!

ROGER?

...

ERRRRRRRAAAAAHHHHH!

ROGER?

YAI YAI YAI

ALL THE ENERGY SHE WAS FORCED TO GENERATE...

HE HAS TAKEN IT INTO HIMSELF.

ROGER! DUMP IT!

DUMP IT INTO THE GROUND!

WAM

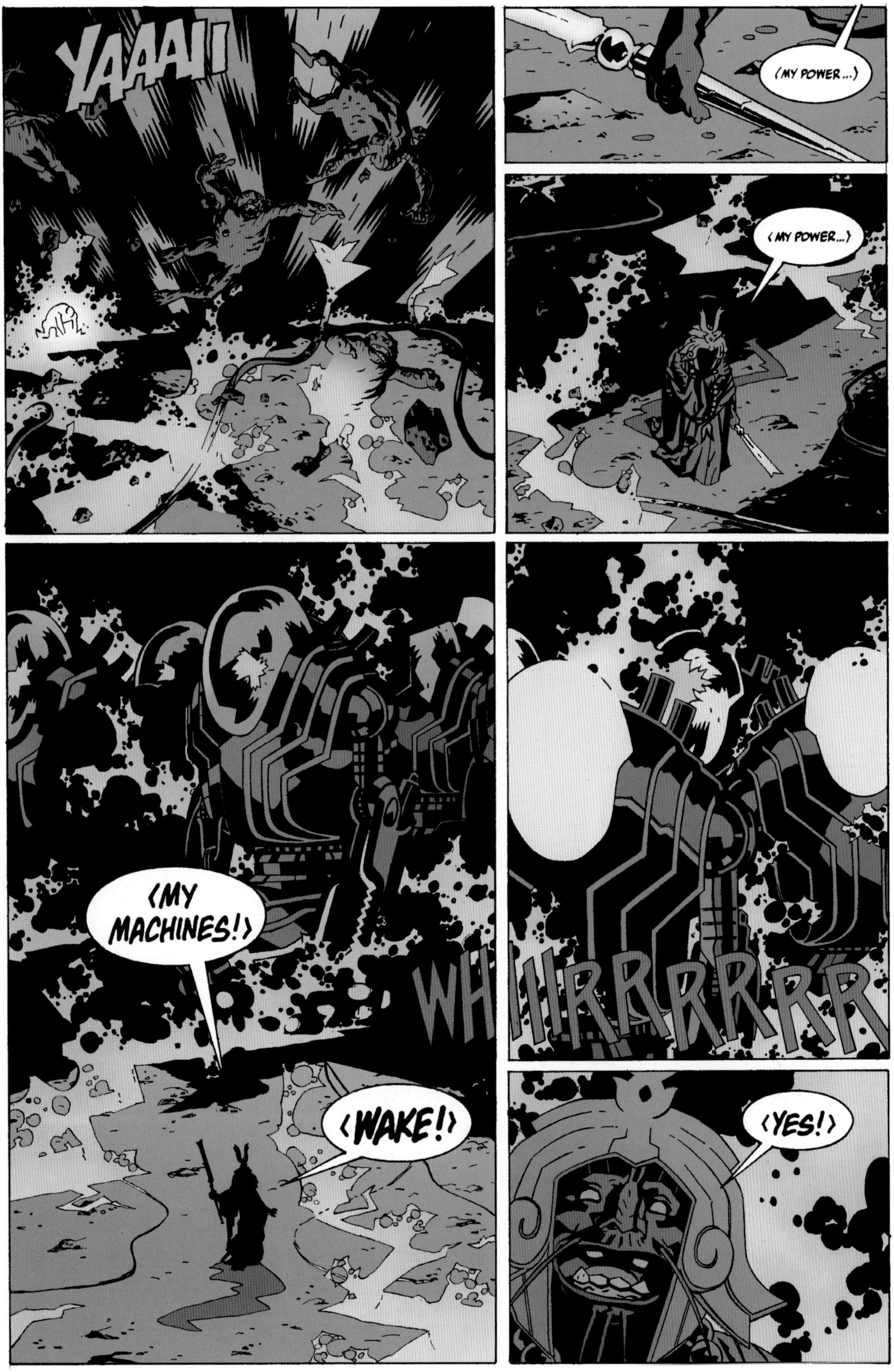
YAAAII
(MY POWER...)
(MY POWER...)
(MY MACHINES!)
(WAKE!)
WHIIRRRRRR
(YES!)

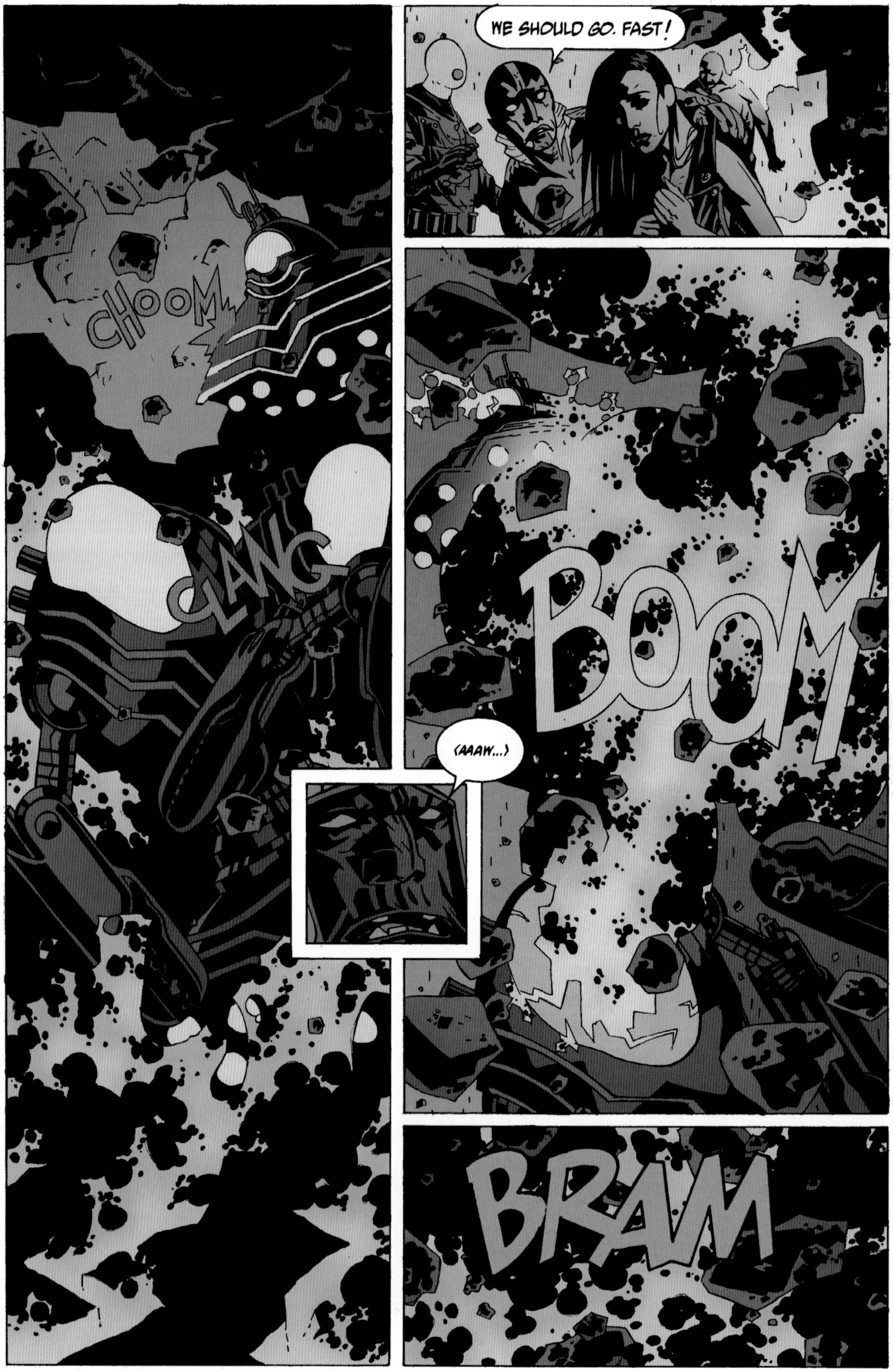
CHOOM
CLANG
WE SHOULD GO. FAST!
BOOM
(AAAW...)
BRAM

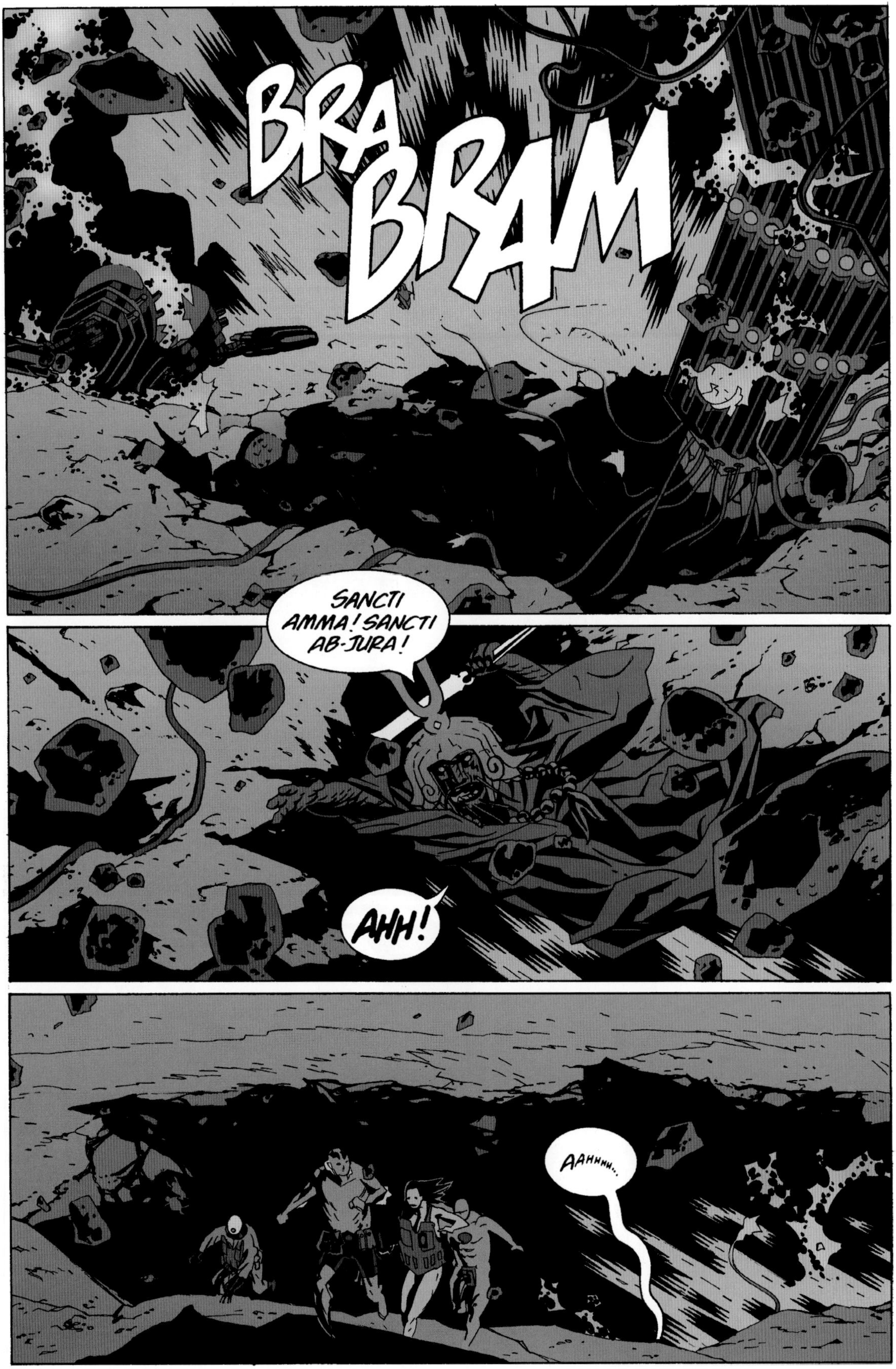
BRA
BRAM
SANCTI AMMA! SANCTI AB-JURA!
AHH!
AAHHHH..

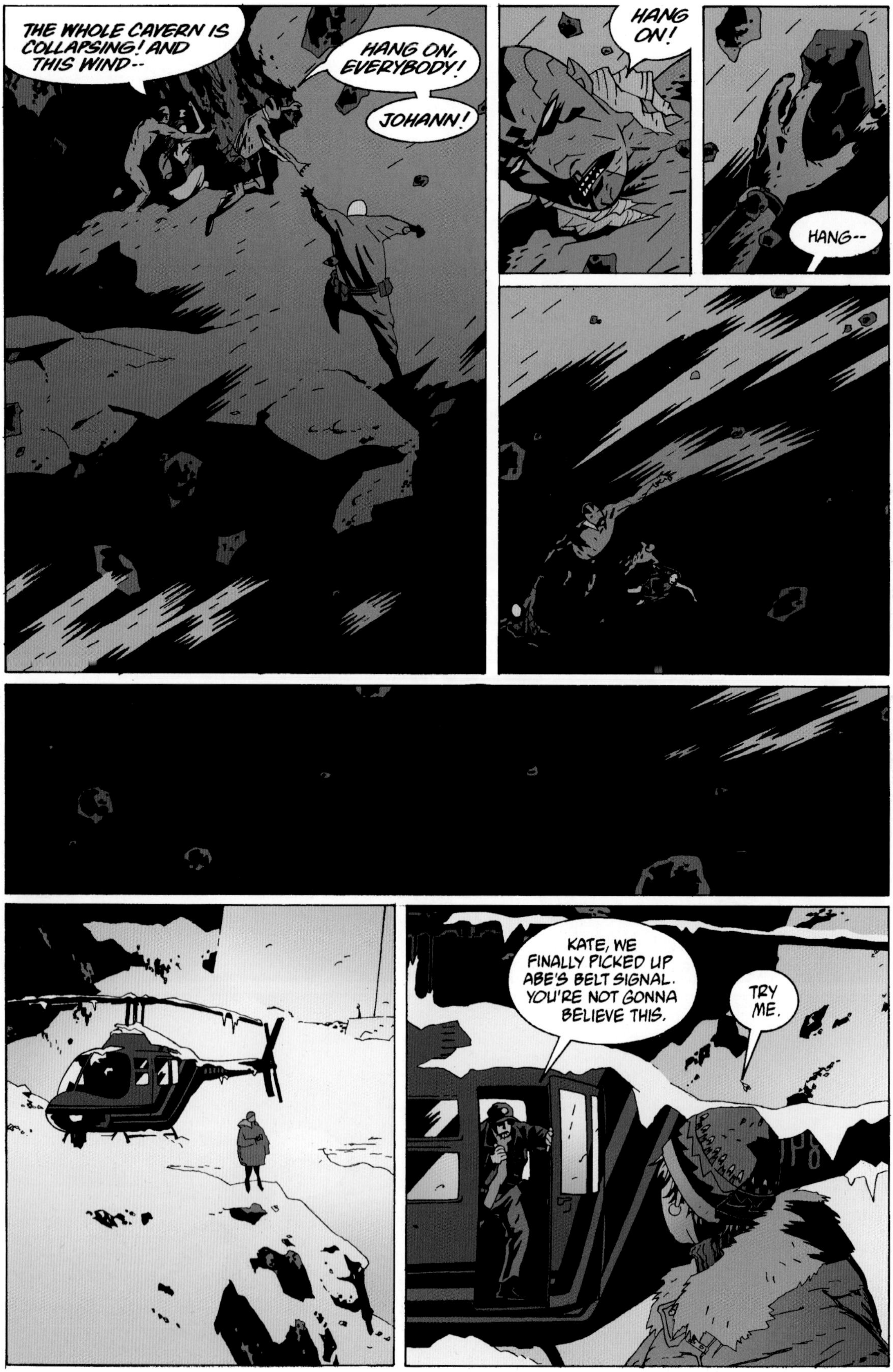
THE WHOLE CAVERN IS COLLAPSING! AND THIS WIND--
HANG ON, EVERYBODY!
JOHANN!
HANG ON!
HANG--
KATE, WE FINALLY PICKED UP ABE'S BELT SIGNAL. YOU'RE NOT GONNA BELIEVE THIS.
TRY ME.

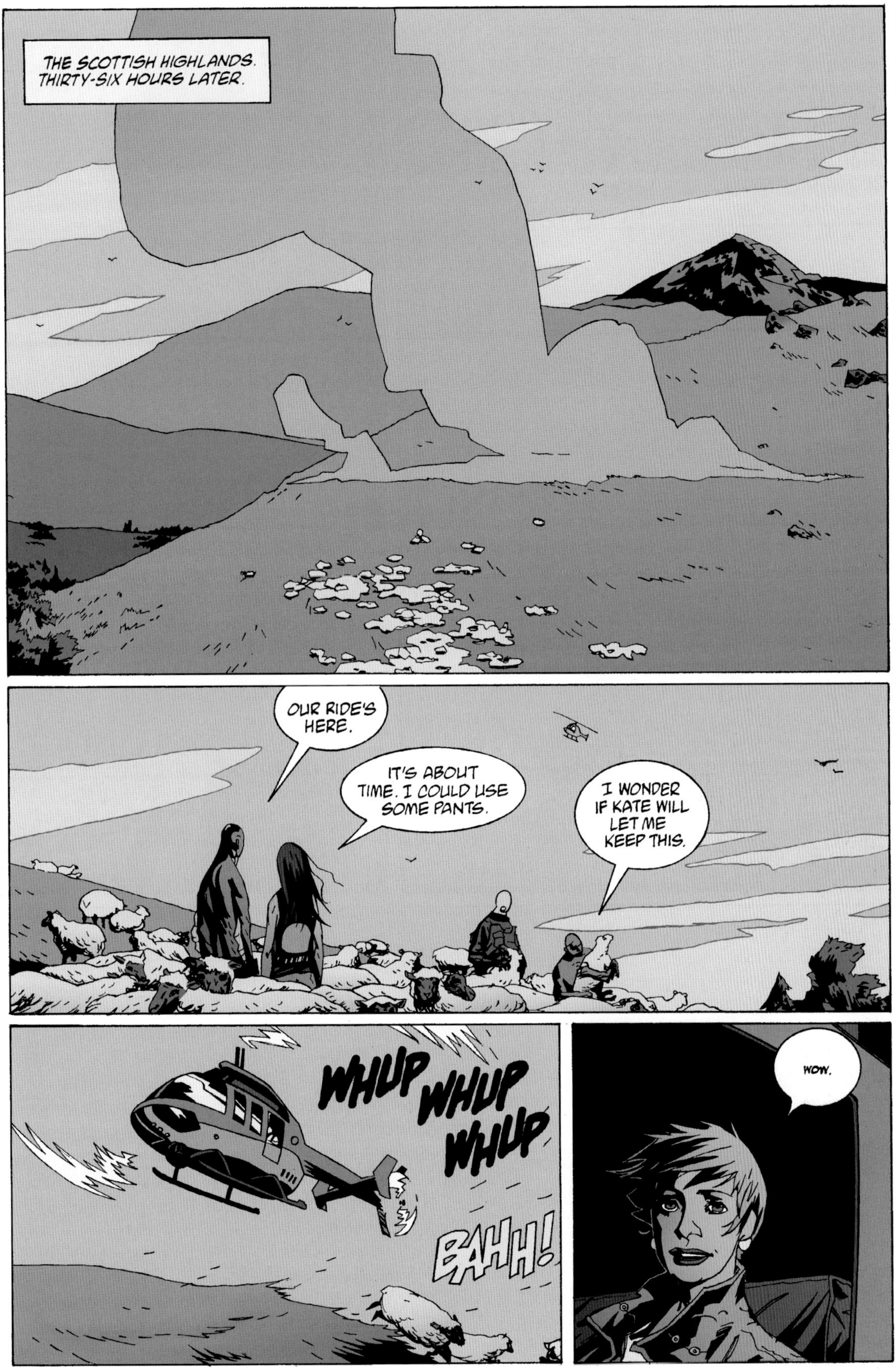
THE SCOTTISH HIGHLANDS.
THIRTY-SIX HOURS LATER.
OUR RIDE'S HERE.
IT'S ABOUT TIME. I COULD USE SOME PANTS.
I WONDER IF KATE WILL LET ME KEEP THIS.
WHUP WHUP WHUP
BAHH!
WOW.

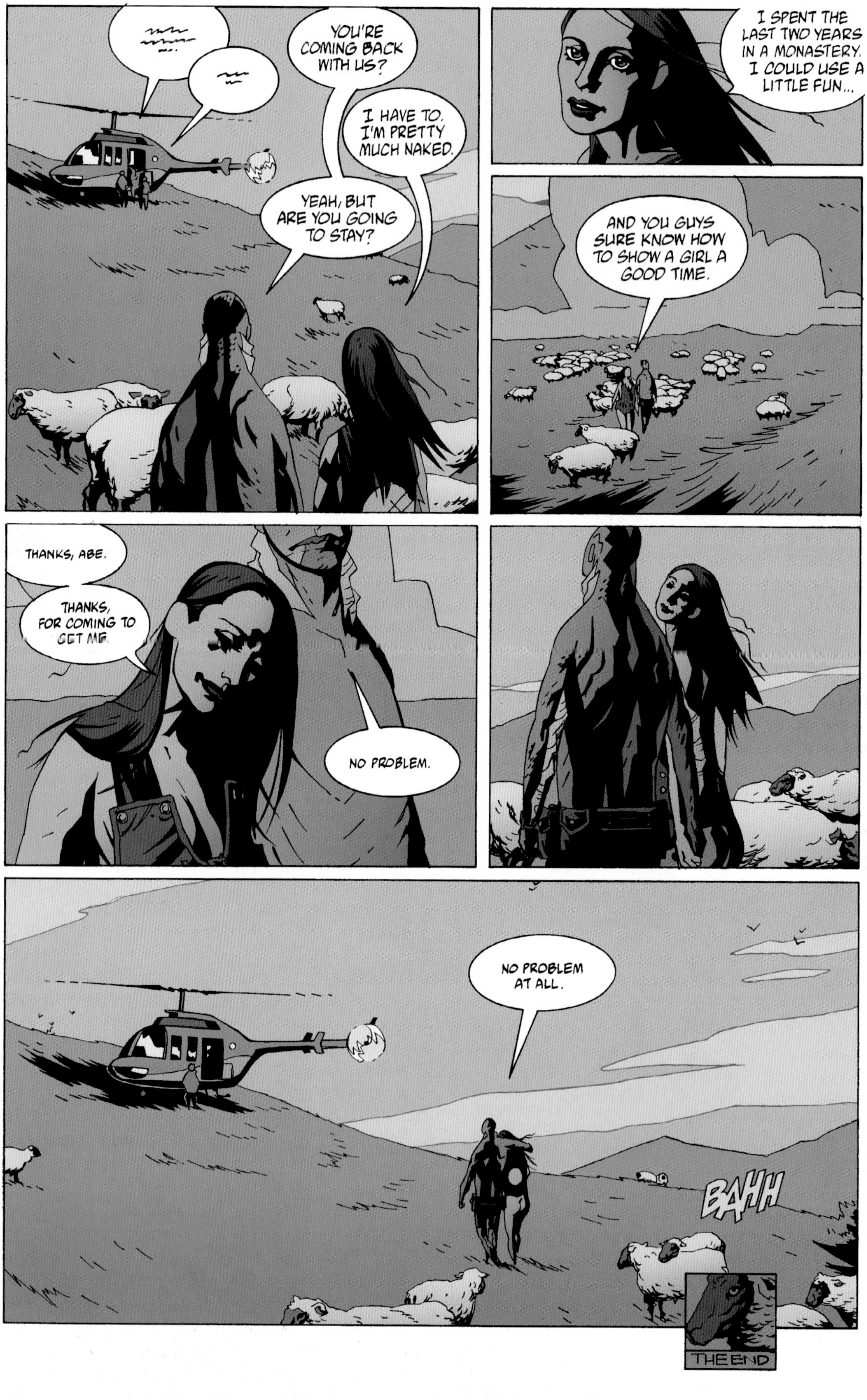
YOU'RE COMING BACK WITH US?
I HAVE TO. I'M PRETTY MUCH NAKED.
YEAH, BUT ARE YOU GOING TO STAY?
I SPENT THE LAST TWO YEARS IN A MONASTERY. I COULD USE A LITTLE FUN...
AND YOU GUYS SURE KNOW HOW TO SHOW A GIRL A GOOD TIME.
THANKS, ABE.
THANKS, FOR COMING TO GET ME.
NO PROBLEM.
NO PROBLEM AT ALL.
BAHH
THE END

HOLLOW EARTH

Mike Mignola had always wanted to expand the world of *Hellboy*, and this collection presents the first efforts in that direction. The preceding story came about after much consideration about what to do with the Bureau after Hellboy's departure. Artist Ryan Sook, who Mike had met at an Oakland, California convention in 1995, had been the clear choice for artist. *Hellboy* novelist Christopher Golden, with his long-time writing partner Tom Sniegoski, pitched the *Hollow Earth* concept, and with its implicit connections to Nazi paranormal research, everything fell into place. Mike contributed ideas for the overall plot, and the ending shows his influence very strongly. After a run on DC's monthly *Spectre* series, Ryan saw *B.P.R.D.* as a chance to have a book all to himself, working with his favorite colorist, Dave Stewart. When schedules became tight, halfway through the story, Curtis Arnold joined the team as inker.

The series came out from January 2002 to June 2002. The following three-page teaser ran in the newspaper-format *Dark Horse Extra* from December 2001 to February 2002. Lettering for the teaser was done by Dan Jackson.

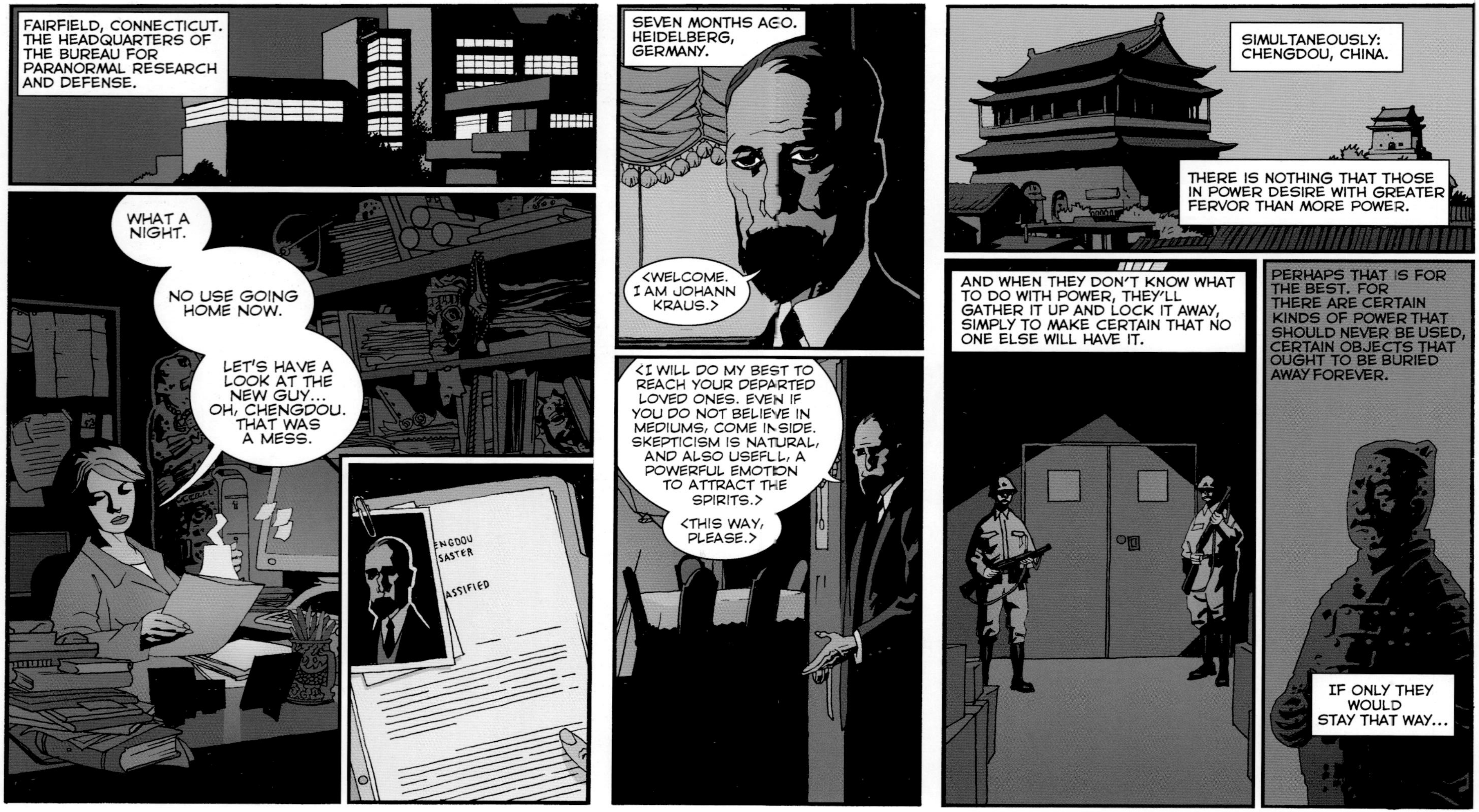
FAIRFIELD, CONNECTICUT. THE HEADQUARTERS OF THE BUREAU FOR PARANORMAL RESEARCH AND DEFENSE.
WHAT A NIGHT.
NO USE GOING HOME NOW.
LET'S HAVE A LOOK AT THE NEW GUY... OH, CHENGDOU. THAT WAS A MESS.
ENGDOU
SASTER
ASSIFIED
SEVEN MONTHS AGO. HEIDELBERG, GERMANY.
<WELCOME. I AM JOHANN KRAUS.>
<I WILL DO MY BEST TO REACH YOUR DEPARTED LOVED ONES. EVEN IF YOU DO NOT BELIEVE IN MEDIUMS, COME INSIDE. SKEPTICISM IS NATURAL, AND ALSO USEFLL, A POWERFUL EMOTION TO ATTRACT THE SPIRITS.>
<THIS WAY, PLEASE.>
SIMULTANEOUSLY: CHENGDOU, CHINA.
THERE IS NOTHING THAT THOSE IN POWER DESIRE WITH GREATER FERVOR THAN MORE POWER.
AND WHEN THEY DON'T KNOW WHAT TO DO WITH POWER, THEY'LL GATHER IT UP AND LOCK IT AWAY, SIMPLY TO MAKE CERTAIN THAT NO ONE ELSE WILL HAVE IT.
PERHAPS THAT IS FOR THE BEST. FOR THERE ARE CERTAIN KINDS OF POWER THAT SHOULD NEVER BE USED, CERTAIN OBJECTS THAT OUGHT TO BE BURIED AWAY FOREVER.
IF ONLY THEY WOULD STAY THAT WAY...

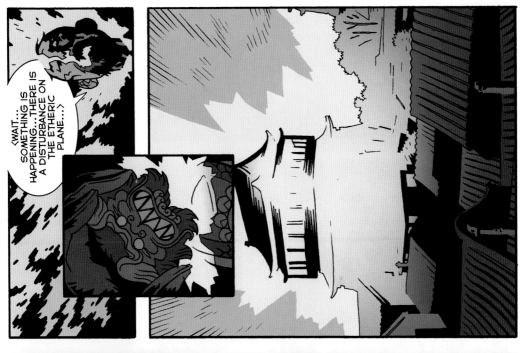

‹WAIT... SOMETHING IS HAPPENING...THERE IS A DISTURBANCE ON THE ETHERIC PLANE...›

AT THAT MOMENT, IN CHENGDOU, CHINA...

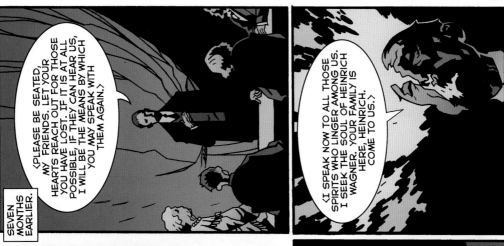

SEVEN MONTHS EARLIER.

‹PLEASE BE SEATED, MY FRIENDS. LET YOUR HEARTS REACH OUT FOR THOSE YOU HAVE LOST. IF IT IS AT ALL POSSIBLE, IF THEY CAN HEAR US, I WILL BE THE MEANS BY WHICH YOU MAY SPEAK WITH THEM AGAIN.›

‹I SPEAK NOW TO ALL THOSE SPIRITS WHO LINGER AMONG US. I SEEK THE SOUL OF HEINRICH WAGNER. YOUR FAMILY IS HERE, HEINRICH. COME TO US.›

A GENUINE PHYSICAL MEDIUM. THAT'S RARE ENOUGH.

POOR BASTARD. HE WAS JUST DOING HIS JOB.

‹JOIN HANDS. WE MUST CREATE A PHYSICAL CIRCUIT, A BEACON TO THOSE NOW DEPARTED.›

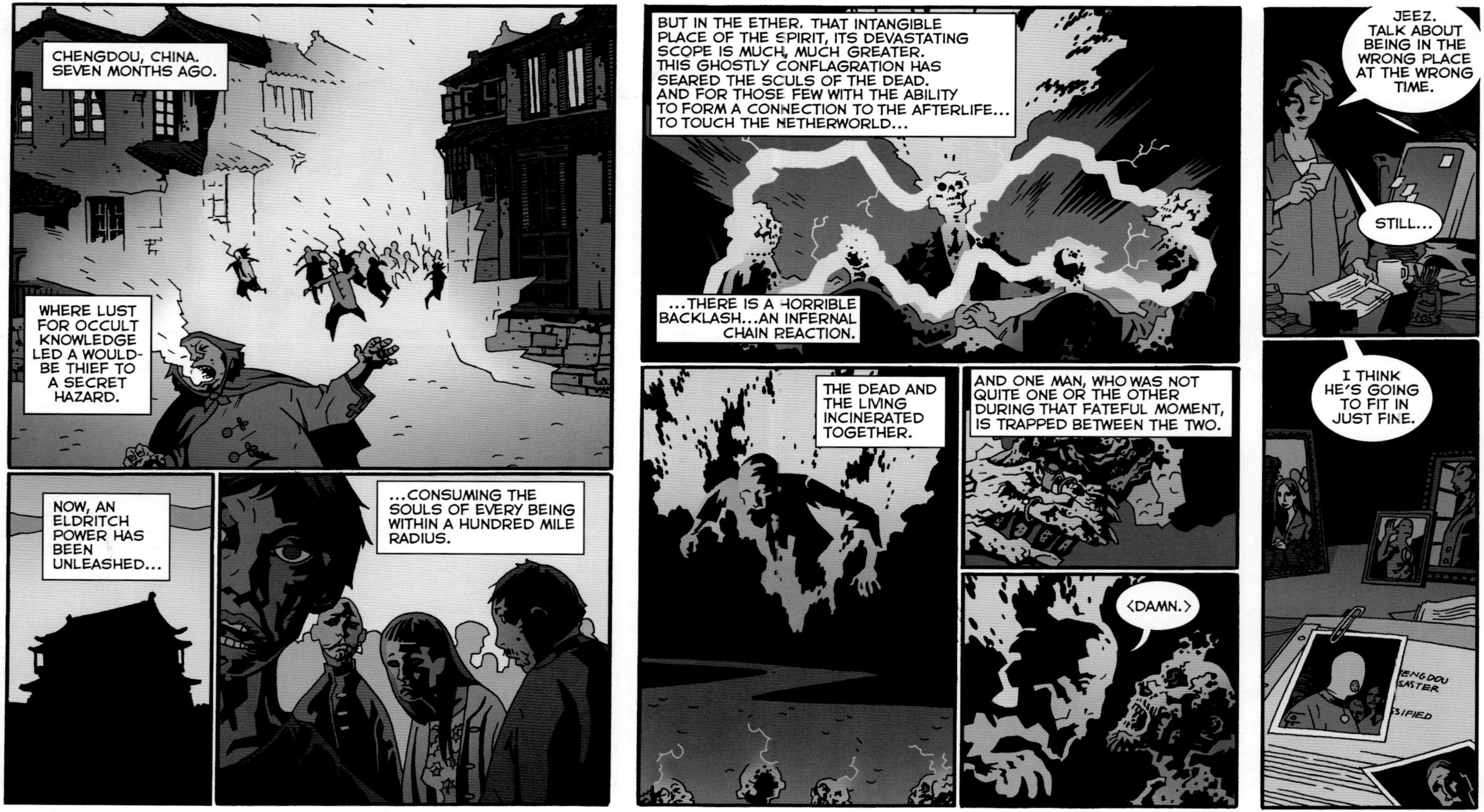
CHENGDOU, CHINA. SEVEN MONTHS AGO.
WHERE LUST FOR OCCULT KNOWLEDGE LED A WOULD-BE THIEF TO A SECRET HAZARD.
NOW, AN ELDRITCH POWER HAS BEEN UNLEASHED...
...CONSUMING THE SOULS OF EVERY BEING WITHIN A HUNDRED MILE RADIUS.
BUT IN THE ETHER. THAT INTANGIBLE PLACE OF THE SPIRIT, ITS DEVASTATING SCOPE IS MUCH, MUCH GREATER. THIS GHOSTLY CONFLAGRATION HAS SEARED THE SOULS OF THE DEAD. AND FOR THOSE FEW WITH THE ABILITY TO FORM A CONNECTION TO THE AFTERLIFE... TO TOUCH THE NETHERWORLD...
...THERE IS A HORRIBLE BACKLASH...AN INFERNAL CHAIN REACTION.
THE DEAD AND THE LIVING INCINERATED TOGETHER.
AND ONE MAN, WHO WAS NOT QUITE ONE OR THE OTHER DURING THAT FATEFUL MOMENT, IS TRAPPED BETWEEN THE TWO.
<DAMN.>
JEEZ. TALK ABOUT BEING IN THE WRONG PLACE AT THE WRONG TIME.
STILL...
I THINK HE'S GOING TO FIT IN JUST FINE.
the end

The Killer
In My Skull

Story by
MIKE MIGNOLA

Pencils by
MATT SMITH

Inks by
RYAN SOOK

Colors by
DAVE STEWART

Letters by
PAT BROSSEAU

Abe Sapien
Versus Science

Story by
MIKE MIGNOLA

Pencils by
MATT SMITH

Inks by
MIKE MIGNOLA

Colors by
DAVE STEWART

Letters by
PAT BROSSEAU

The Killer
In My Skull

This backup to Mike's *Box Full of Evil* (1999) featured the first appearance of Lobster Johnson, a character who became a sudden favorite among *Hellboy* fans, and returned to play a significant if not mystifying part in the next big series, *Conqueror Worm*. Had there been a *BPRD* in the thirties, Lobster Johnson would no doubt have been a member. Ryan's work on inks here was his first contribution to a *Hellboy* comic.

Abe Sapien
Versus Science

The backup to the second issue of *Box Full of Evil* provided more insight into the popular fishman's character than any story to date, but mainly served to reanimate Roger the Homunculus in time for *Conqueror Worm* and *Hollow Earth*.

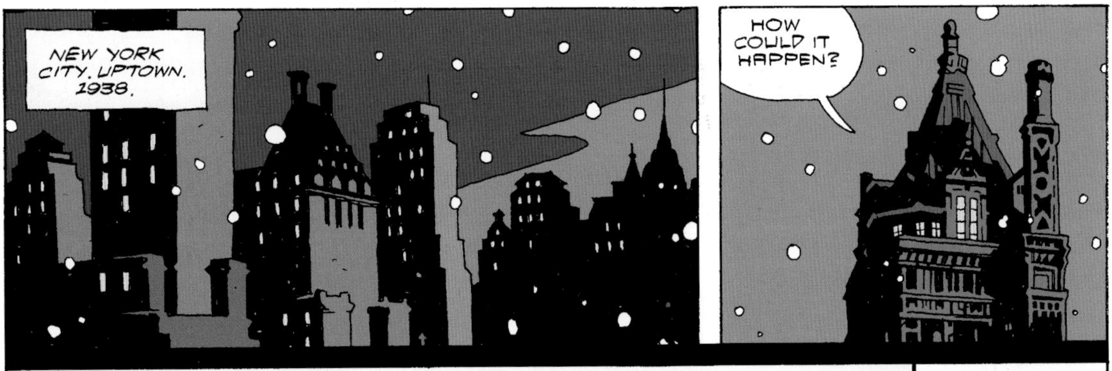
NEW YORK CITY. UPTOWN. 1938.
HOW COULD IT HAPPEN?

The Killer in My Skull

Introducing **LOBSTER JOHNSON**

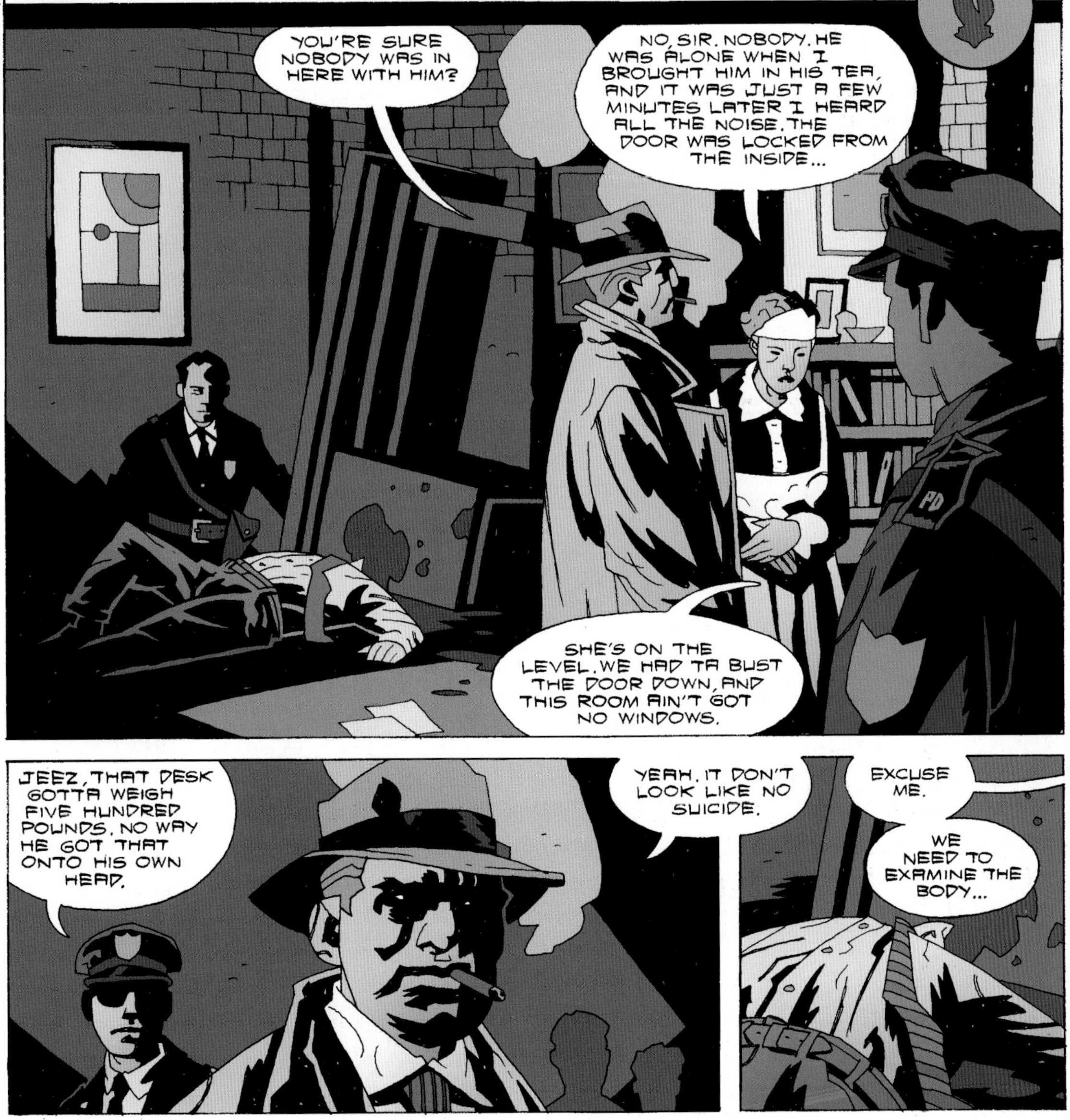
YOU'RE SURE NOBODY WAS IN HERE WITH HIM?
NO, SIR. NOBODY. HE WAS ALONE WHEN I BROUGHT HIM IN HIS TEA, AND IT WAS JUST A FEW MINUTES LATER I HEARD ALL THE NOISE. THE DOOR WAS LOCKED FROM THE INSIDE...
SHE'S ON THE LEVEL. WE HAD TA BUST THE DOOR DOWN, AND THIS ROOM AIN'T GOT NO WINDOWS.
JEEZ, THAT DESK GOTTA WEIGH FIVE HUNDRED POUNDS. NO WAY HE GOT THAT ONTO HIS OWN HEAD.
YEAH. IT DON'T LOOK LIKE NO SUICIDE.
EXCUSE ME.
WE NEED TO EXAMINE THE BODY...

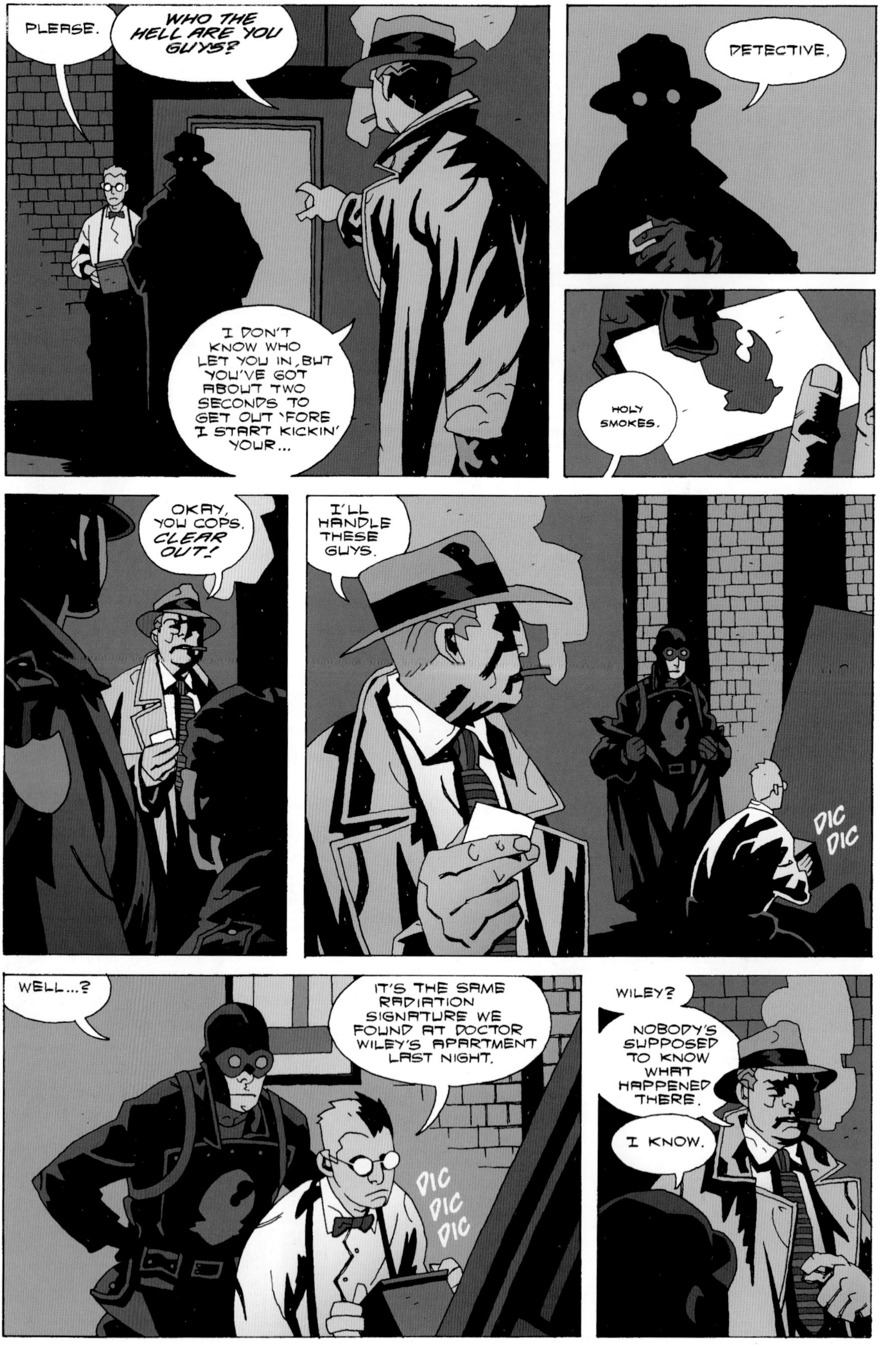
PLEASE.
WHO THE HELL ARE YOU GUYS?
I DON'T KNOW WHO LET YOU IN, BUT YOU'VE GOT ABOUT TWO SECONDS TO GET OUT 'FORE I START KICKIN' YOUR...
DETECTIVE.
HOLY SMOKES.
OKAY, YOU COPS. CLEAR OUT!
I'LL HANDLE THESE GUYS.
DIC DIC
WELL...?
IT'S THE SAME RADIATION SIGNATURE WE FOUND AT DOCTOR WILEY'S APARTMENT LAST NIGHT.
DIC DIC DIC
WILEY?
NOBODY'S SUPPOSED TO KNOW WHAT HAPPENED THERE.
I KNOW.

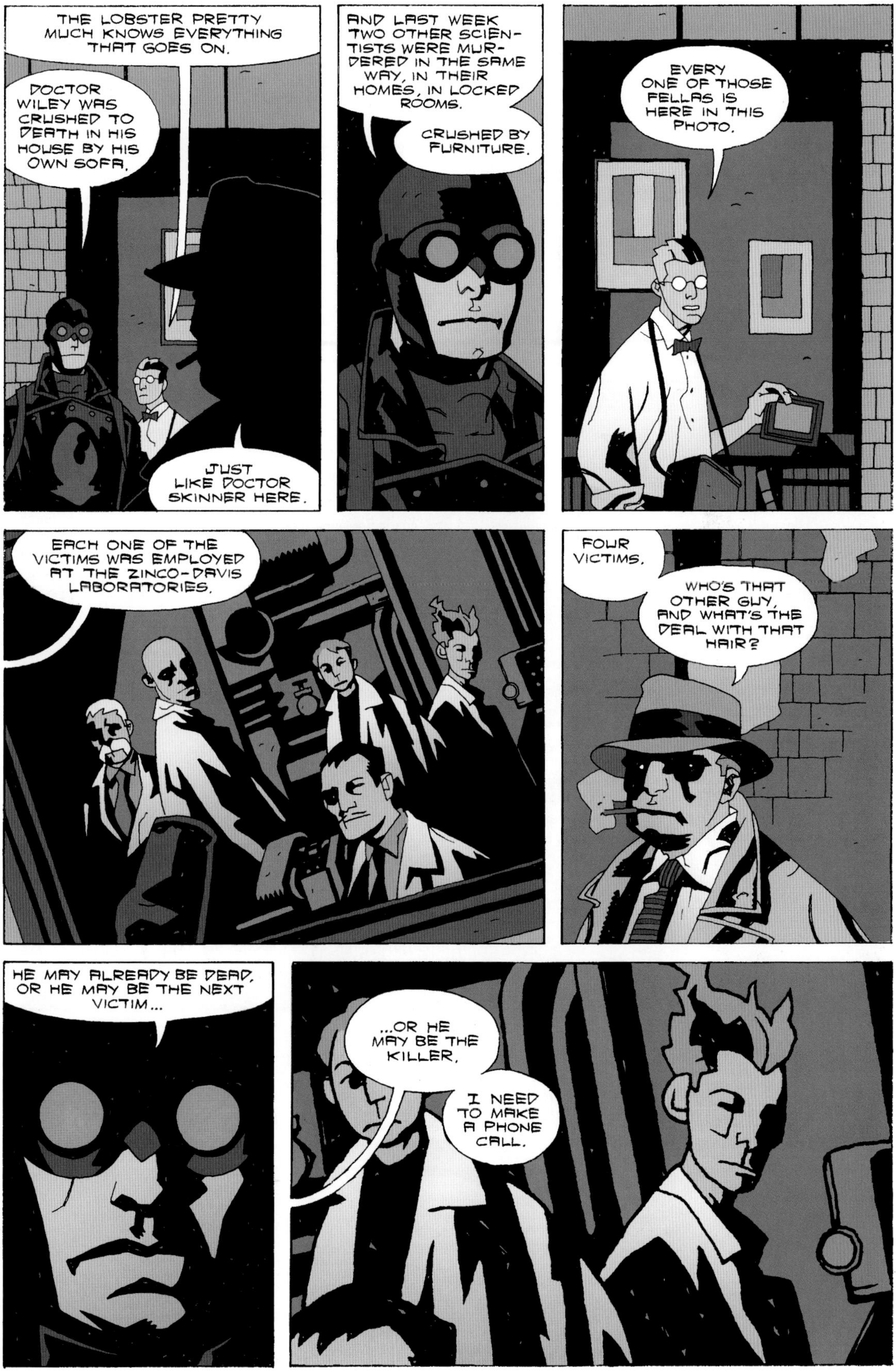
THE LOBSTER PRETTY MUCH KNOWS EVERYTHING THAT GOES ON.
DOCTOR WILEY WAS CRUSHED TO DEATH IN HIS HOUSE BY HIS OWN SOFA.
JUST LIKE DOCTOR SKINNER HERE.
AND LAST WEEK TWO OTHER SCIEN-TISTS WERE MUR-DERED IN THE SAME WAY, IN THEIR HOMES, IN LOCKED ROOMS.
CRUSHED BY FURNITURE.
EVERY ONE OF THOSE FELLAS IS HERE IN THIS PHOTO.
EACH ONE OF THE VICTIMS WAS EMPLOYED AT THE ZINCO-DAVIS LABORATORIES.
FOUR VICTIMS.
WHO'S THAT OTHER GUY, AND WHAT'S THE DEAL WITH THAT HAIR?
HE MAY ALREADY BE DEAD, OR HE MAY BE THE NEXT VICTIM...
...OR HE MAY BE THE KILLER.
I NEED TO MAKE A PHONE CALL.

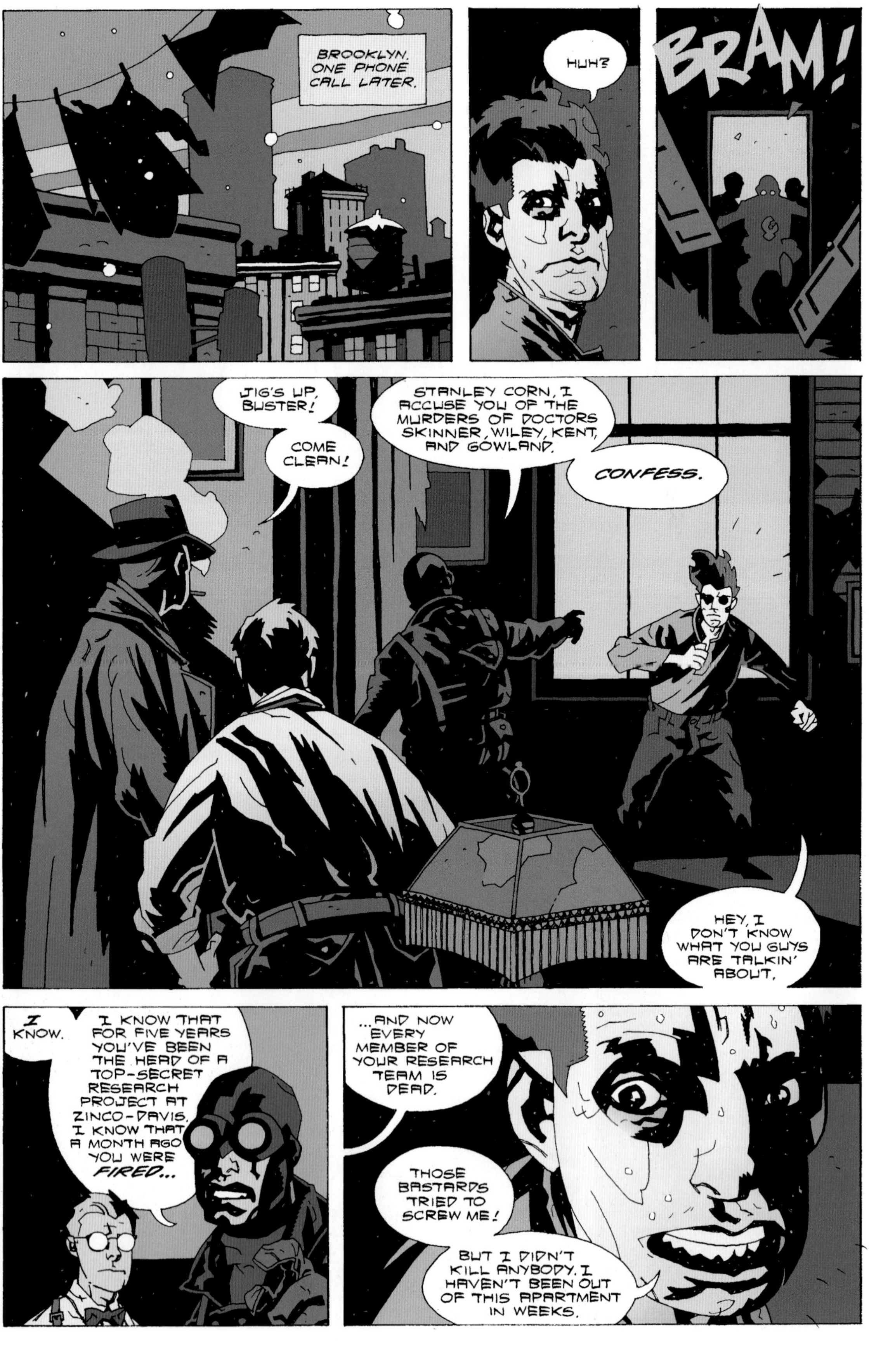
BROOKLYN. ONE PHONE CALL LATER.
HUH?
BRAM!
JIG'S UP, BUSTER!
COME CLEAN!
STANLEY CORN, I ACCUSE YOU OF THE MURDERS OF DOCTORS SKINNER, WILEY, KENT, AND GOWLAND.
CONFESS.
HEY, I DON'T KNOW WHAT YOU GUYS ARE TALKIN' ABOUT.
I KNOW.
I KNOW THAT FOR FIVE YEARS YOU'VE BEEN THE HEAD OF A TOP-SECRET RESEARCH PROJECT AT ZINCO-DAVIS. I KNOW THAT A MONTH AGO YOU WERE FIRED...
...AND NOW EVERY MEMBER OF YOUR RESEARCH TEAM IS DEAD.
THOSE BASTARDS TRIED TO SCREW ME!
BUT I DIDN'T KILL ANYBODY. I HAVEN'T BEEN OUT OF THIS APARTMENT IN WEEKS.

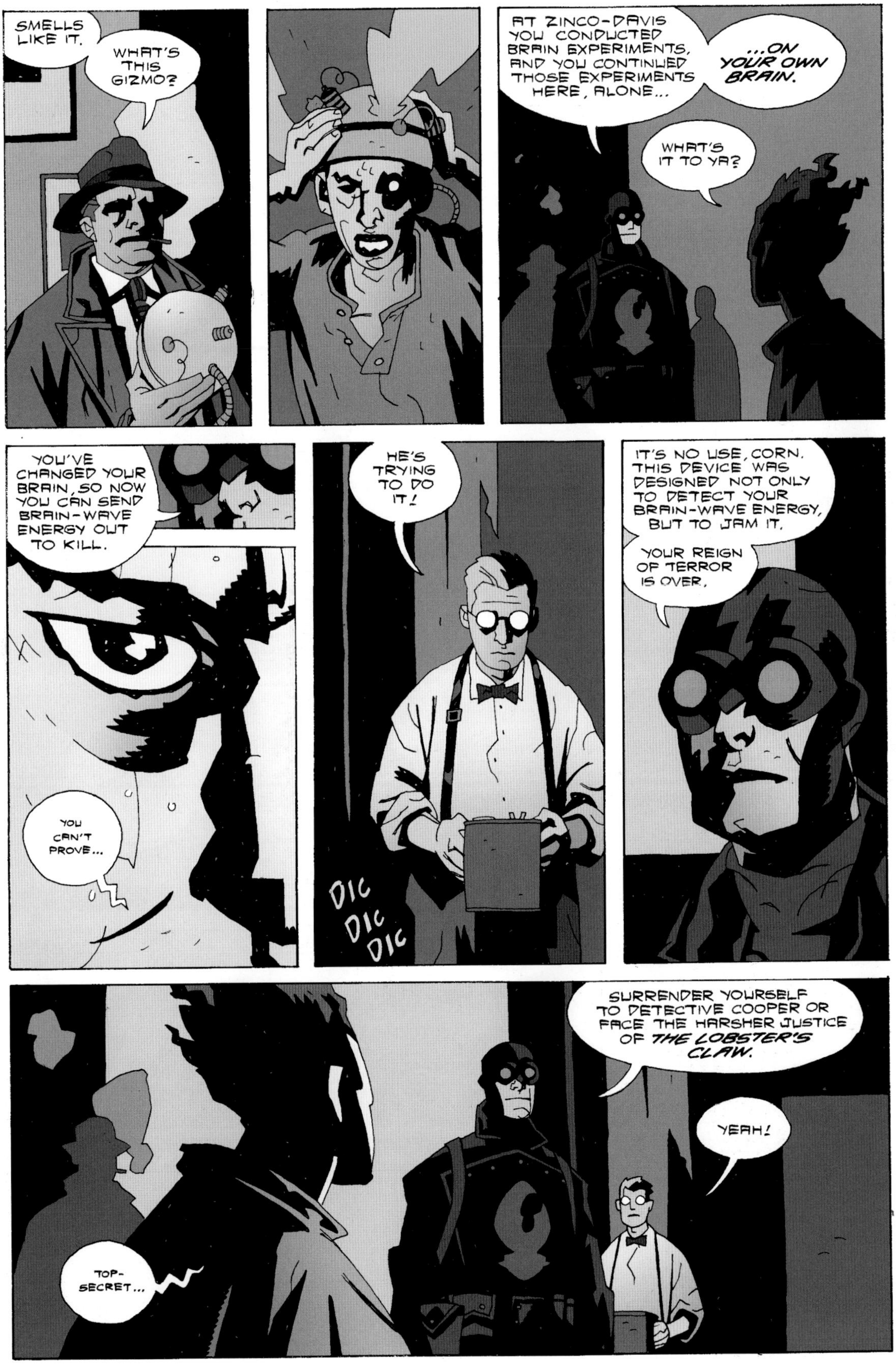
SMELLS LIKE IT.
WHAT'S THIS GIZMO?
AT ZINCO-DAVIS YOU CONDUCTED BRAIN EXPERIMENTS, AND YOU CONTINUED THOSE EXPERIMENTS HERE, ALONE...
...ON YOUR OWN BRAIN.
WHAT'S IT TO YA?
YOU'VE CHANGED YOUR BRAIN, SO NOW YOU CAN SEND BRAIN-WAVE ENERGY OUT TO KILL.
YOU CAN'T PROVE...
HE'S TRYING TO DO IT!
DIC DIC DIC
IT'S NO USE, CORN. THIS DEVICE WAS DESIGNED NOT ONLY TO DETECT YOUR BRAIN-WAVE ENERGY, BUT TO JAM IT.
YOUR REIGN OF TERROR IS OVER.
SURRENDER YOURSELF TO DETECTIVE COOPER OR FACE THE HARSHER JUSTICE OF THE LOBSTER'S CLAW.
YEAH!
TOP-SECRET...

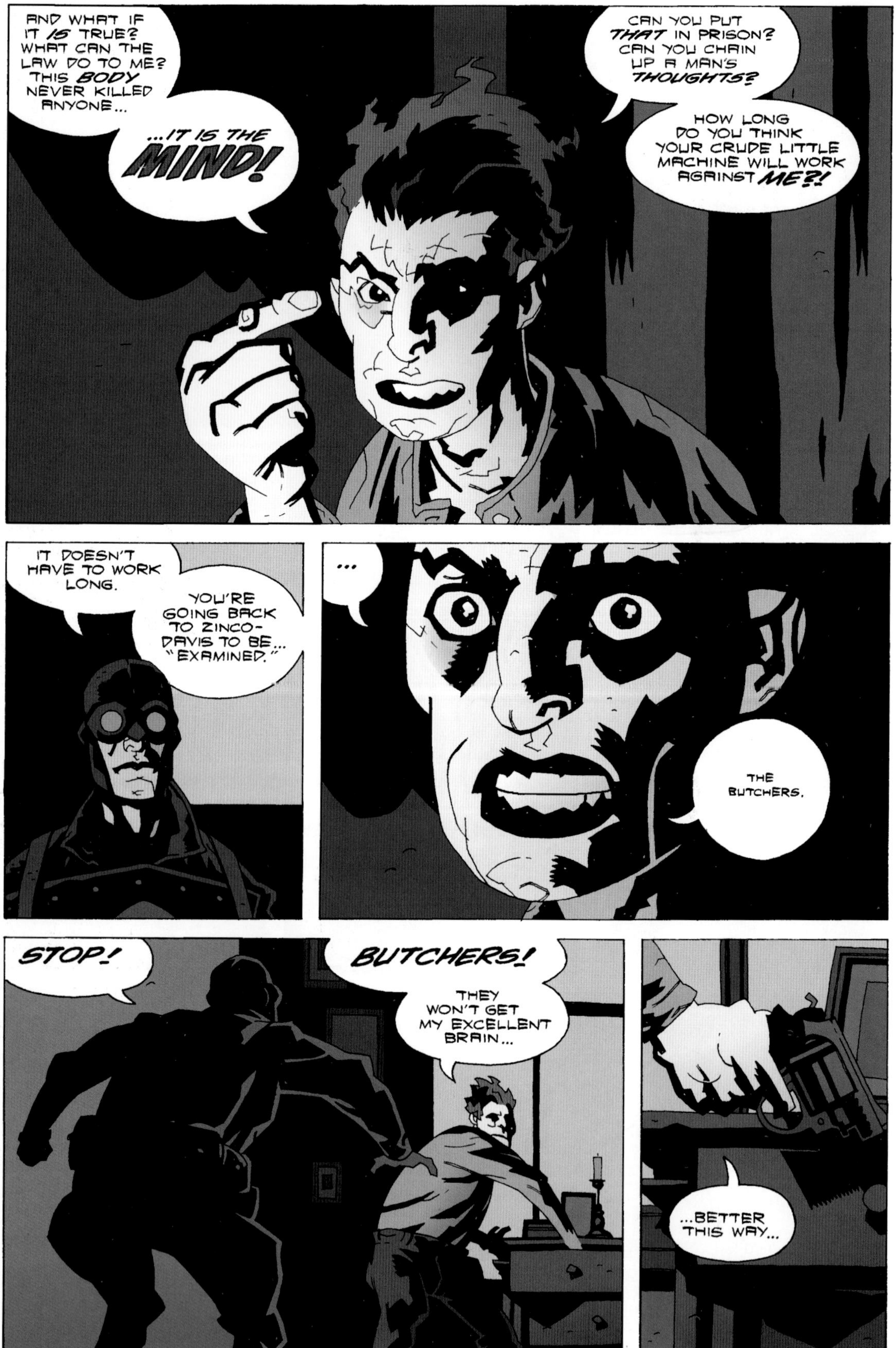
AND WHAT IF IT *IS* TRUE? WHAT CAN THE LAW DO TO ME? THIS *BODY* NEVER KILLED ANYONE...
...IT IS THE MIND!
CAN YOU PUT *THAT* IN PRISON? CAN YOU CHAIN UP A MAN'S *THOUGHTS?*
HOW LONG DO YOU THINK YOUR CRUDE LITTLE MACHINE WILL WORK AGAINST *ME?!*
IT DOESN'T HAVE TO WORK LONG.
YOU'RE GOING BACK TO ZINCO-DAVIS TO BE... "EXAMINED."
...
THE BUTCHERS.
STOP!
BUTCHERS!
THEY WON'T GET MY EXCELLENT BRAIN...
...BETTER THIS WAY...

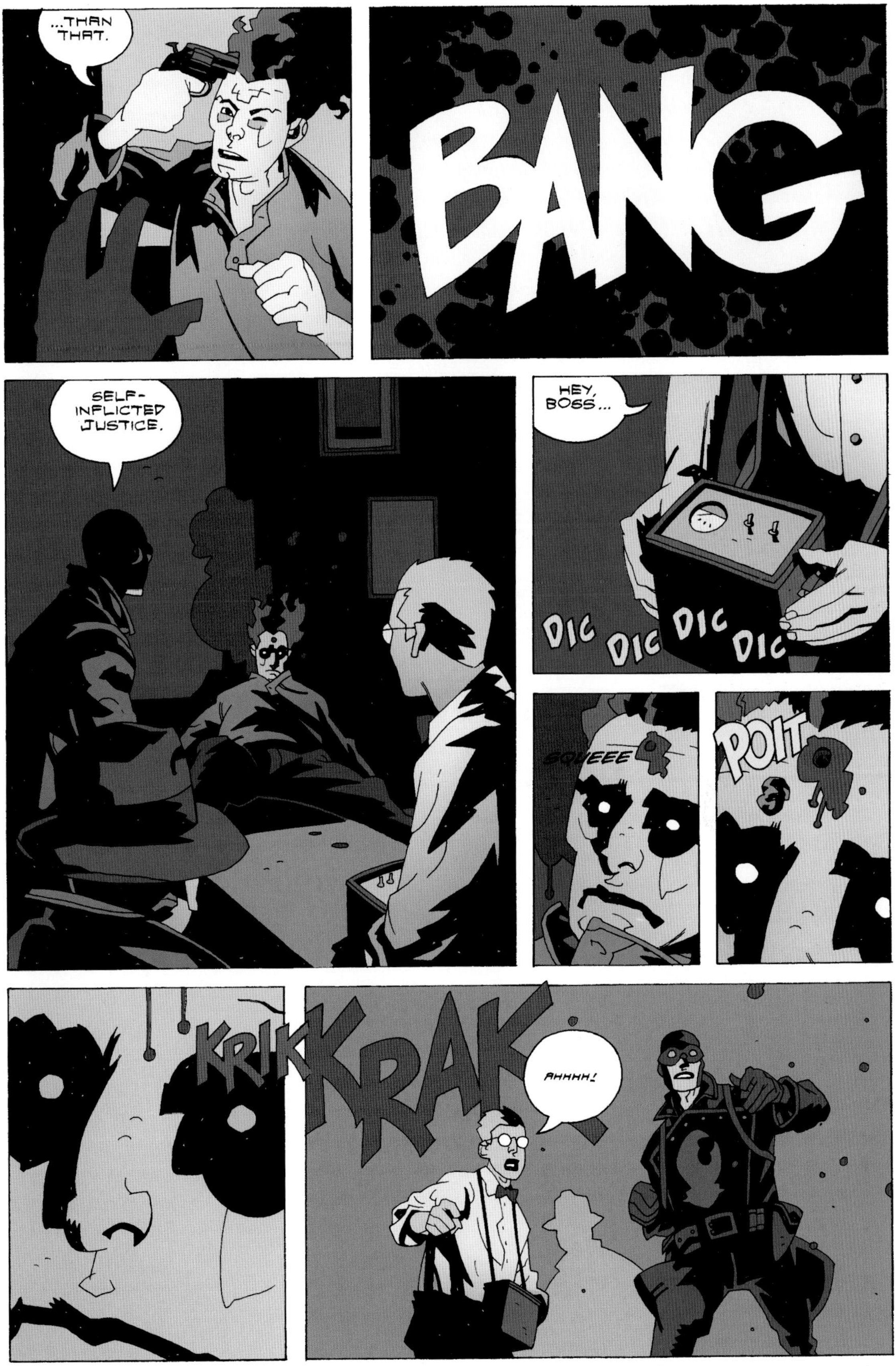
...THAN THAT.
BANG
SELF-INFLICTED JUSTICE.
HEY, BOSS...
DIC DIC DIC DIC
SQUEEE
POIT
KRIK KRAK
AHHHH!

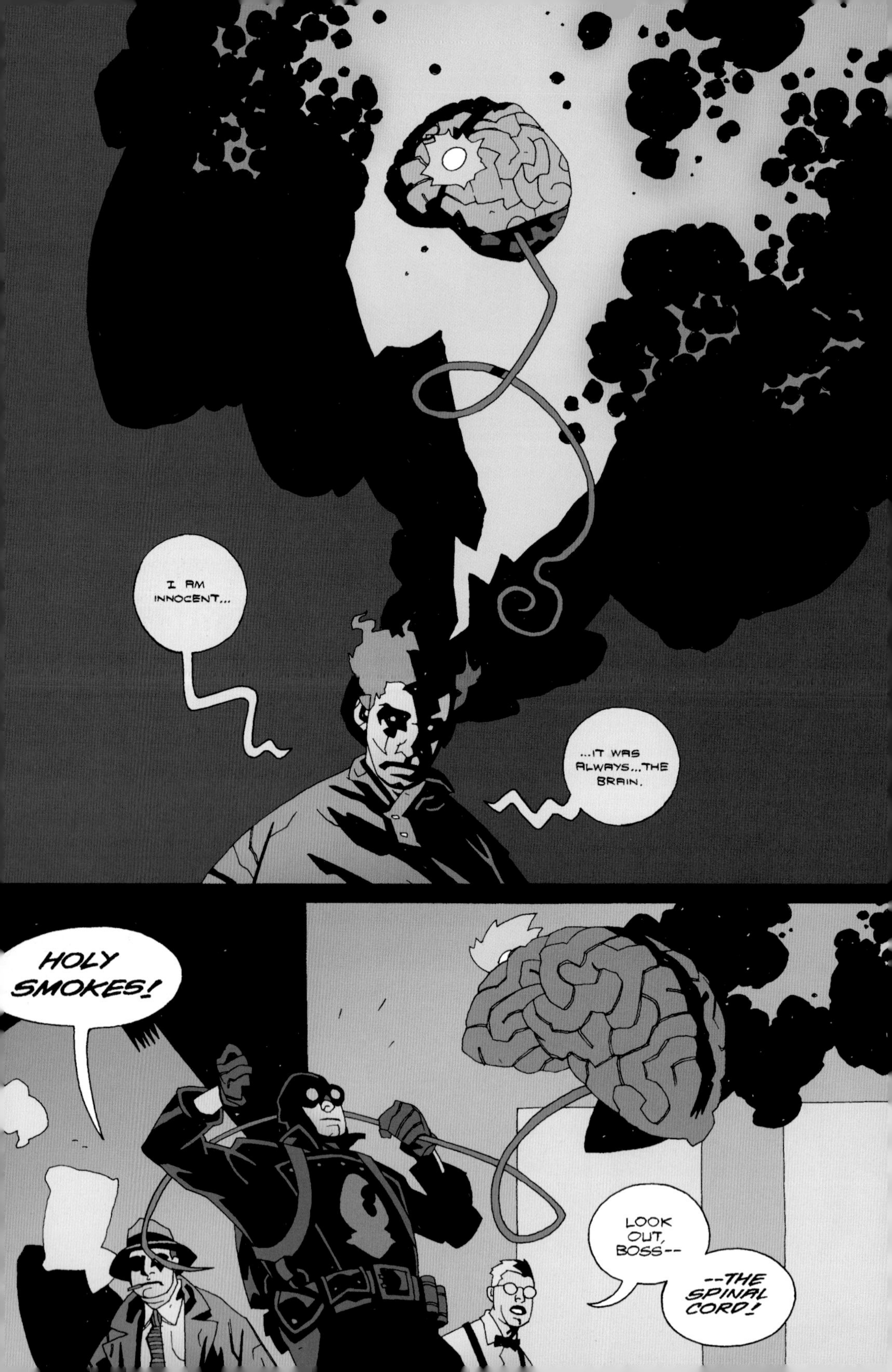

I AM INNOCENT...
...IT WAS ALWAYS...THE BRAIN.
HOLY SMOKES!
LOOK OUT, BOSS--
--THE SPINAL CORD!

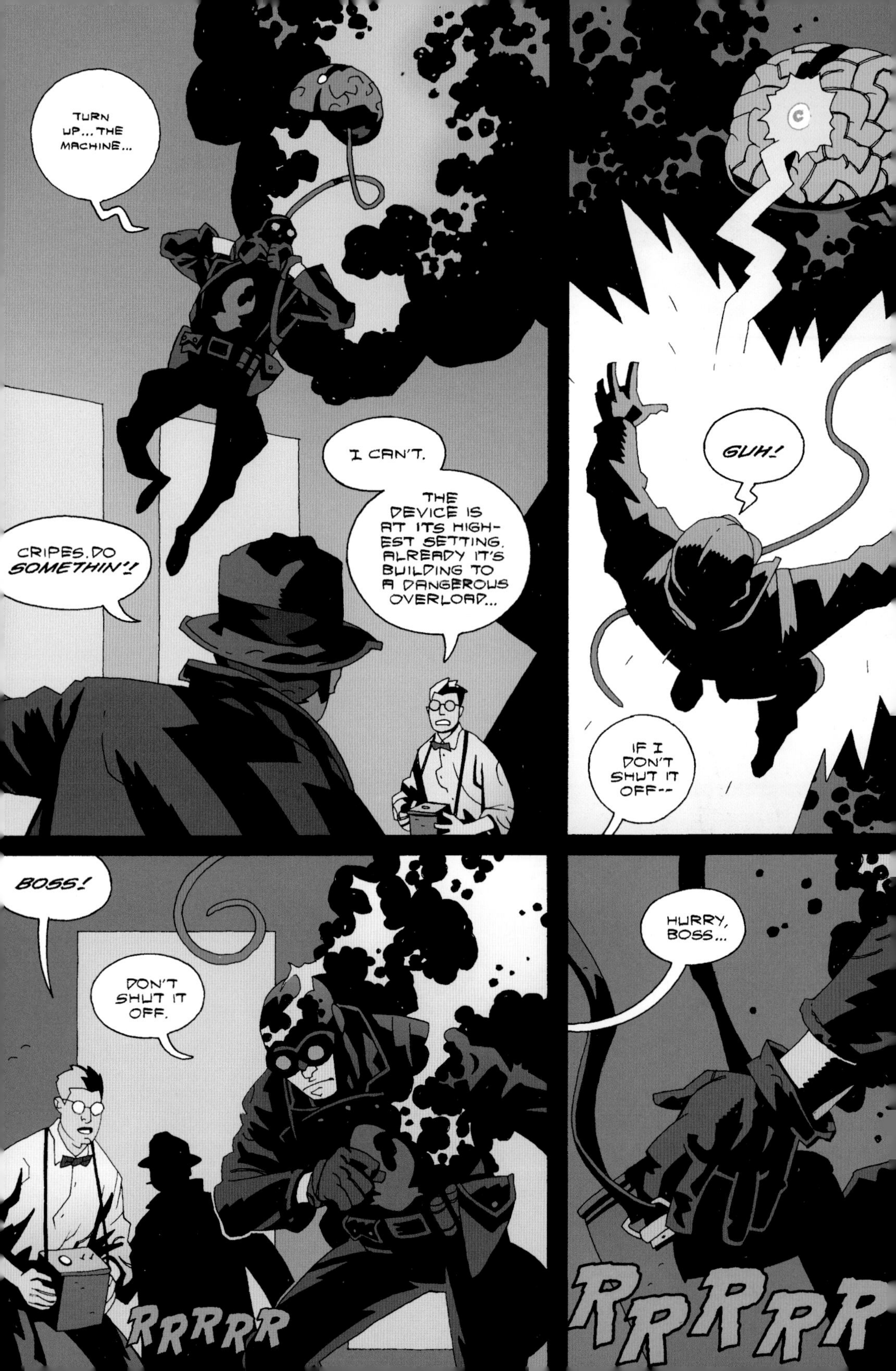
TURN UP... THE MACHINE...
I CAN'T.
THE DEVICE IS AT ITS HIGHEST SETTING. ALREADY IT'S BUILDING TO A DANGEROUS OVERLOAD...
CRIPES. DO *SOMETHIN'!*
GUH!
IF I DON'T SHUT IT OFF--
BOSS!
DON'T SHUT IT OFF.
RRRRRR
HURRY, BOSS...
RRRRRR

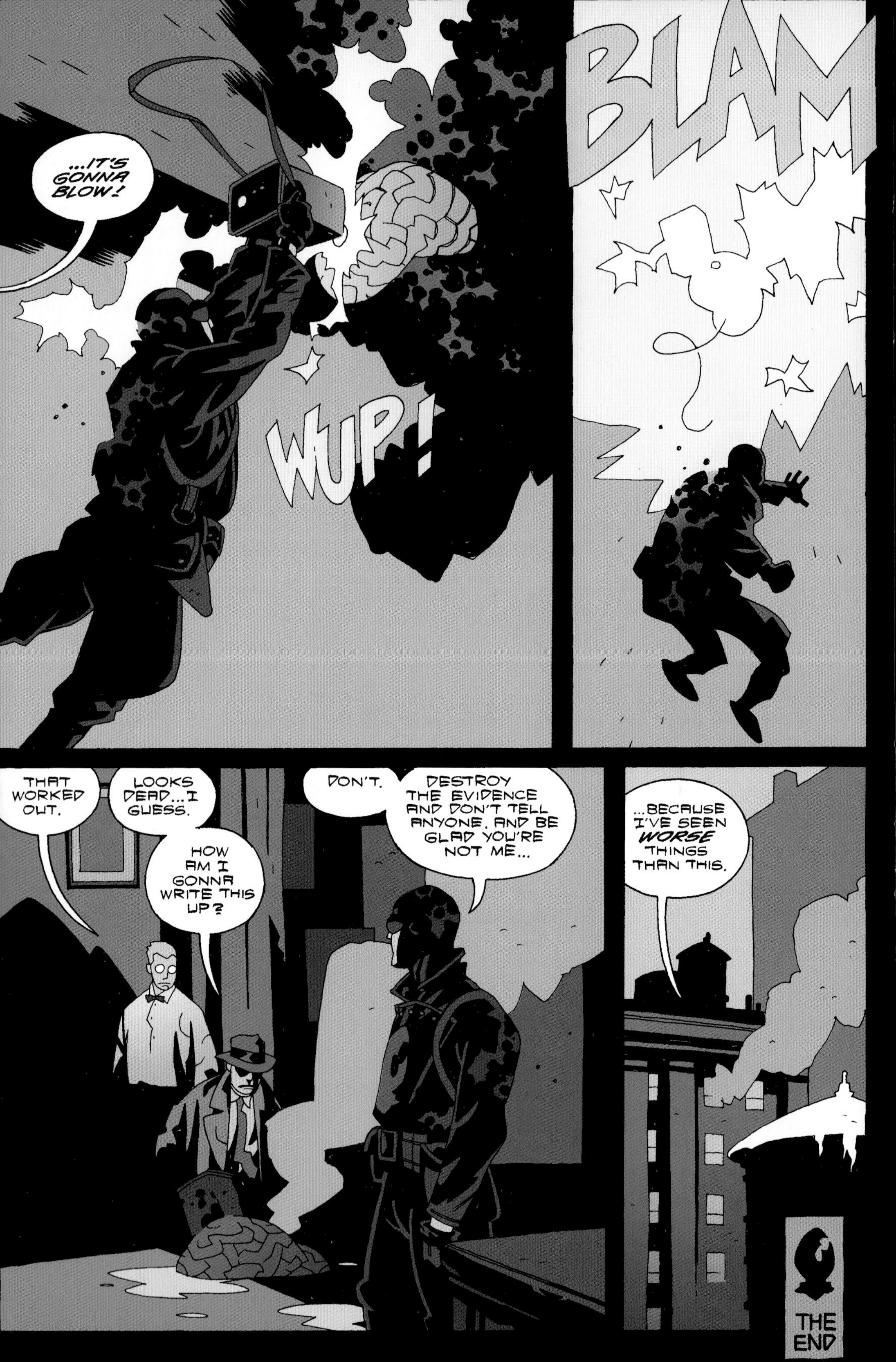
...IT'S GONNA BLOW!
BLAM
WUP!
THAT WORKED OUT.
LOOKS DEAD...I GUESS.
HOW AM I GONNA WRITE THIS UP?
DON'T.
DESTROY THE EVIDENCE AND DON'T TELL ANYONE. AND BE GLAD YOU'RE NOT ME...
...BECAUSE I'VE SEEN WORSE THINGS THAN THIS.
THE END

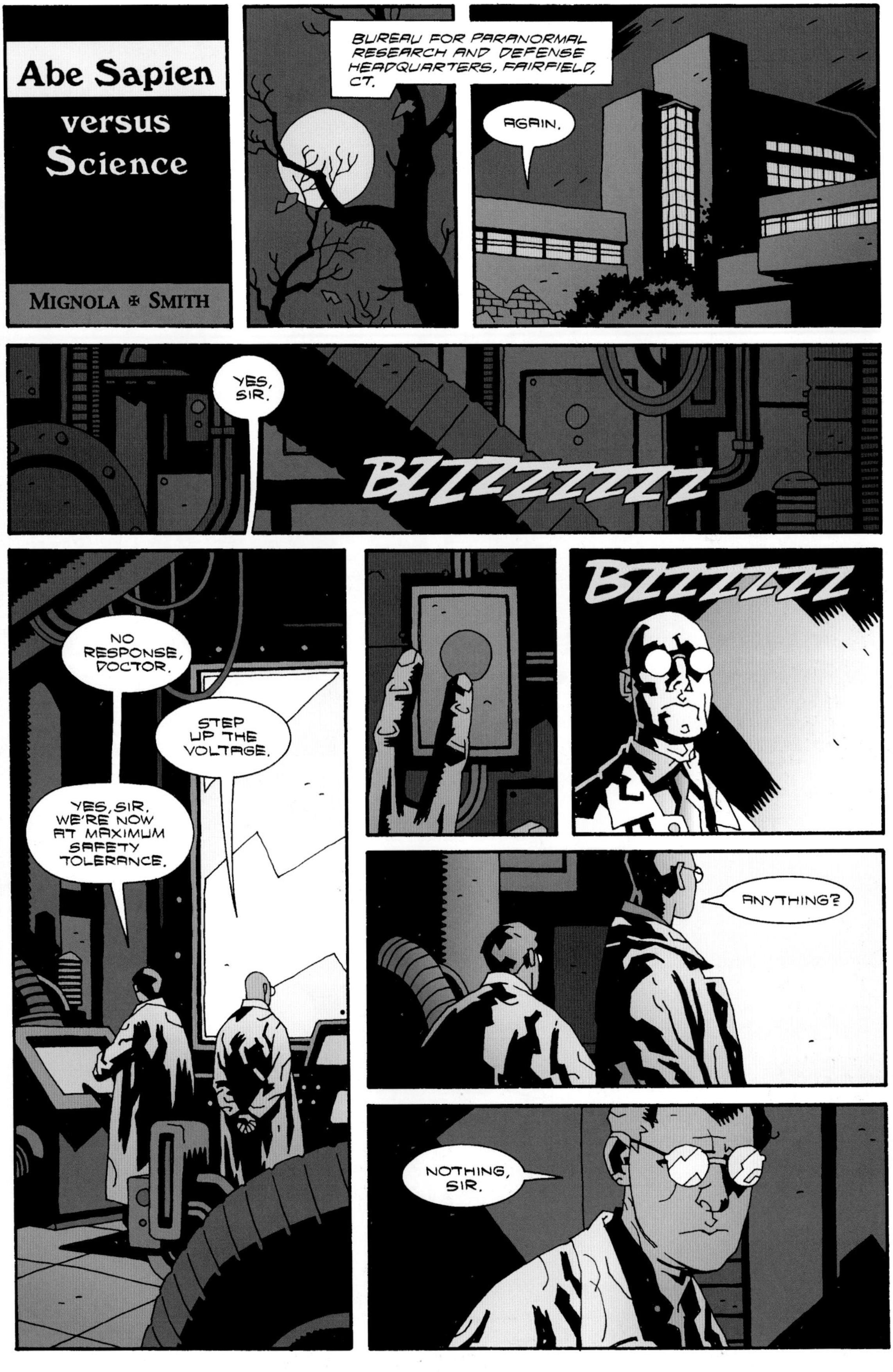
Abe Sapien
versus
Science
MIGNOLA ✠ SMITH
BUREAU FOR PARANORMAL RESEARCH AND DEFENSE HEADQUARTERS, FAIRFIELD, CT.
AGAIN.
YES, SIR.
BZZZZZZZZZ
NO RESPONSE, DOCTOR.
STEP UP THE VOLTAGE.
YES, SIR. WE'RE NOW AT MAXIMUM SAFETY TOLERANCE.
BZZZZZZZ
ANYTHING?
NOTHING, SIR.

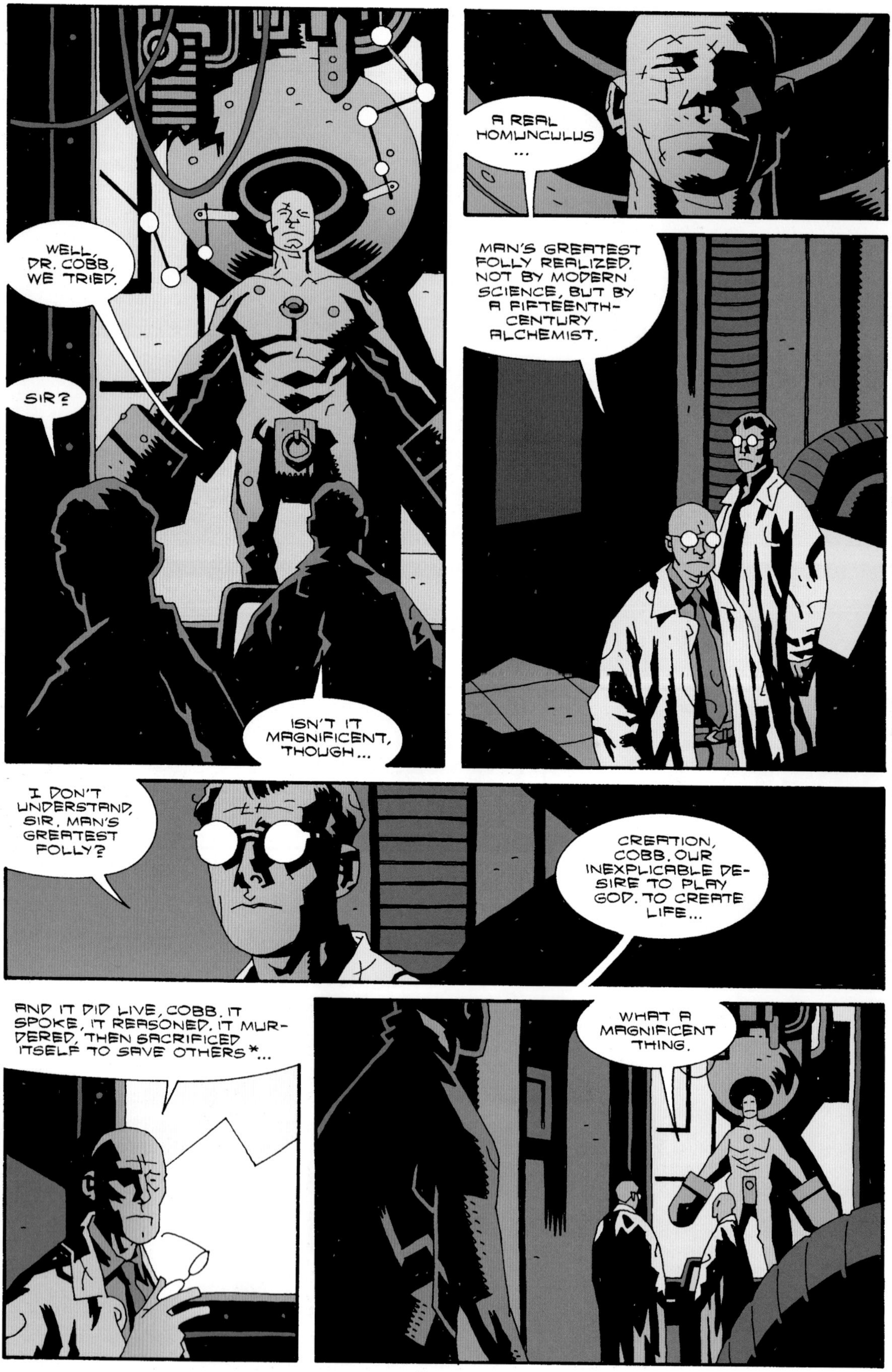
WELL, DR. COBB, WE TRIED.
SIR?
ISN'T IT MAGNIFICENT, THOUGH...
A REAL HOMUNCULUS ...
MAN'S GREATEST FOLLY REALIZED. NOT BY MODERN SCIENCE, BUT BY A FIFTEENTH-CENTURY ALCHEMIST.
I DON'T UNDERSTAND, SIR. MAN'S GREATEST FOLLY?
CREATION, COBB. OUR INEXPLICABLE DESIRE TO PLAY GOD. TO CREATE LIFE...
AND IT DID LIVE, COBB. IT SPOKE, IT REASONED. IT MURDERED, THEN SACRIFICED ITSELF TO SAVE OTHERS*...
WHAT A MAGNIFICENT THING.

*HELLBOY: WAKE THE DEVIL AND ALMOST COLOSSUS

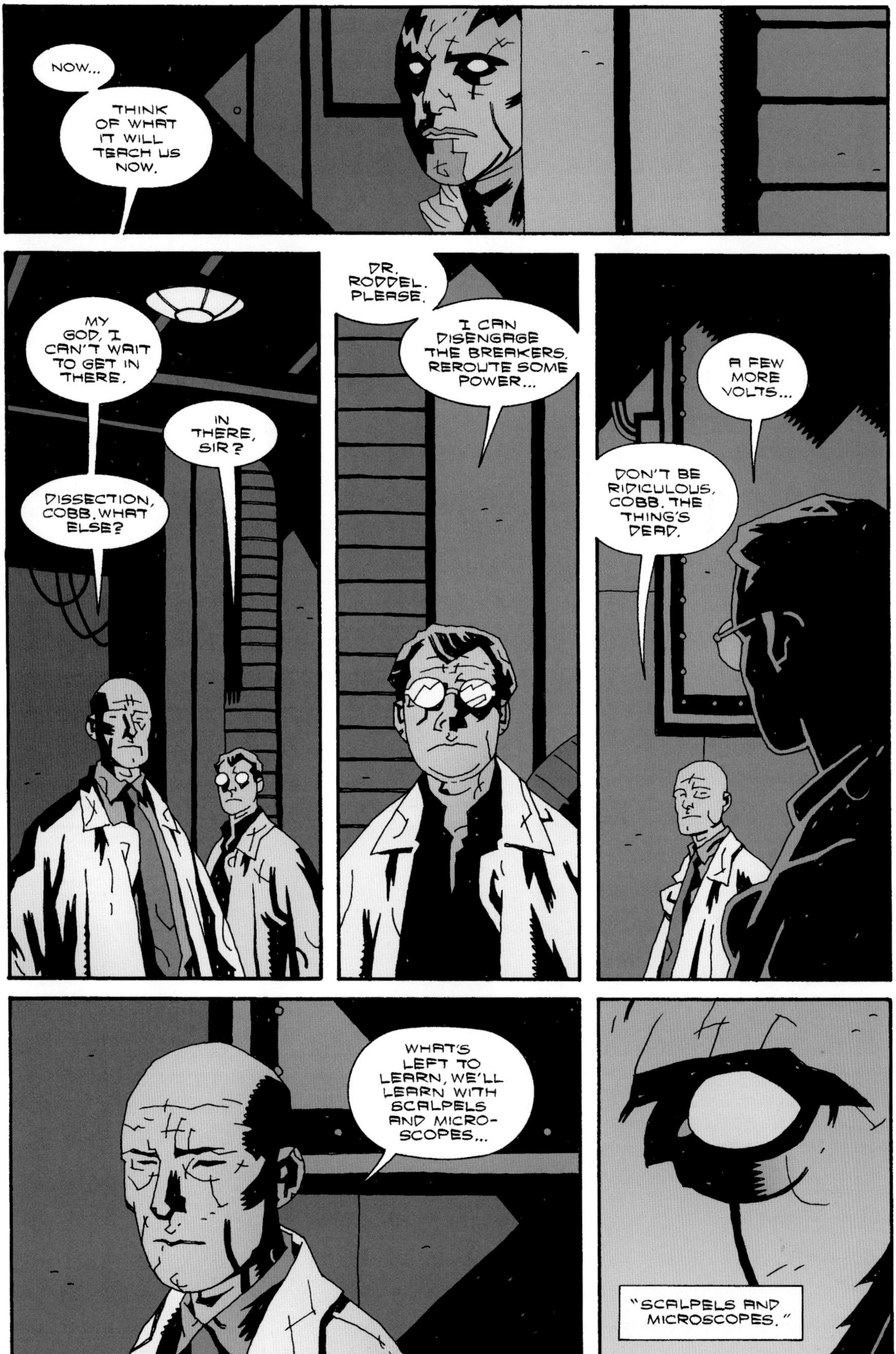

NOW...
THINK OF WHAT IT WILL TEACH US NOW.
MY GOD, I CAN'T WAIT TO GET IN THERE.
IN THERE, SIR?
DISSECTION, COBB, WHAT ELSE?
DR. RODDEL. PLEASE.
I CAN DISENGAGE THE BREAKERS, REROUTE SOME POWER...
A FEW MORE VOLTS...
DON'T BE RIDICULOUS, COBB. THE THING'S DEAD.
WHAT'S LEFT TO LEARN, WE'LL LEARN WITH SCALPELS AND MICRO-SCOPES...
"SCALPELS AND MICROSCOPES."

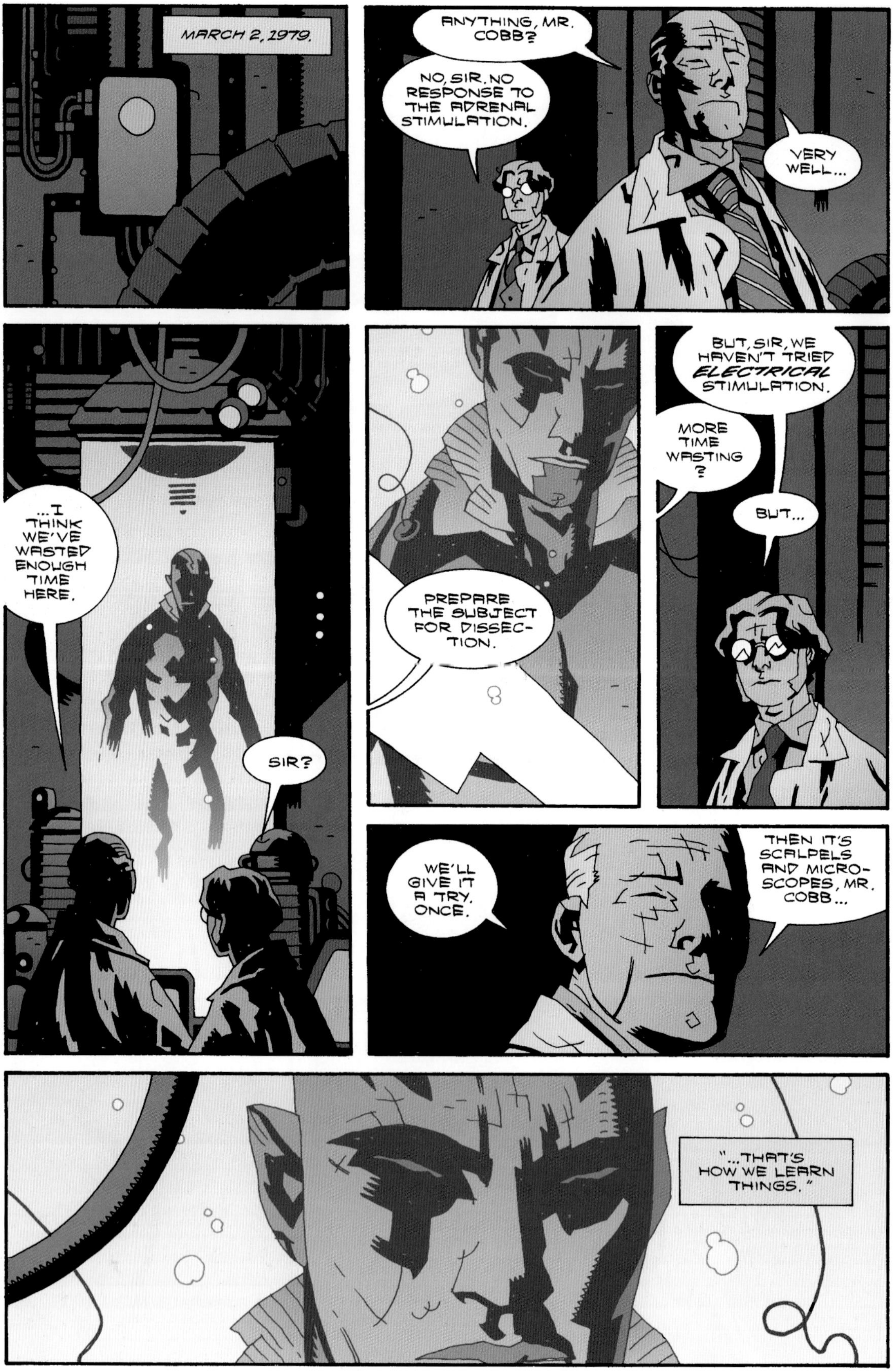
MARCH 2, 1979.
ANYTHING, MR. COBB?
NO, SIR. NO RESPONSE TO THE ADRENAL STIMULATION.
VERY WELL...
...I THINK WE'VE WASTED ENOUGH TIME HERE.
SIR?
PREPARE THE SUBJECT FOR DISSECTION.
BUT, SIR, WE HAVEN'T TRIED ELECTRICAL STIMULATION.
MORE TIME WASTING?
BUT...
WE'LL GIVE IT A TRY. ONCE.
THEN IT'S SCALPELS AND MICROSCOPES, MR. COBB...
"...THAT'S HOW WE LEARN THINGS."

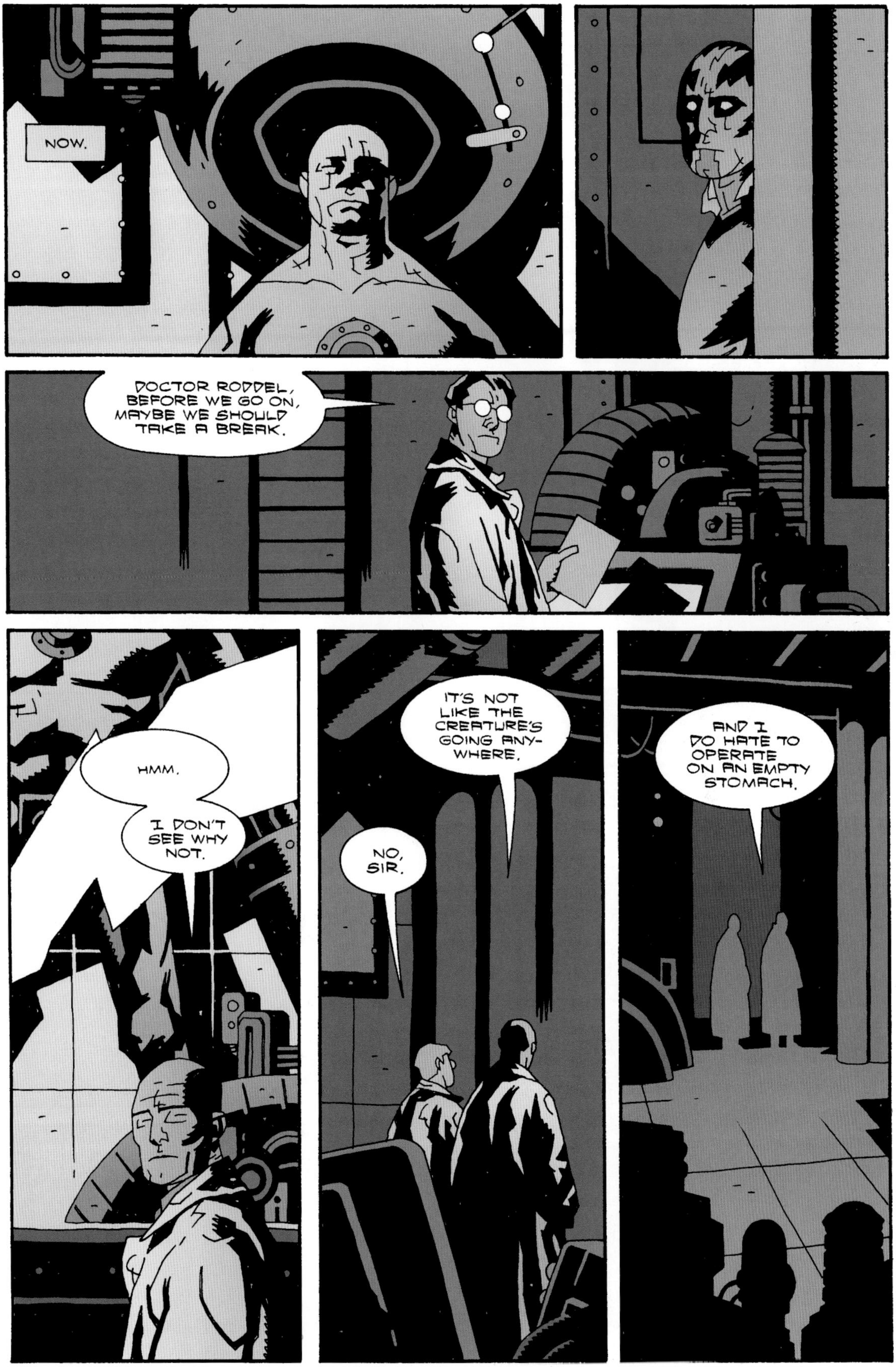
NOW.
DOCTOR RODDEL, BEFORE WE GO ON, MAYBE WE SHOULD TAKE A BREAK.
HMM.
I DON'T SEE WHY NOT.
IT'S NOT LIKE THE CREATURE'S GOING ANY-WHERE.
NO, SIR.
AND I DO HATE TO OPERATE ON AN EMPTY STOMACH.

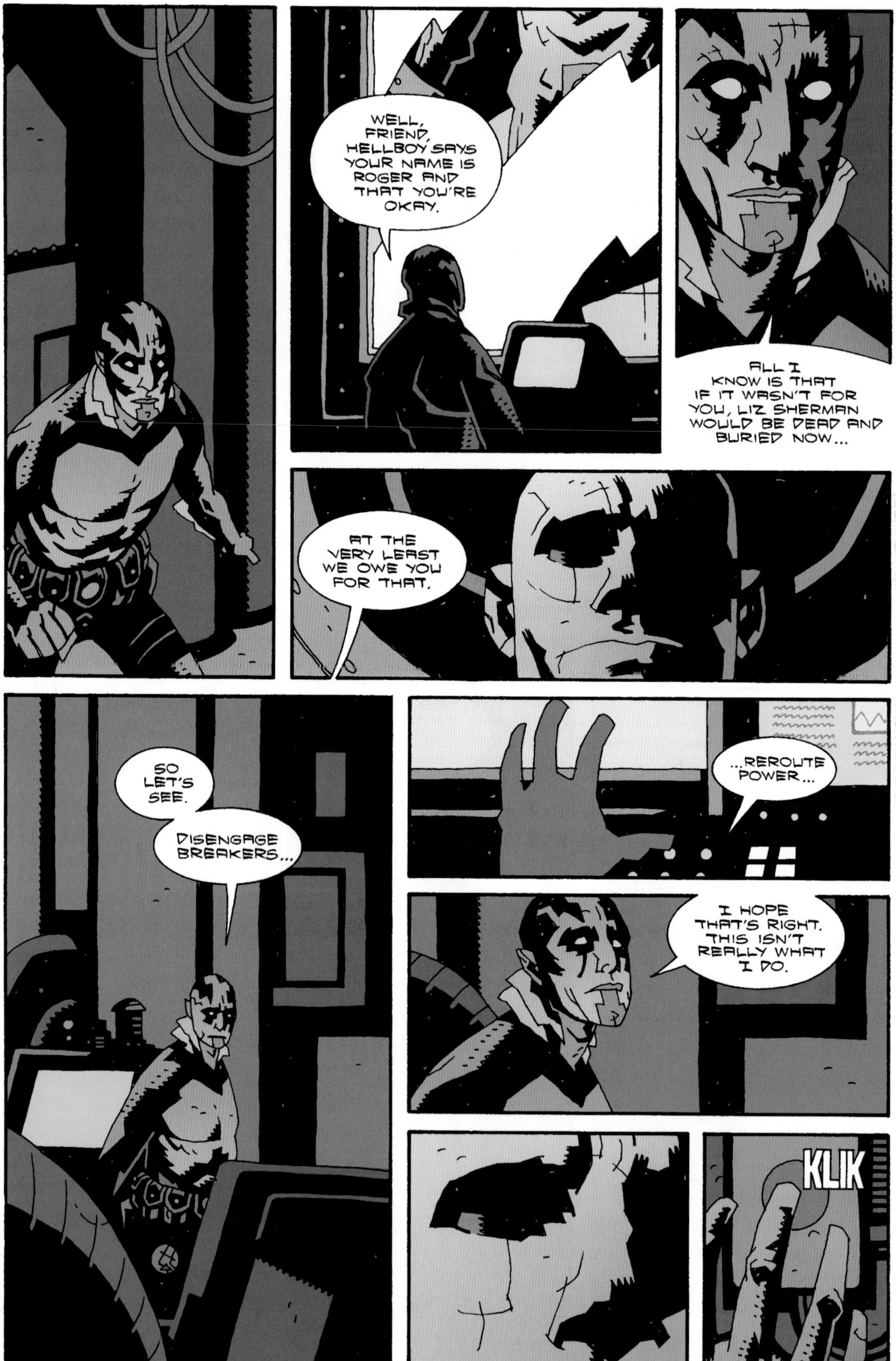
WELL, FRIEND, HELLBOY SAYS YOUR NAME IS ROGER AND THAT YOU'RE OKAY.
ALL I KNOW IS THAT IF IT WASN'T FOR YOU, LIZ SHERMAN WOULD BE DEAD AND BURIED NOW...
AT THE VERY LEAST WE OWE YOU FOR THAT.
SO LET'S SEE.
DISENGAGE BREAKERS...
...REROUTE POWER...
I HOPE THAT'S RIGHT. THIS ISN'T REALLY WHAT I DO.
KLIK

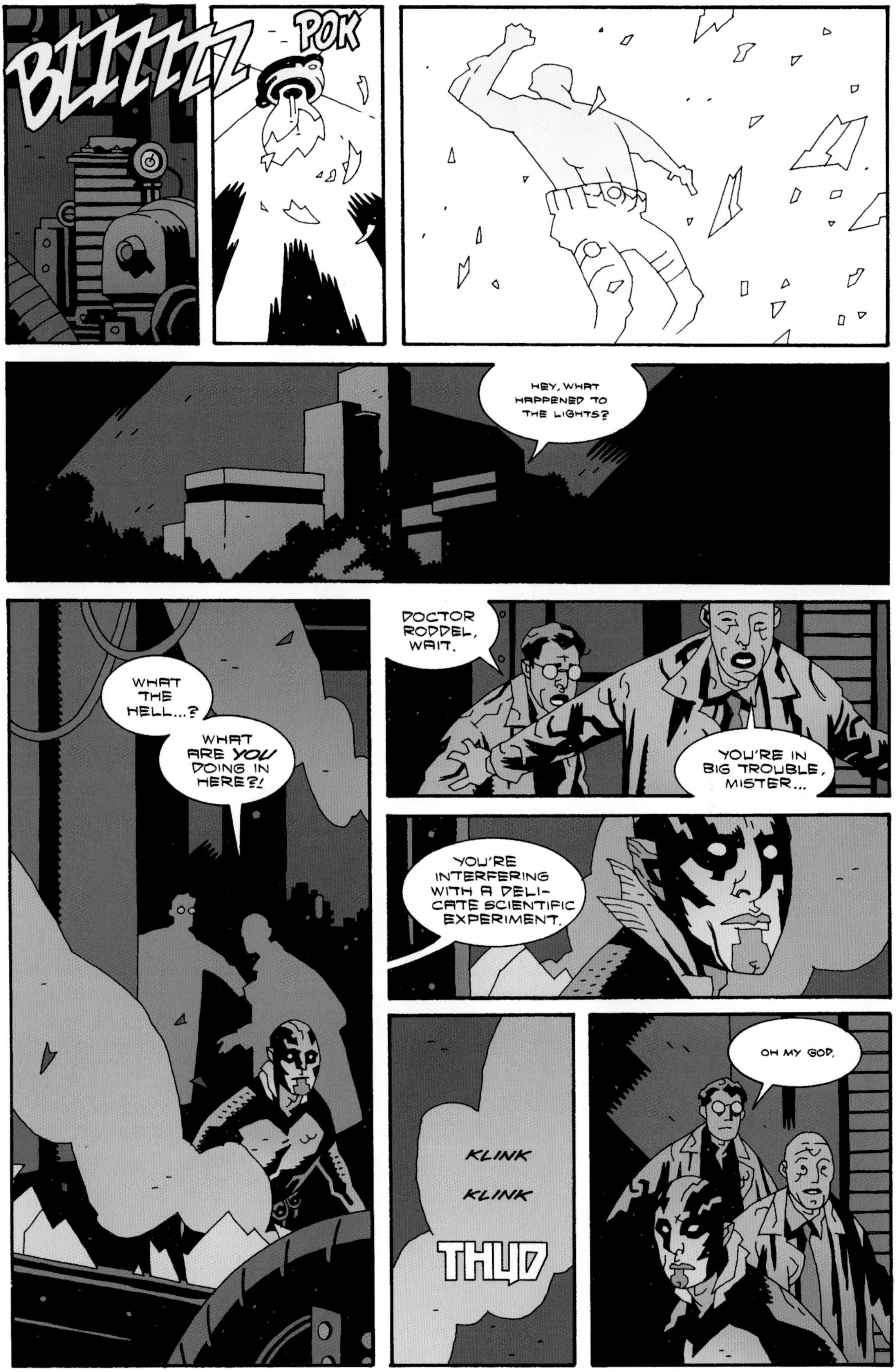
BZZZZZ
POK
HEY, WHAT HAPPENED TO THE LIGHTS?
WHAT THE HELL...?
WHAT ARE YOU DOING IN HERE?!
DOCTOR RODDEL, WAIT.
YOU'RE IN BIG TROUBLE, MISTER...
YOU'RE INTERFERING WITH A DELICATE SCIENTIFIC EXPERIMENT.
KLINK
KLINK
THUD
OH MY GOD.

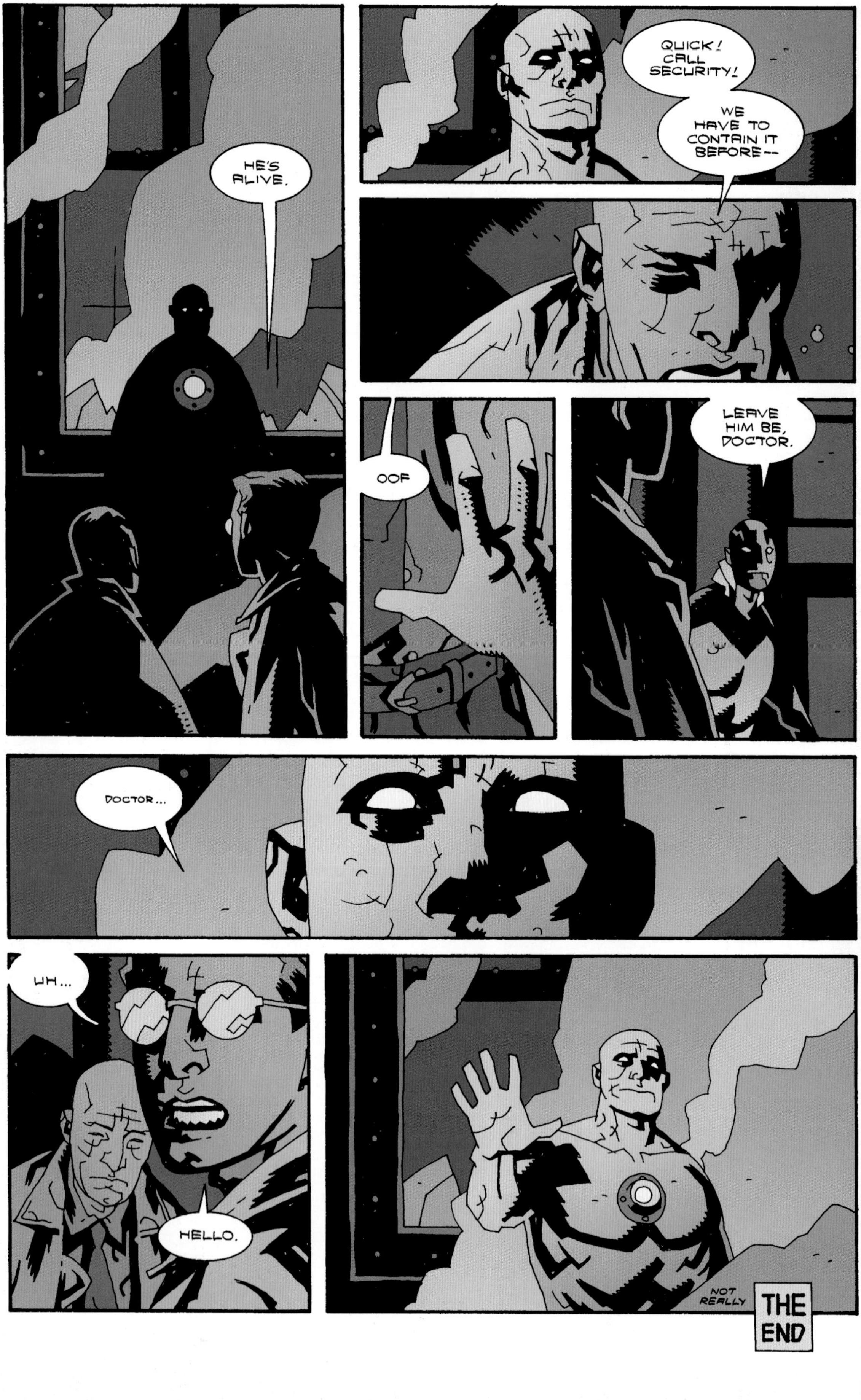
HE'S ALIVE.
QUICK! CALL SECURITY!
WE HAVE TO CONTAIN IT BEFORE--
OOF
LEAVE HIM BE, DOCTOR.
DOCTOR...
UH...
HELLO.
NOT REALLY
THE END

DRUMS OF THE DEAD

DRUMS OF THE DEAD

Story by
BRIAN MCDONALD

Art by
DEREK THOMPSON

Colors by
JAMES SINCLAIR

Letters by
PAT BROSSEAU

Mike had been considering using artist Derek Thompson for a *Hellboy*-related story. Brian McDonald, whose *Harry the Cop* comic had won him recognition around the industry, had been talking to me about various projects. When Mike and I put it together that these two guys were friends, we decided to go ahead and do our first *Hellboy* comic without Hellboy.

—Scott Allie

Portland, Oregon

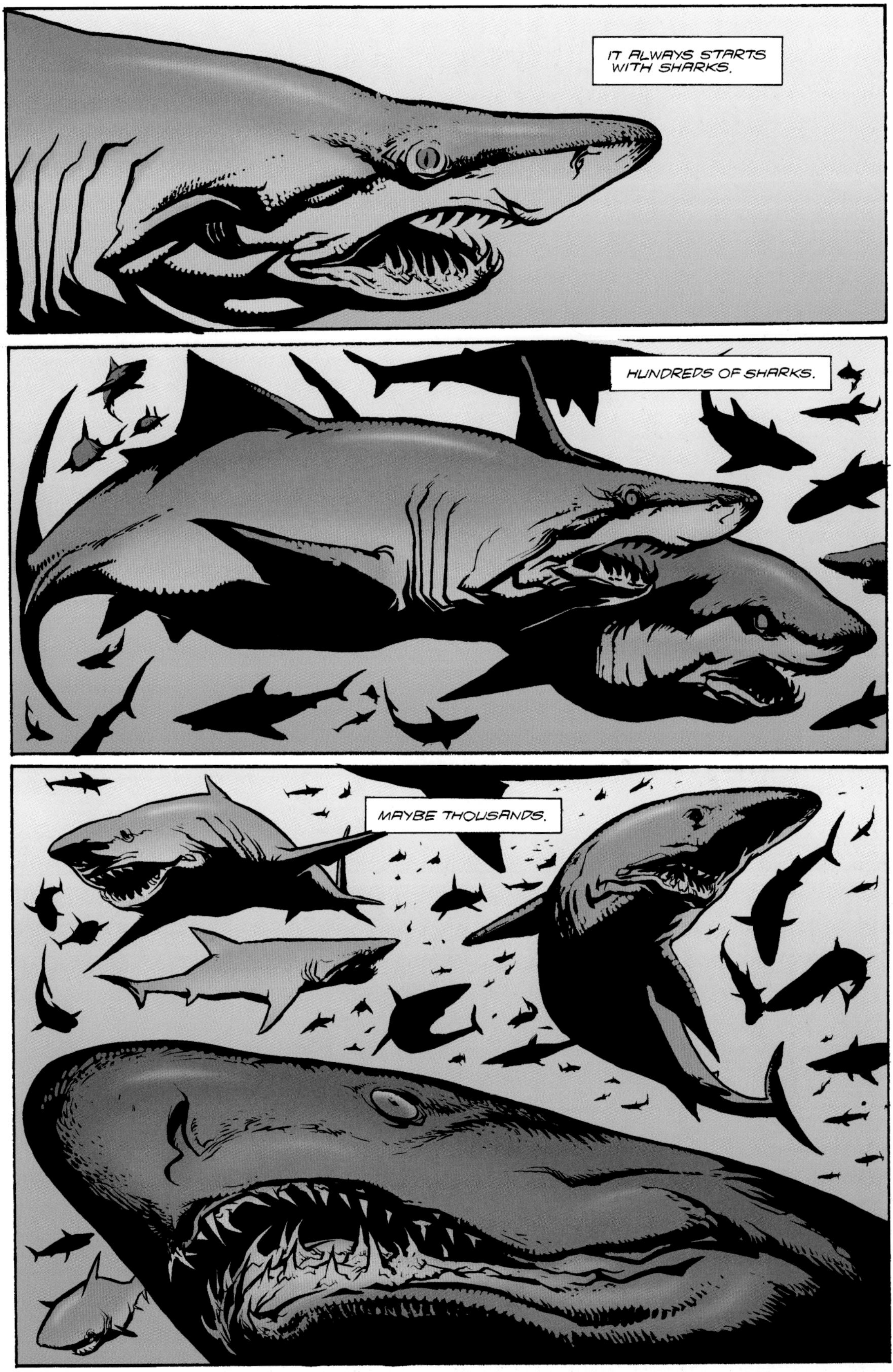
IT ALWAYS STARTS WITH SHARKS.
HUNDREDS OF SHARKS.
MAYBE THOUSANDS.

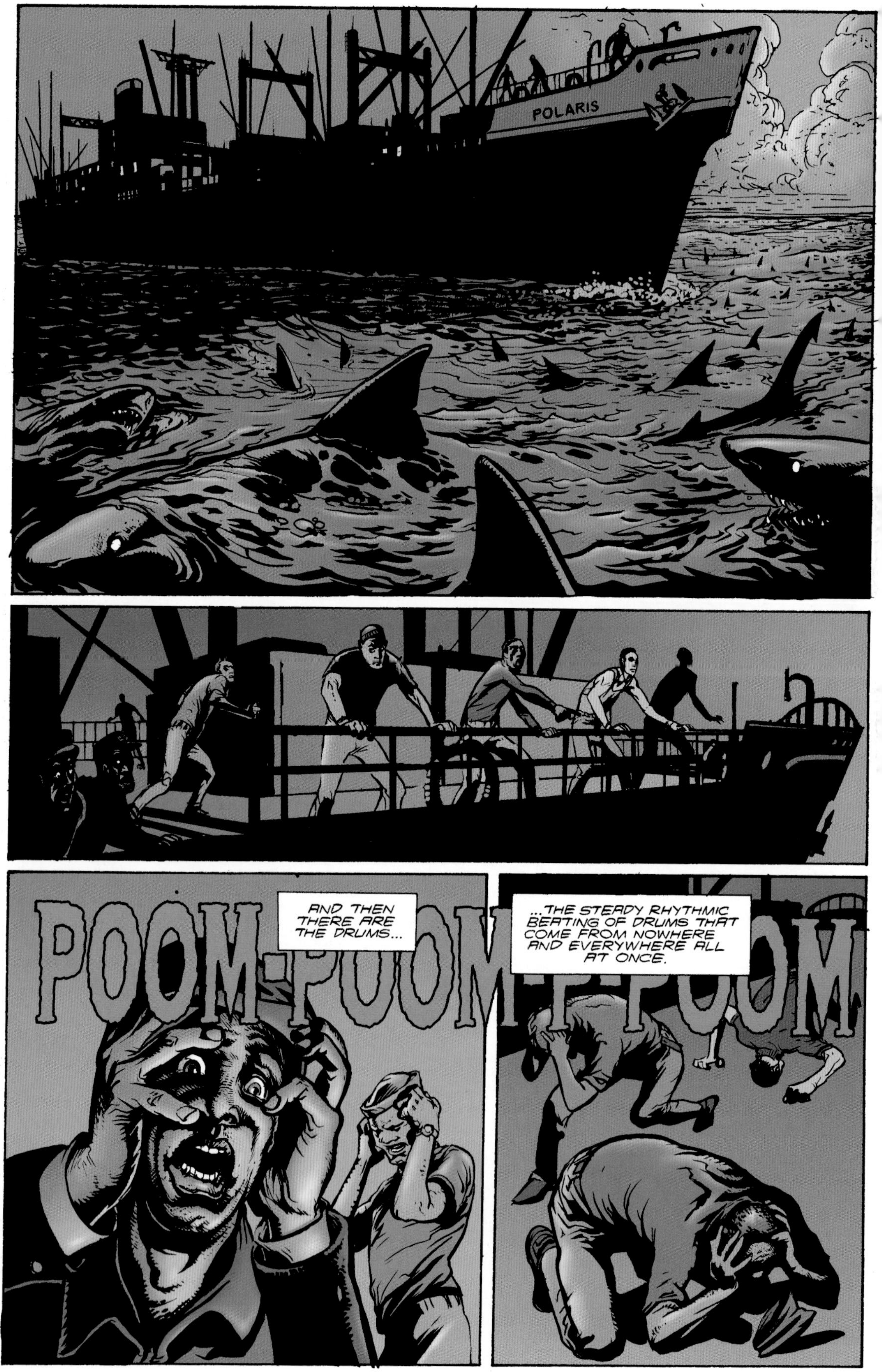
POLARIS
POOM-POOM-P-POOM
AND THEN THERE ARE THE DRUMS...
...THE STEADY RHYTHMIC BEATING OF DRUMS THAT COME FROM NOWHERE AND EVERYWHERE ALL AT ONCE.

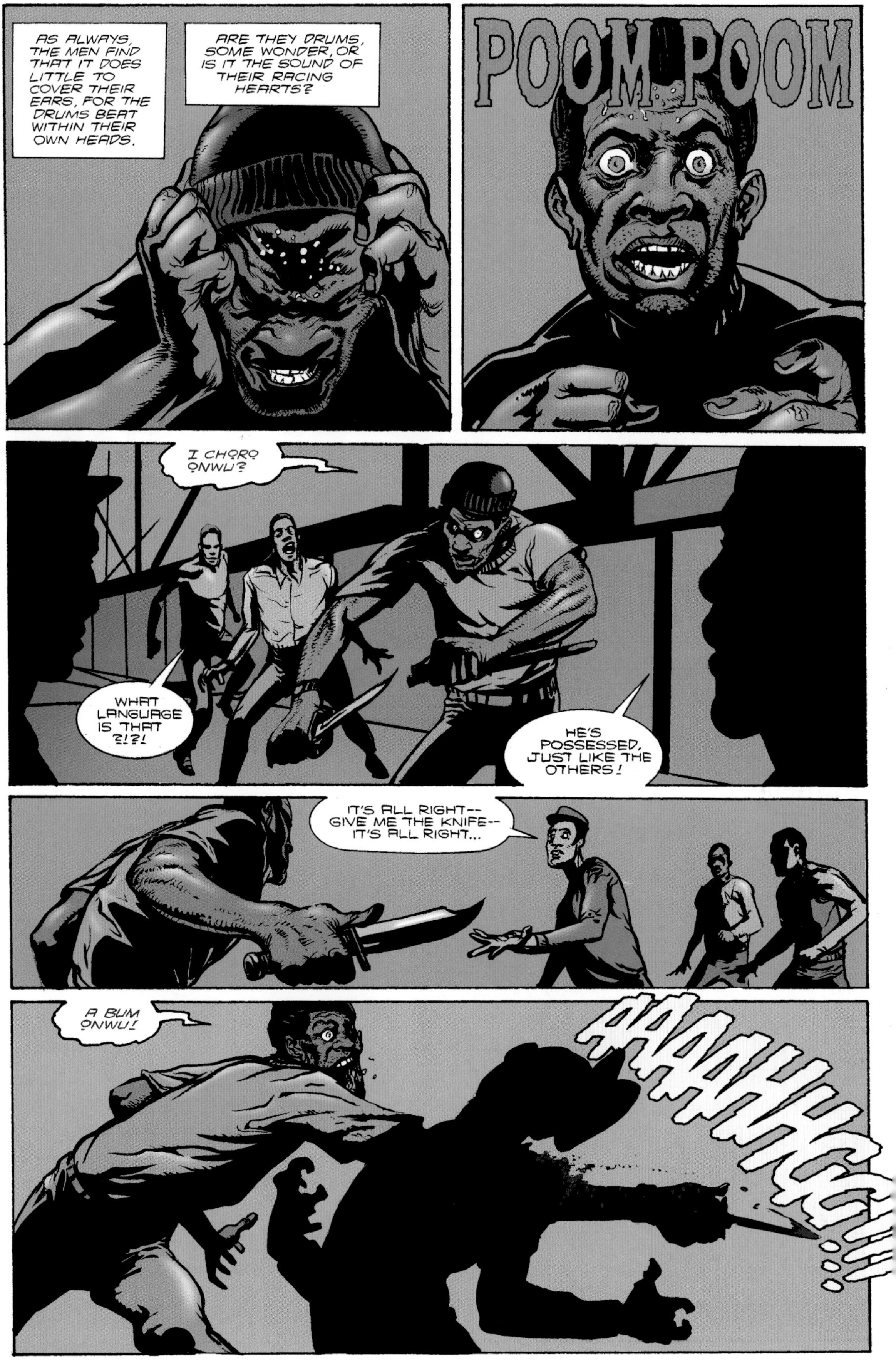
AS ALWAYS, THE MEN FIND THAT IT DOES LITTLE TO COVER THEIR EARS, FOR THE DRUMS BEAT WITHIN THEIR OWN HEADS.
ARE THEY DRUMS, SOME WONDER, OR IS IT THE SOUND OF THEIR RACING HEARTS?
POOM POOM
I CHỌRỌ ỌNWU?
WHAT LANGUAGE IS THAT ?!?!
HE'S POSSESSED, JUST LIKE THE OTHERS!
IT'S ALL RIGHT-- GIVE ME THE KNIFE-- IT'S ALL RIGHT...
A BUM ỌNWU!
AAAHHGGHH!!

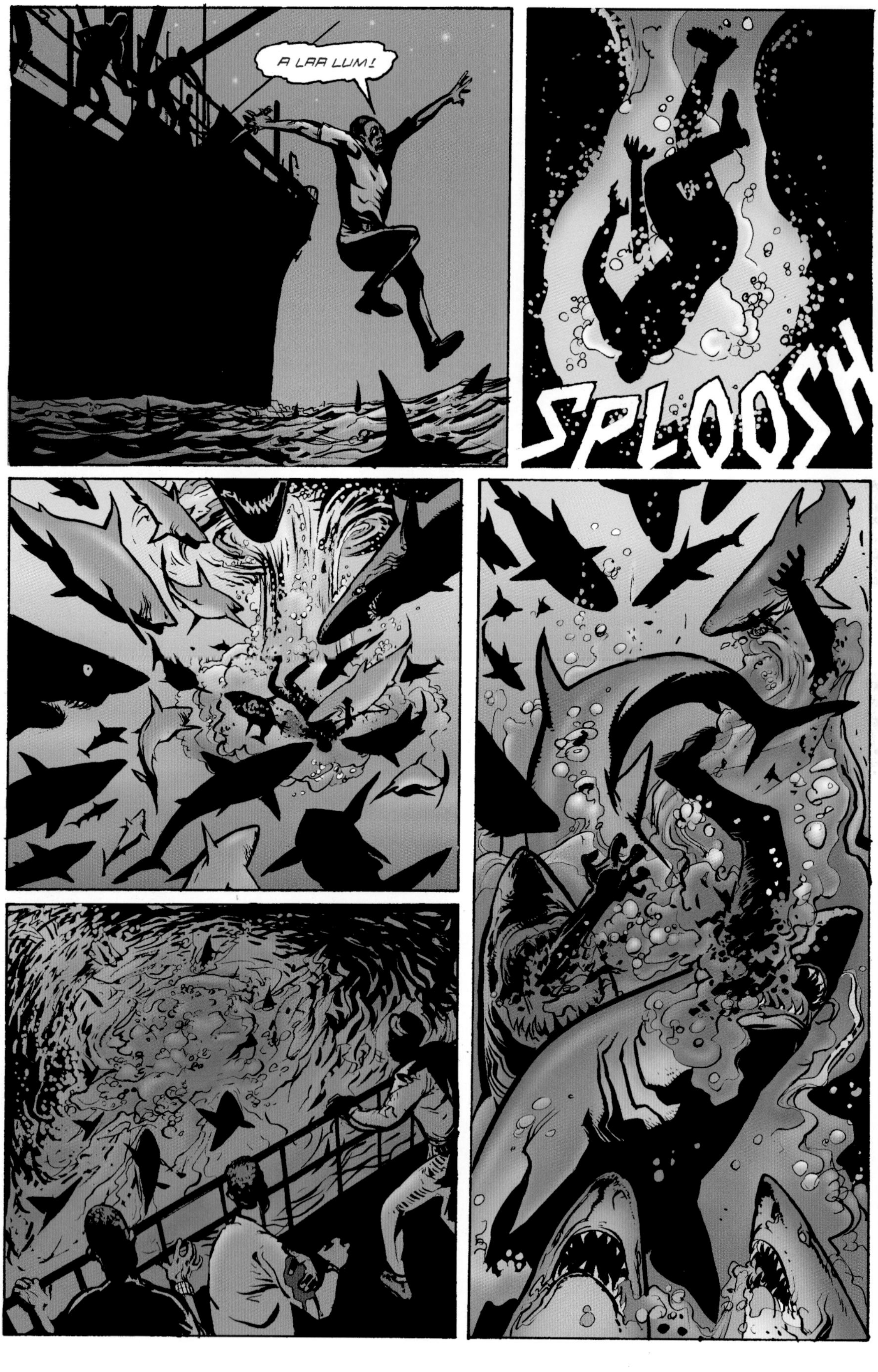
A LAA LUM!
SPLOOSH

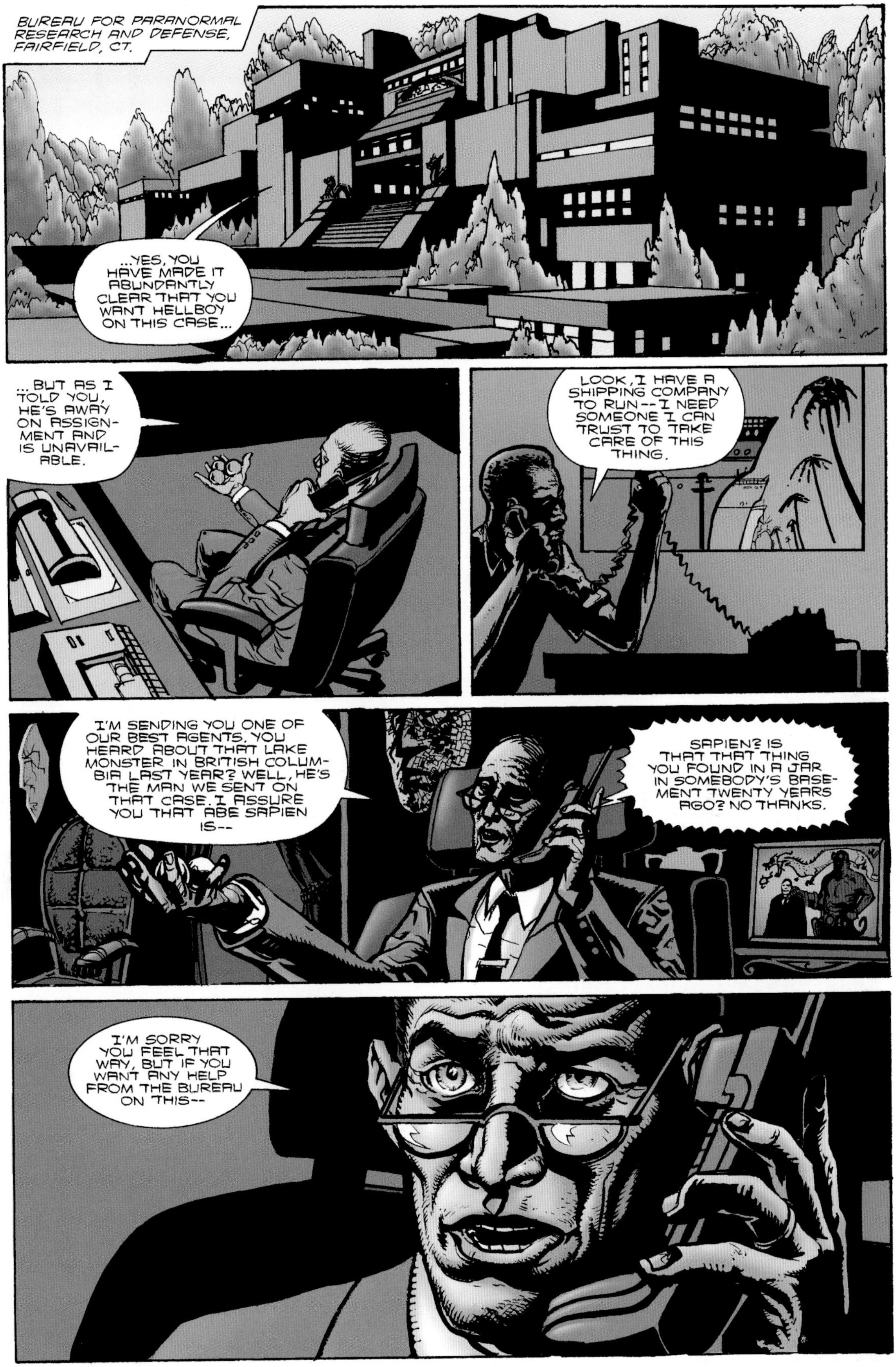
BUREAU FOR PARANORMAL RESEARCH AND DEFENSE, FAIRFIELD, CT.
...YES, YOU HAVE MADE IT ABUNDANTLY CLEAR THAT YOU WANT HELLBOY ON THIS CASE...
...BUT AS I TOLD YOU, HE'S AWAY ON ASSIGN-MENT AND IS UNAVAIL-ABLE.
LOOK, I HAVE A SHIPPING COMPANY TO RUN--I NEED SOMEONE I CAN TRUST TO TAKE CARE OF THIS THING.
I'M SENDING YOU ONE OF OUR BEST AGENTS. YOU HEARD ABOUT THAT LAKE MONSTER IN BRITISH COLUM-BIA LAST YEAR? WELL, HE'S THE MAN WE SENT ON THAT CASE. I ASSURE YOU THAT ABE SAPIEN IS--
SAPIEN? IS THAT THAT THING YOU FOUND IN A JAR IN SOMEBODY'S BASE-MENT TWENTY YEARS AGO? NO THANKS.
I'M SORRY YOU FEEL THAT WAY, BUT IF YOU WANT ANY HELP FROM THE BUREAU ON THIS--

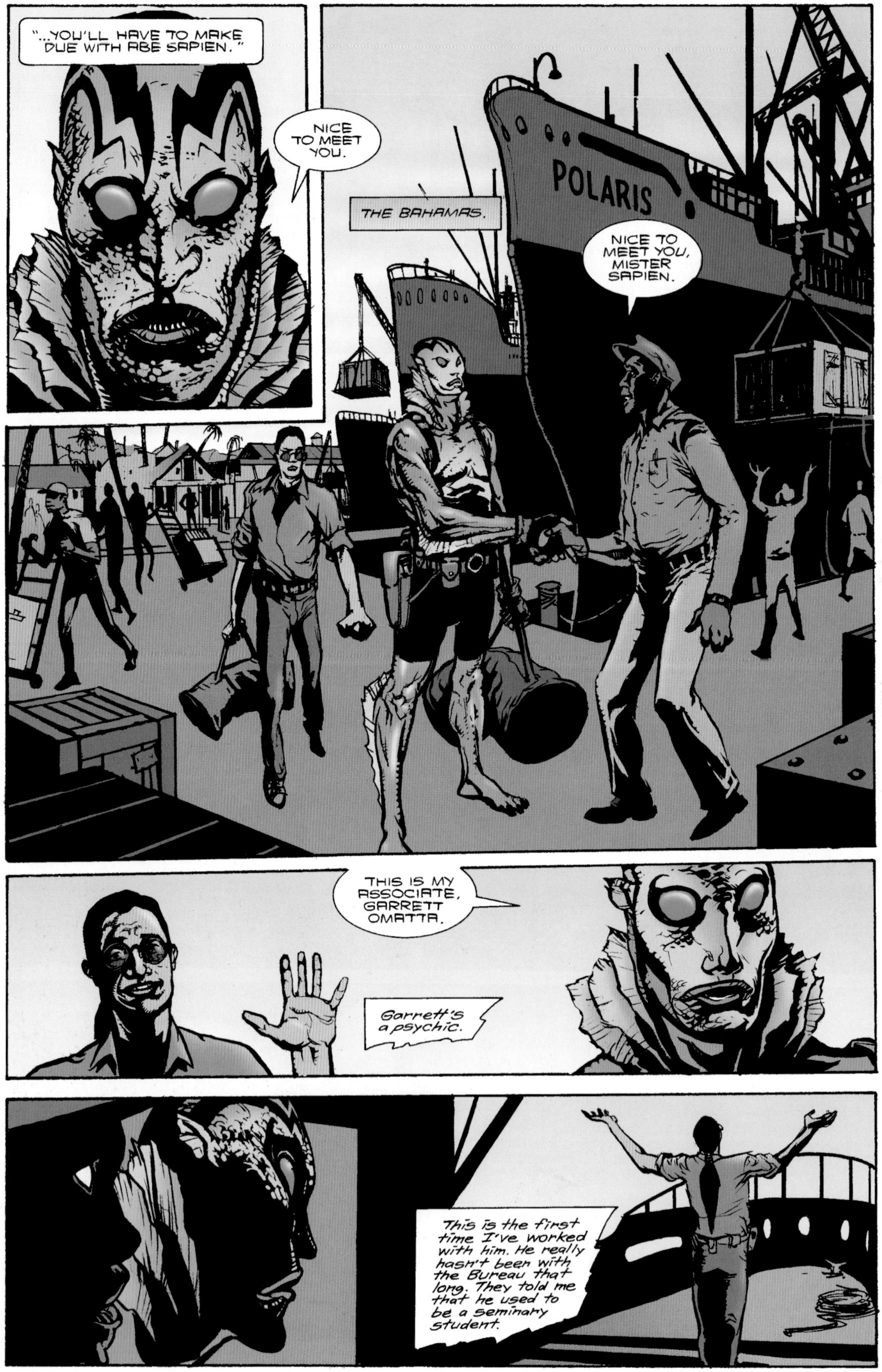
"...YOU'LL HAVE TO MAKE DUE WITH ABE SAPIEN."
NICE TO MEET YOU.
THE BAHAMAS.
NICE TO MEET YOU, MISTER SAPIEN.
POLARIS
THIS IS MY ASSOCIATE, GARRETT OMATTA.
Garrett's a psychic.
This is the first time I've worked with him. He really hasn't been with the Bureau that long. They told me that he used to be a seminary student.

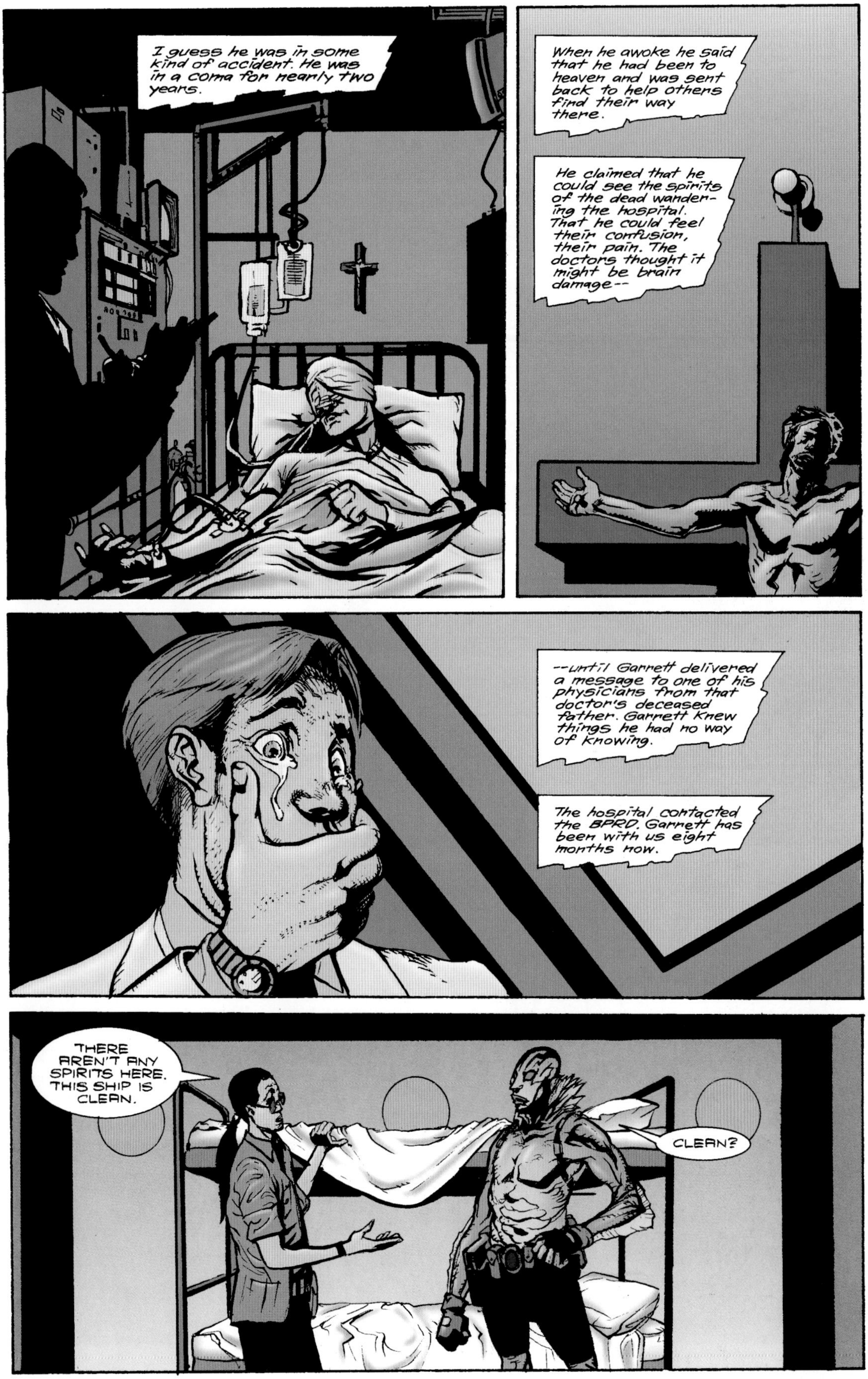
I guess he was in some kind of accident. He was in a coma for nearly two years.
When he awoke he said that he had been to heaven and was sent back to help others find their way there.
He claimed that he could see the spirits of the dead wandering the hospital. That he could feel their confusion, their pain. The doctors thought it might be brain damage--
--until Garrett delivered a message to one of his physicians from that doctor's deceased father. Garrett knew things he had no way of knowing.
The hospital contacted the BPRD. Garrett has been with us eight months now.
THERE AREN'T ANY SPIRITS HERE. THIS SHIP IS CLEAN.
CLEAN?

The captain says that these occurrences have been happening on this ship, and others, for years. He says that they are getting worse.

But after six days at sea we have experienced no overt paranormal activity.

Garrett has been feeling increasingly disturbed since we've been at sea. He has an intense feeling of claustrophobia whenever we are below deck, and a sense of intense confusion and loneliness.

FEEL ANYTHING?

NO, I'M FINE RIGHT NOW.

THAT REMINDS ME—HOW ARE *YOU* FEELING?

ME? OH, I'M OKAY AS LONG AS I TAKE MY DRAMAMINE.

I STILL CAN'T GET OVER THE FACT THAT YOU, OF ALL PEOPLE, GET SEASICK.

BEING *IN* THE WATER IS NOT THE SAME THING AS BEING *ON* THE WATER.

ABOUT THIS CASE—YOU KNOW WE COULD BE DEALING WITH VOODOO HERE. AFTER ALL, THIS SHIP DOES TRAVEL FROM THE BAHAMAS TO WEST AFRICA.

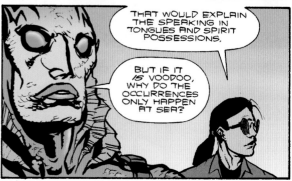

THAT WOULD EXPLAIN THE SPEAKING IN TONGUES AND SPIRIT POSSESSIONS.

BUT IF IT *IS* VOODOO, WHY DO THE OCCURRENCES ONLY HAPPEN AT SEA?

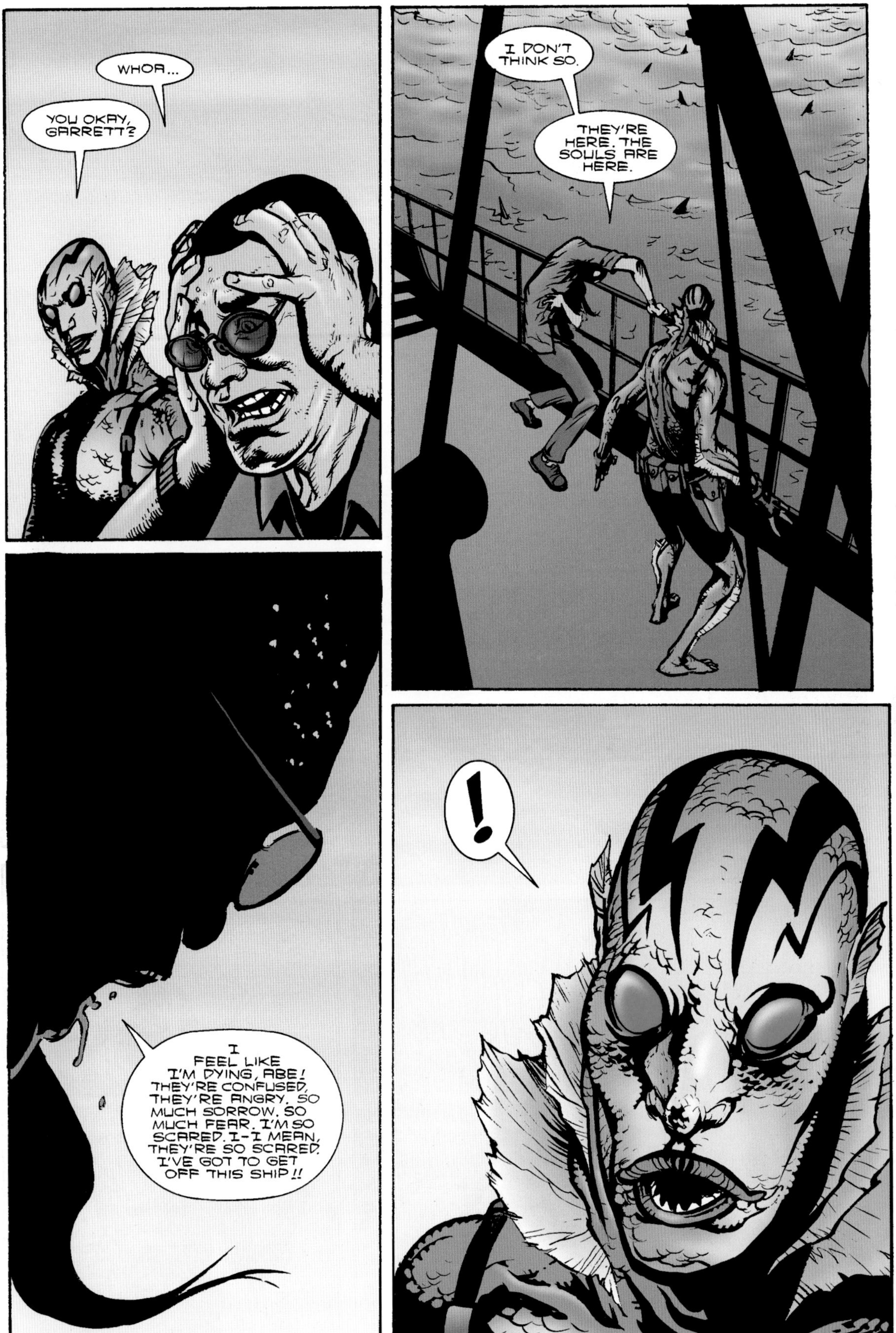
WHOA...
YOU OKAY, GARRETT?
I DON'T THINK SO.
THEY'RE HERE. THE SOULS ARE HERE.
I FEEL LIKE I'M DYING, ABE! THEY'RE CONFUSED, THEY'RE ANGRY. SO MUCH SORROW. SO MUCH FEAR. I'M SO SCARED. I-I MEAN, THEY'RE SO SCARED. I'VE GOT TO GET OFF THIS SHIP!!
!

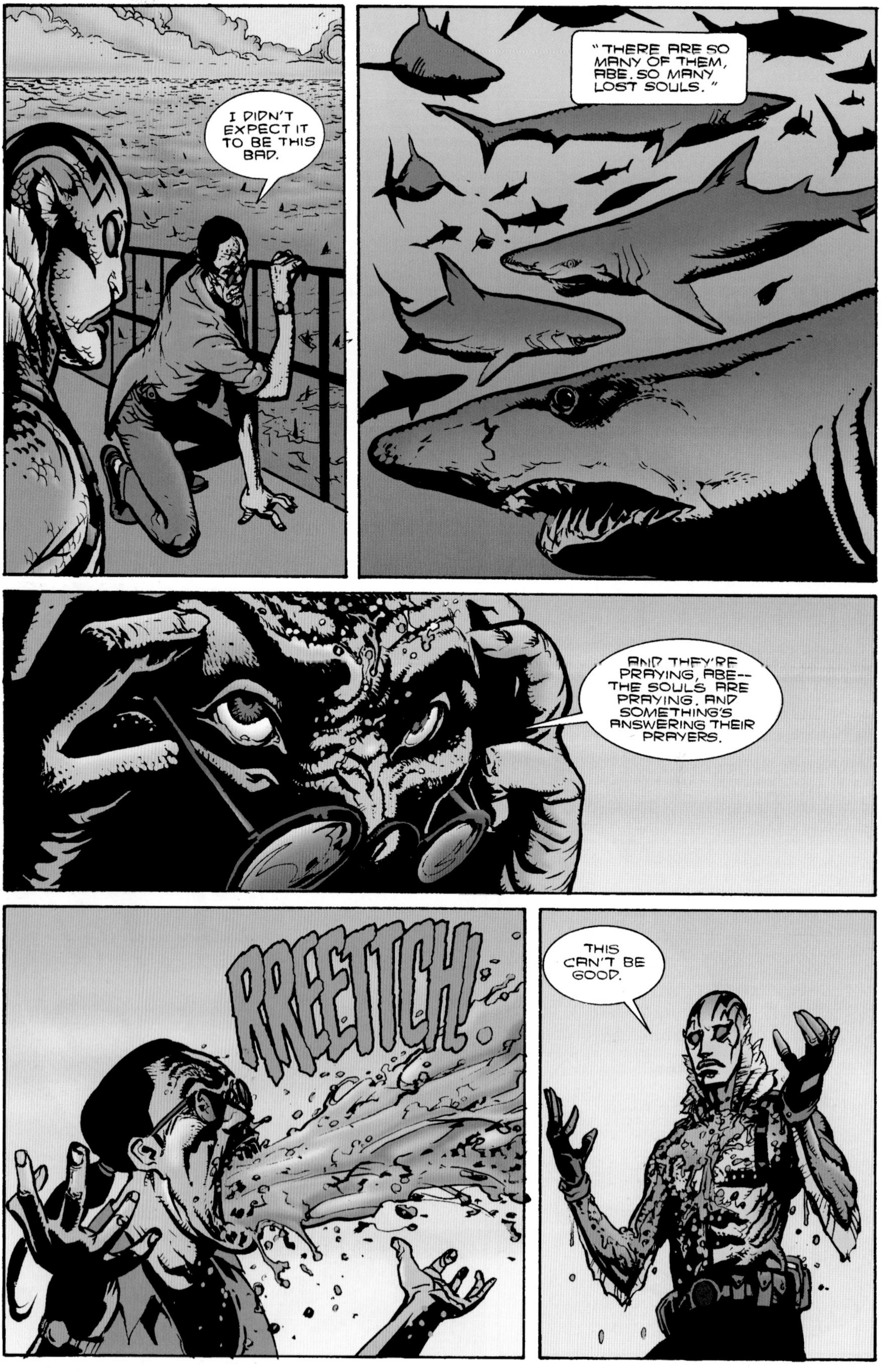
I DIDN'T EXPECT IT TO BE THIS BAD.
"THERE ARE SO MANY OF THEM, ABE. SO MANY LOST SOULS."
AND THEY'RE PRAYING, ABE-- THE SOULS ARE PRAYING. AND SOMETHING'S ANSWERING THEIR PRAYERS.
RREETTCH!
THIS CAN'T BE GOOD.

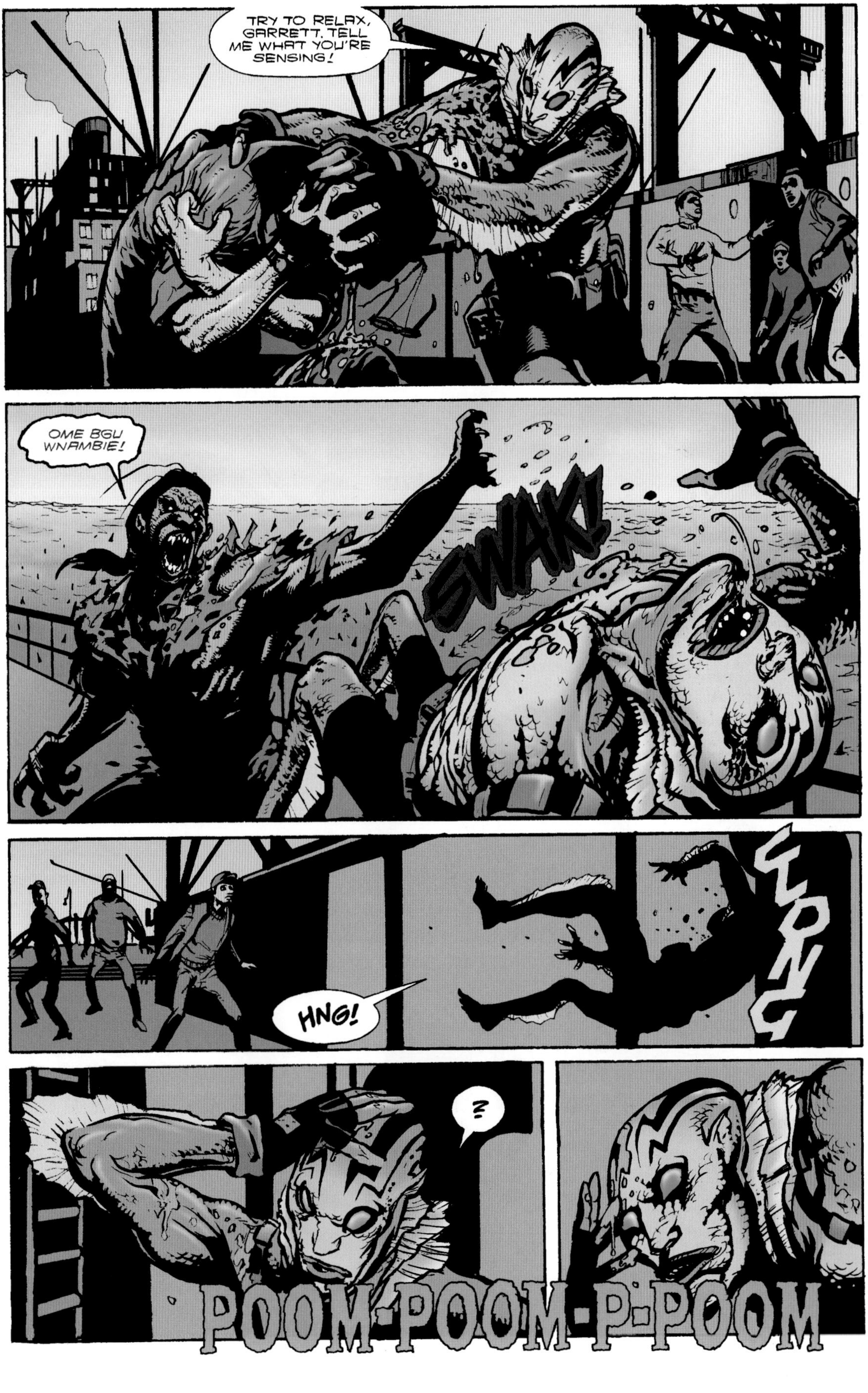
TRY TO RELAX, GARRETT. TELL ME WHAT YOU'RE SENSING!
OME BGU WNAMBIE!
SWAK!
HNG!
WONG
?
POOM-POOM-P-POOM

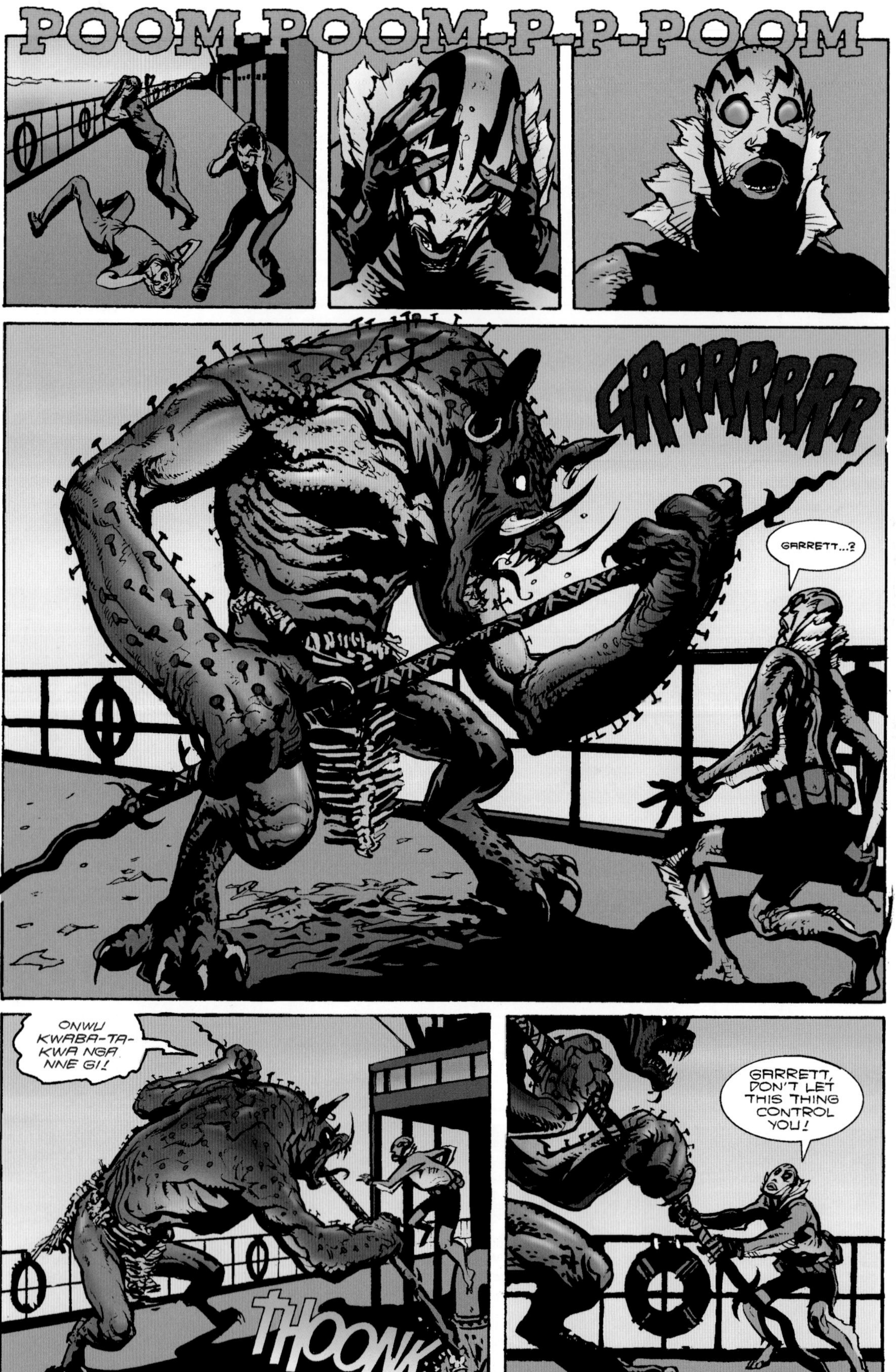
POOM-POOM-P-P-POOM
GRRRRRRR
GARRETT...?
ONWU KWABA-TA-KWA NGA NNE GI!
THOONK
GARRETT, DON'T LET THIS THING CONTROL YOU!

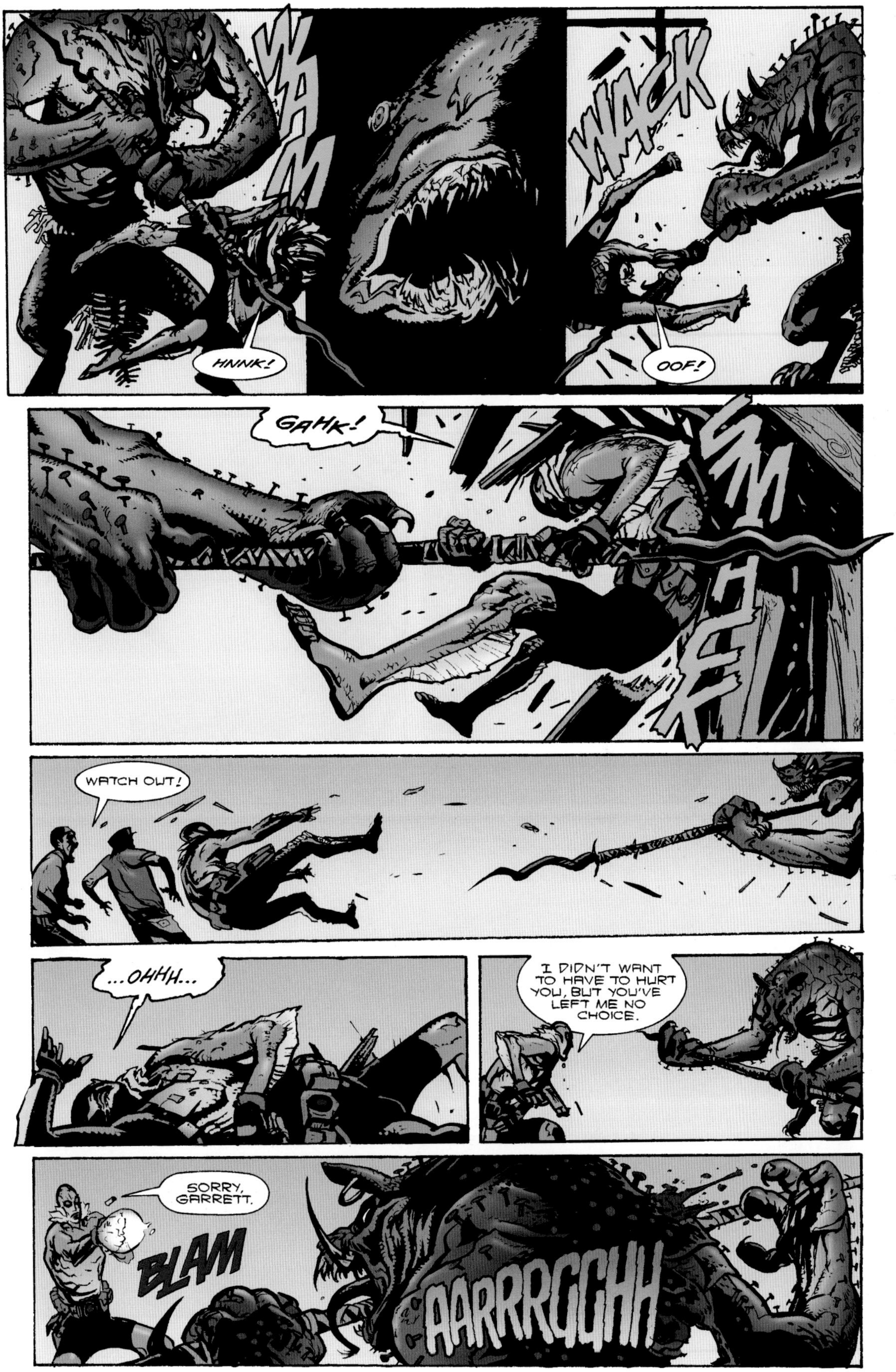
WAM
HNNK!
WACK
OOF!
GAHK!
SMACK
WATCH OUT!
...OHHH...
I DIDN'T WANT TO HAVE TO HURT YOU, BUT YOU'VE LEFT ME NO CHOICE.
SORRY, GARRETT.
BLAM
AARRRGGHH

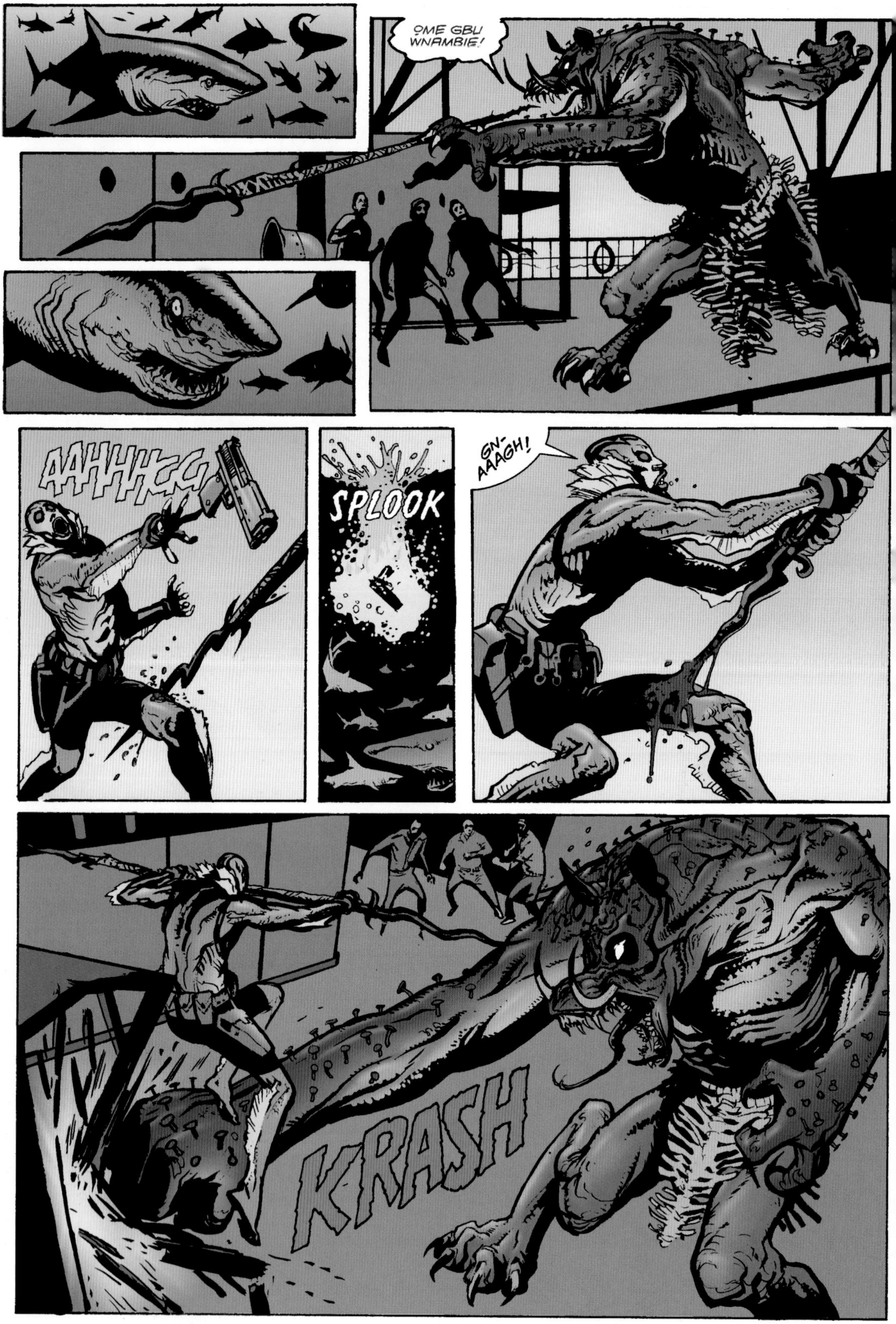

OME GBU WNAMBIE!
AAHHHGG
SPLOOK
GN-AAAGH!
KRASH

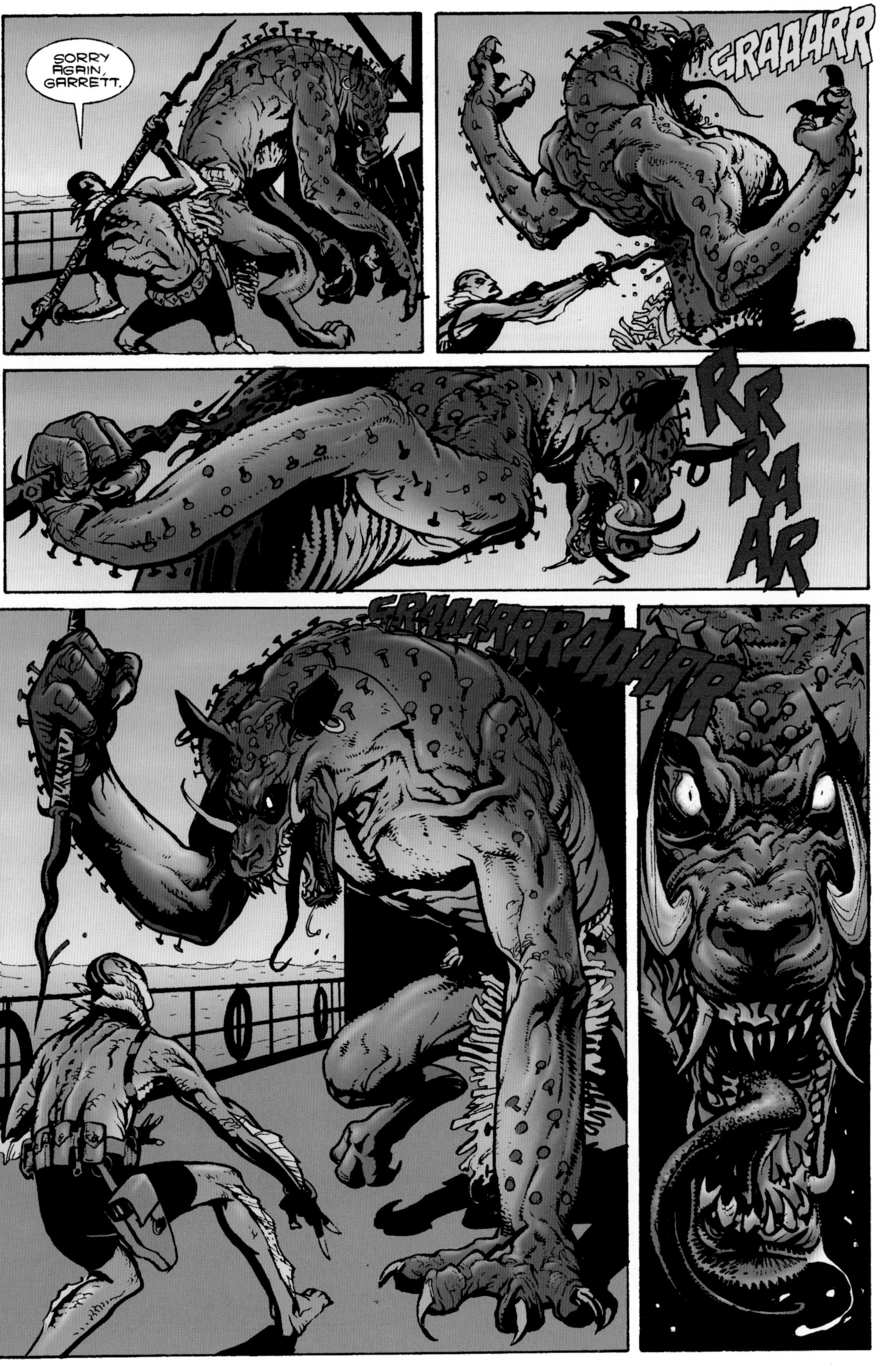
SORRY AGAIN, GARRETT.
GRAAARR
RRRAAAR
GRAAARRRAAAARR

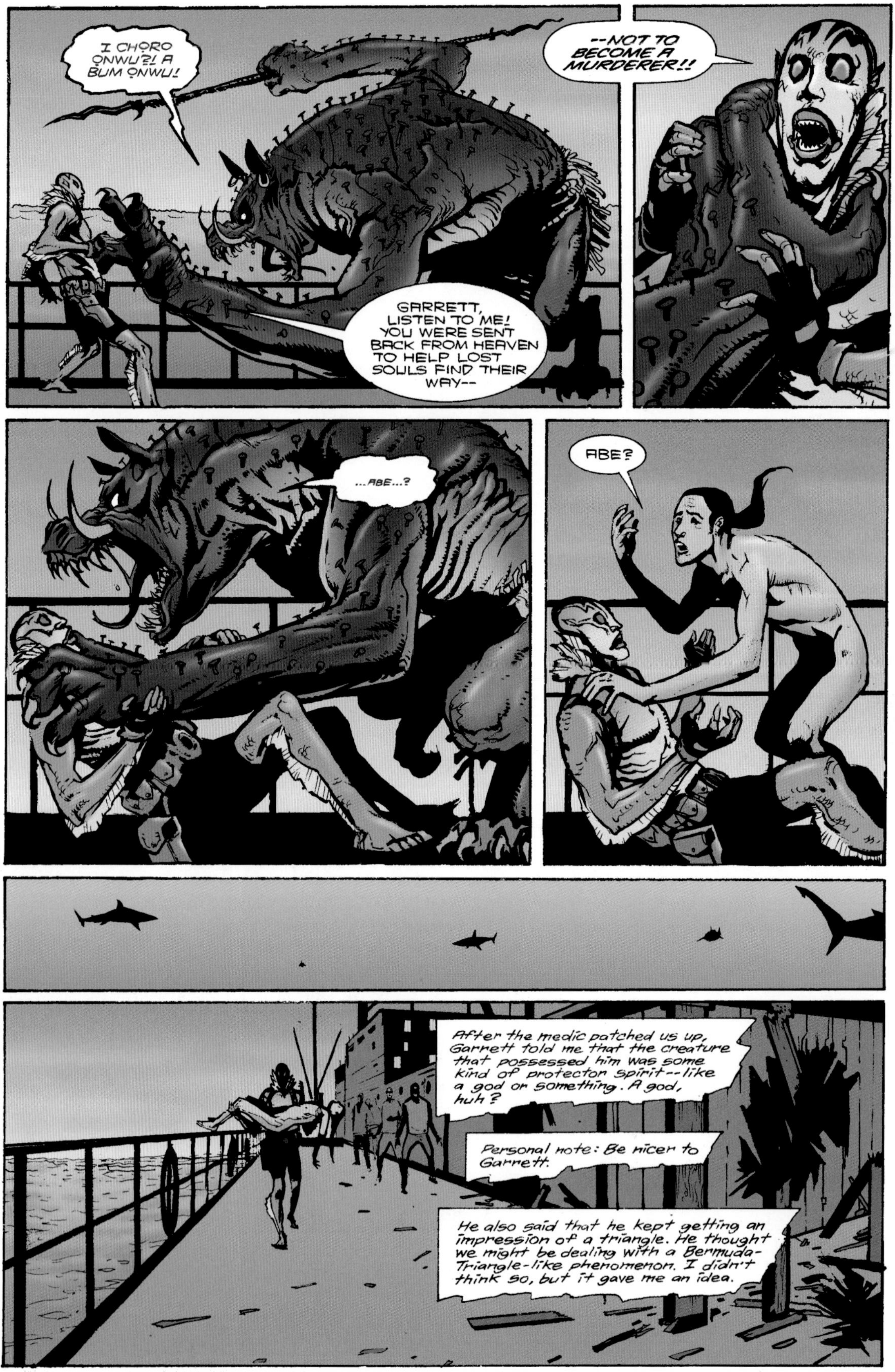
I CHỌRO ỌNWU?! A BUM ỌNWU!
--NOT TO BECOME A MURDERER!!
GARRETT, LISTEN TO ME! YOU WERE SENT BACK FROM HEAVEN TO HELP LOST SOULS FIND THEIR WAY--
...ABE...?
ABE?
After the medic patched us up, Garrett told me that the creature that possessed him was some kind of protector spirit--like a god or something. A god, huh?
Personal note: Be nicer to Garrett.
He also said that he kept getting an impression of a triangle. He thought we might be dealing with a Bermuda-Triangle-like phenomenon. I didn't think so, but it gave me an idea.

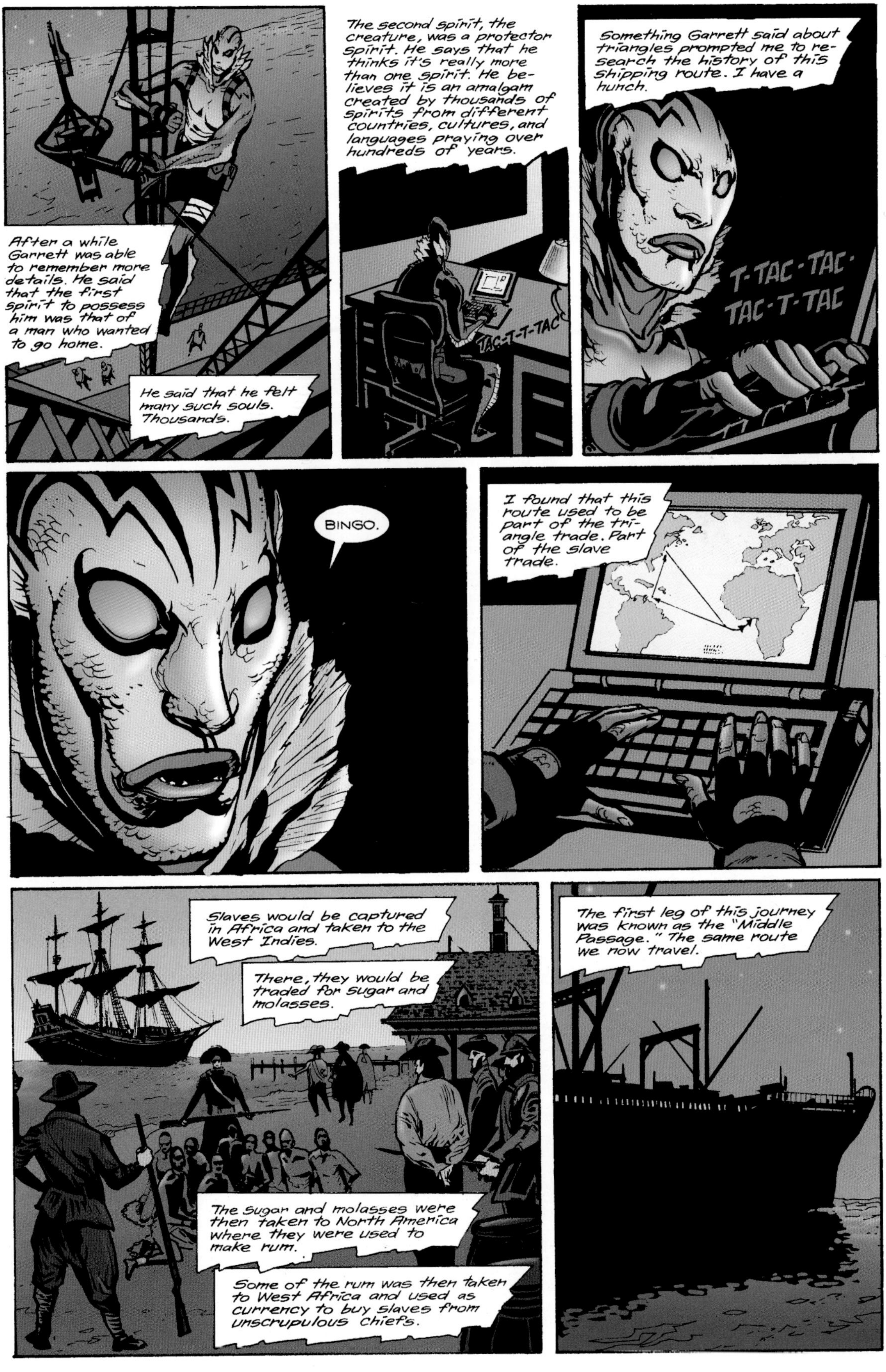
After a while Garrett was able to remember more details. He said that the first spirit to possess him was that of a man who wanted to go home.
He said that he felt many such souls. Thousands.
The second spirit, the creature, was a protector spirit. He says that he thinks it's really more than one spirit. He believes it is an amalgam created by thousands of spirits from different countries, cultures, and languages praying over hundreds of years.
TAC-T-T-TAC
Something Garrett said about triangles prompted me to research the history of this shipping route. I have a hunch.
T-TAC-TAC-
TAC-T-TAC
BINGO.
I found that this route used to be part of the triangle trade. Part of the slave trade.
Slaves would be captured in Africa and taken to the West Indies.
There, they would be traded for sugar and molasses.
The sugar and molasses were then taken to North America where they were used to make rum.
Some of the rum was then taken to West Africa and used as currency to buy slaves from unscrupulous chiefs.
The first leg of this journey was known as the "Middle Passage." The same route we now travel.

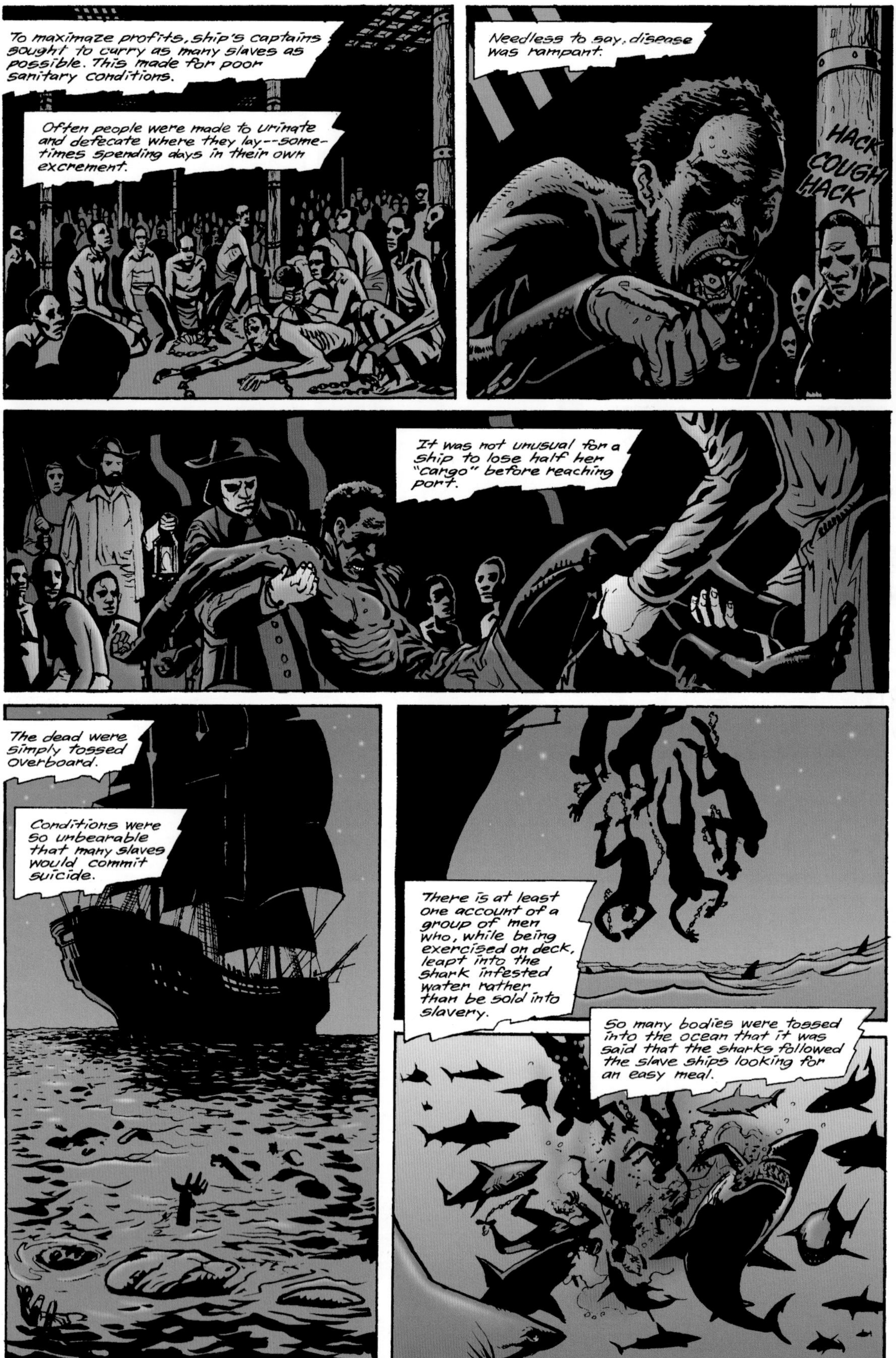

To maximaze profits, ship's captains sought to carry as many slaves as possible. This made for poor sanitary conditions.
Often people were made to urinate and defecate where they lay--sometimes spending days in their own excrement.
Needless to say, disease was rampant.
HACK
COUGH
HACK
It was not unusual for a ship to lose half her "cargo" before reaching port.
The dead were simply tossed overboard.
Conditions were so unbearable that many slaves would commit suicide.
There is at least one account of a group of men who, while being exercised on deck, leapt into the shark infested water rather than be sold into slavery.
So many bodies were tossed into the ocean that it was said that the sharks followed the slave ships looking for an easy meal.

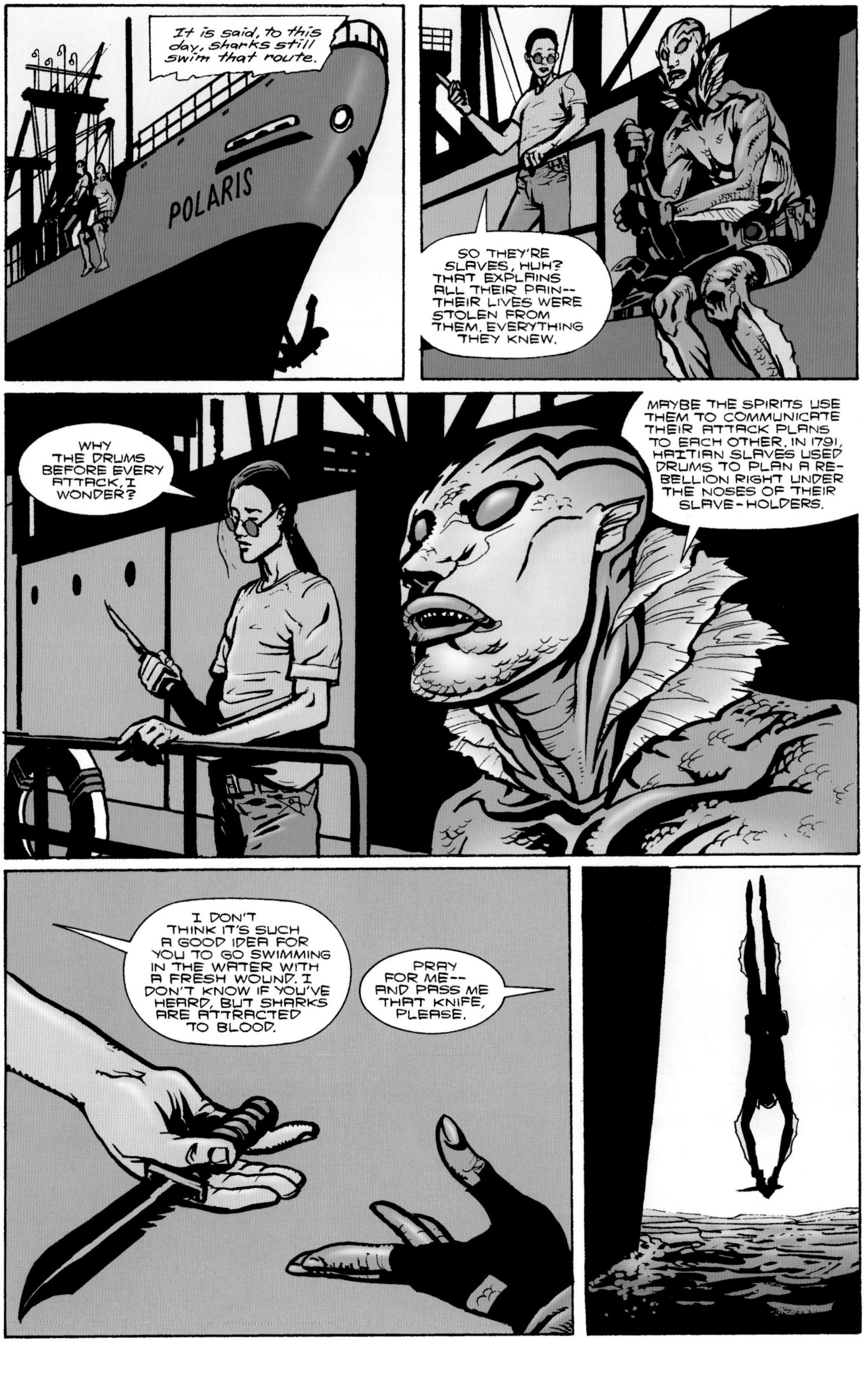
It is said, to this day, sharks still swim that route.
POLARIS
SO THEY'RE SLAVES, HUH? THAT EXPLAINS ALL THEIR PAIN-- THEIR LIVES WERE STOLEN FROM THEM. EVERYTHING THEY KNEW.
WHY THE DRUMS BEFORE EVERY ATTACK, I WONDER?
MAYBE THE SPIRITS USE THEM TO COMMUNICATE THEIR ATTACK PLANS TO EACH OTHER. IN 1791, HAITIAN SLAVES USED DRUMS TO PLAN A RE-BELLION RIGHT UNDER THE NOSES OF THEIR SLAVE-HOLDERS.
I DON'T THINK IT'S SUCH A GOOD IDEA FOR YOU TO GO SWIMMING IN THE WATER WITH A FRESH WOUND. I DON'T KNOW IF YOU'VE HEARD, BUT SHARKS ARE ATTRACTED TO BLOOD.
PRAY FOR ME-- AND PASS ME THAT KNIFE, PLEASE.

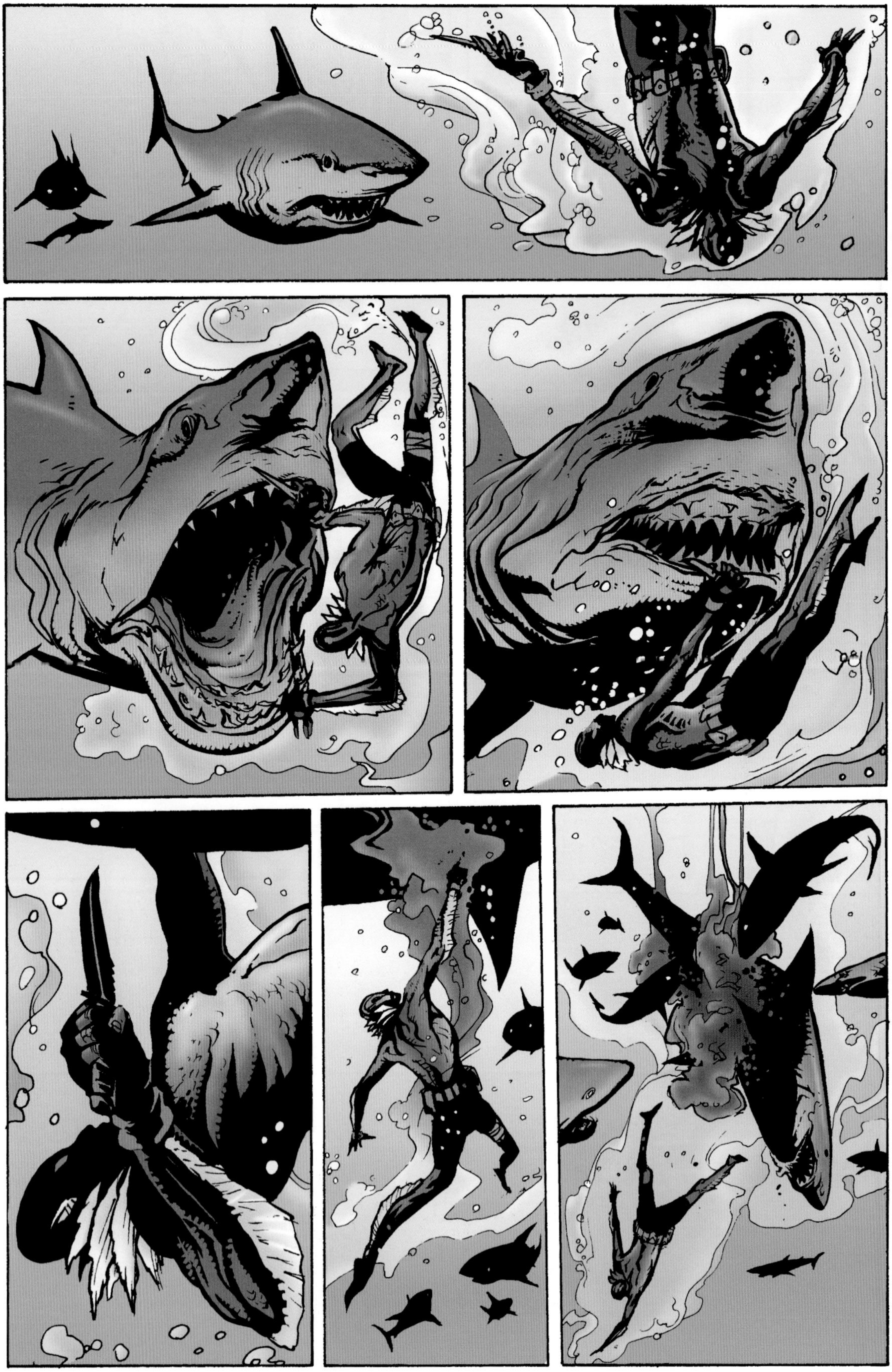

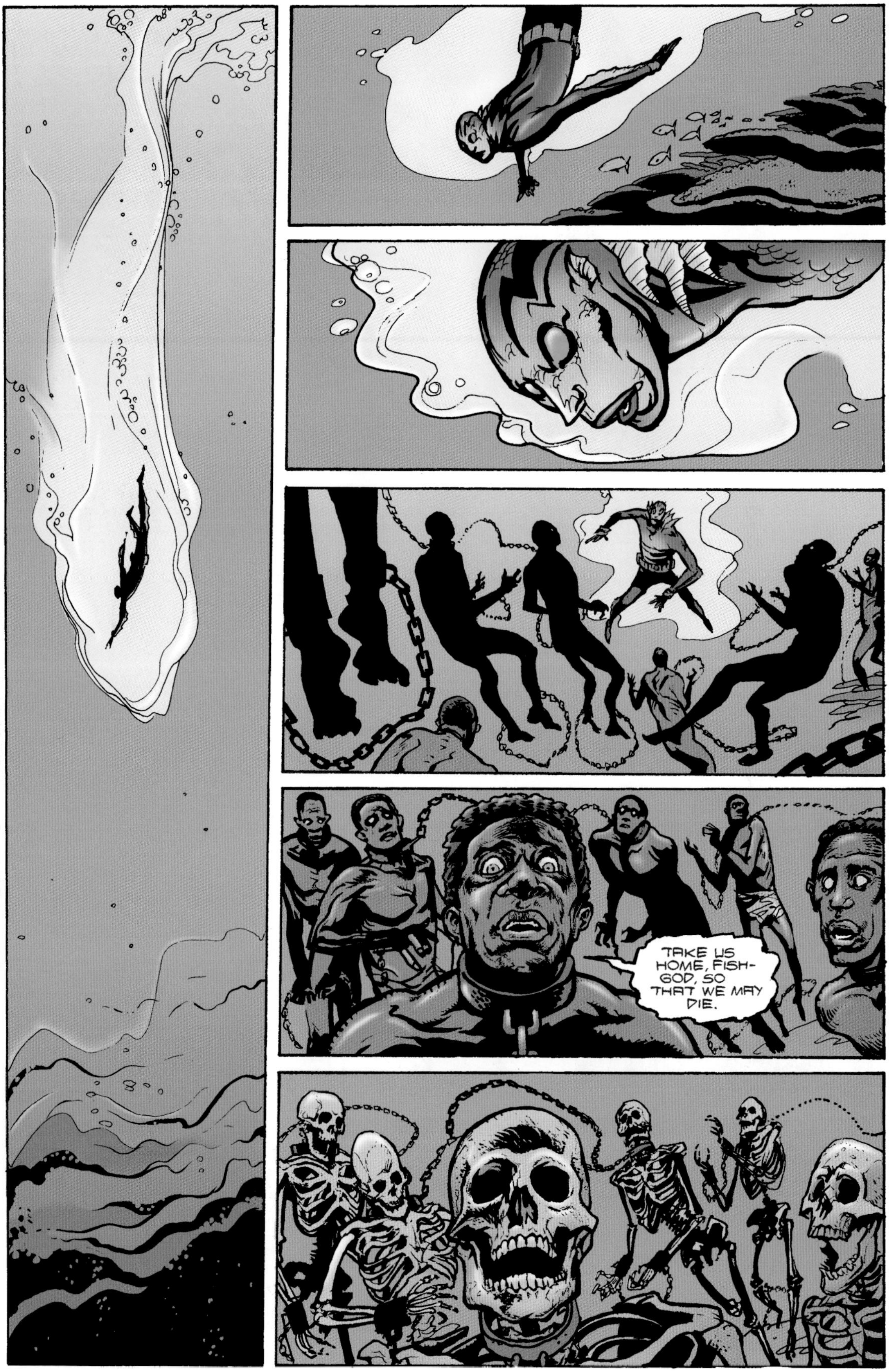
TAKE US HOME, FISH-GOD, SO THAT WE MAY DIE.

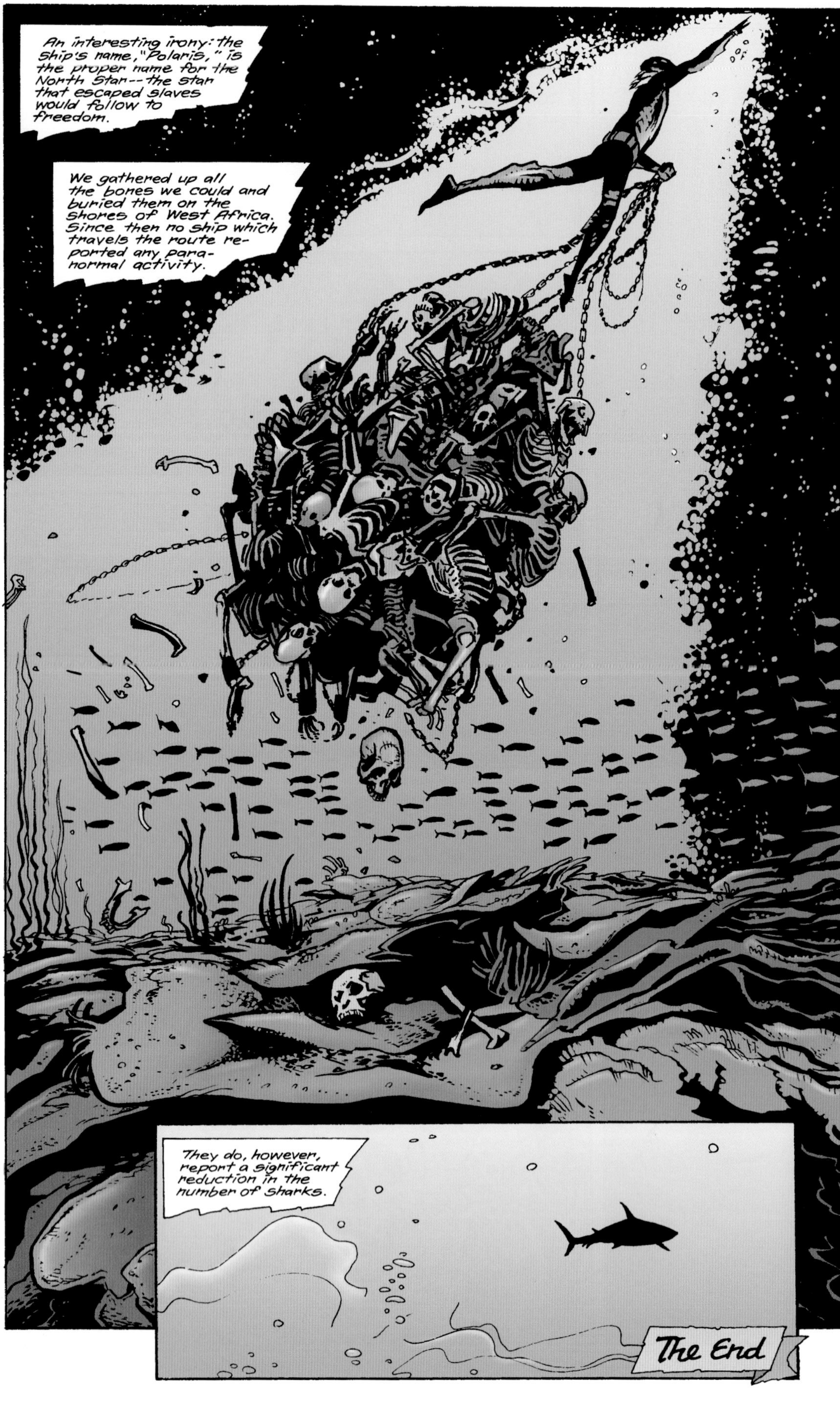
An interesting irony: the ship's name, "Polaris," is the proper name for the North Star--the star that escaped slaves would follow to freedom.
We gathered up all the bones we could and buried them on the shores of West Africa. Since then no ship which travels the route reported any paranormal activity.
They do, however, report a significant reduction in the number of sharks.
The End

B.P.R.D.
SKETCHBOOK

BPRD: Hollow Earth provided the opportunity for a unique collaboration between Mike and Ryan Sook. Since Ryan would be working with characters Mike had developed over eight years, the two decided to collaborate on new designs and the look of the Hyperborean underworld. Excerpts from both artists' sketchbooks are presented on the following pages.

Hyperborean weapons by Mignola.

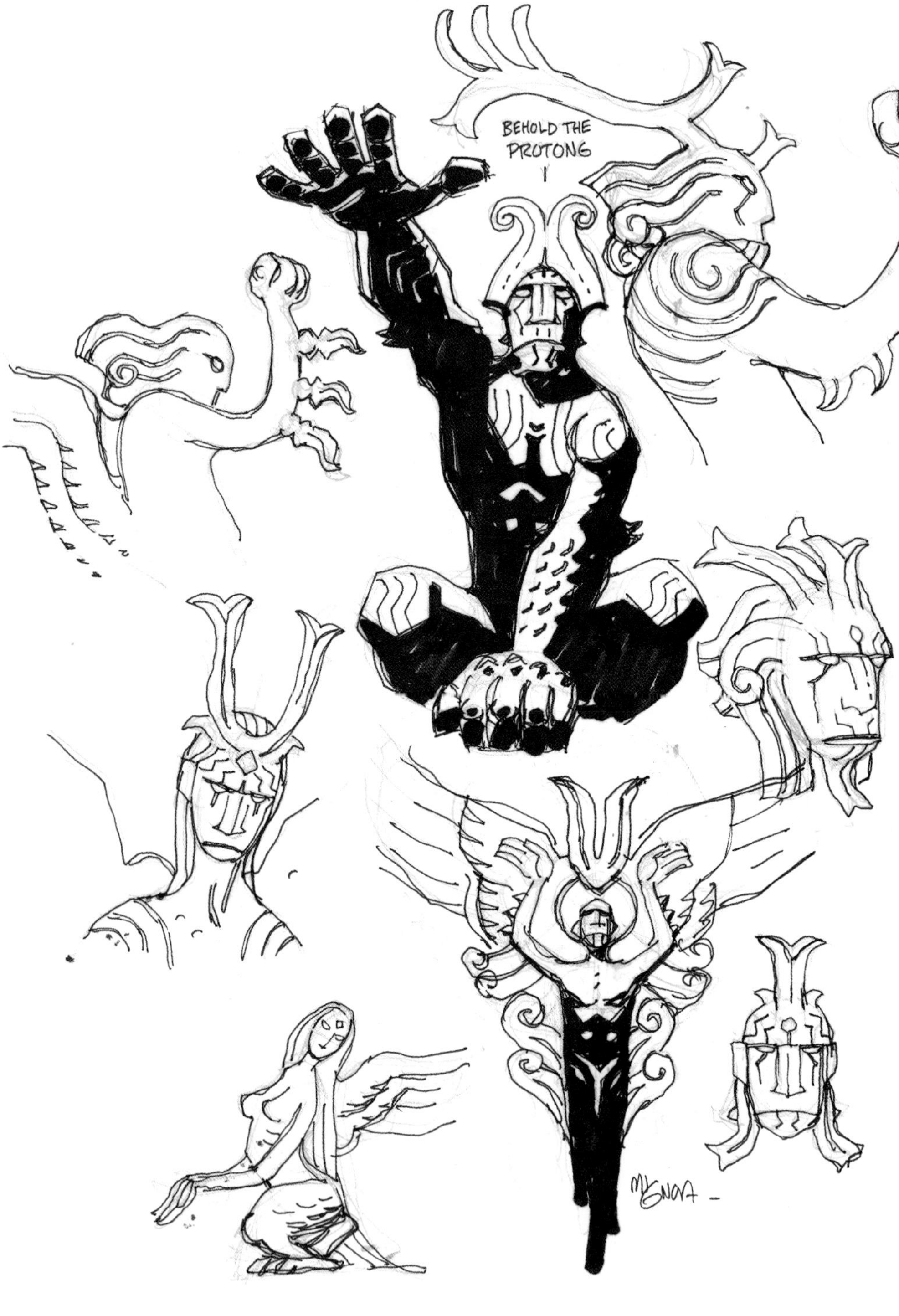
BEHOLD THE PROTONG
MIGNOLA

Mike suggested basing the look of all things Hyperborean on the sculptures and drawings of Polish artist Stanislav Szukalski (1893-1987).

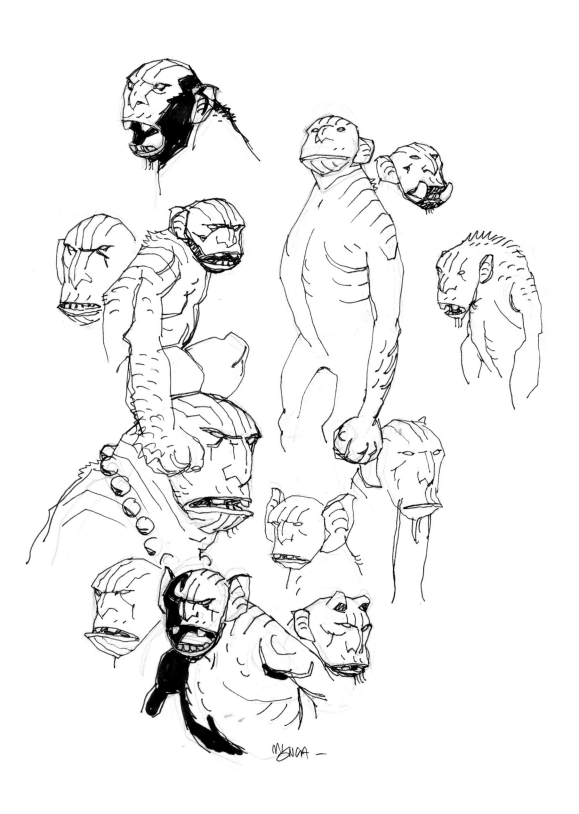

Mignola's studies for the
underworld inhabitants.

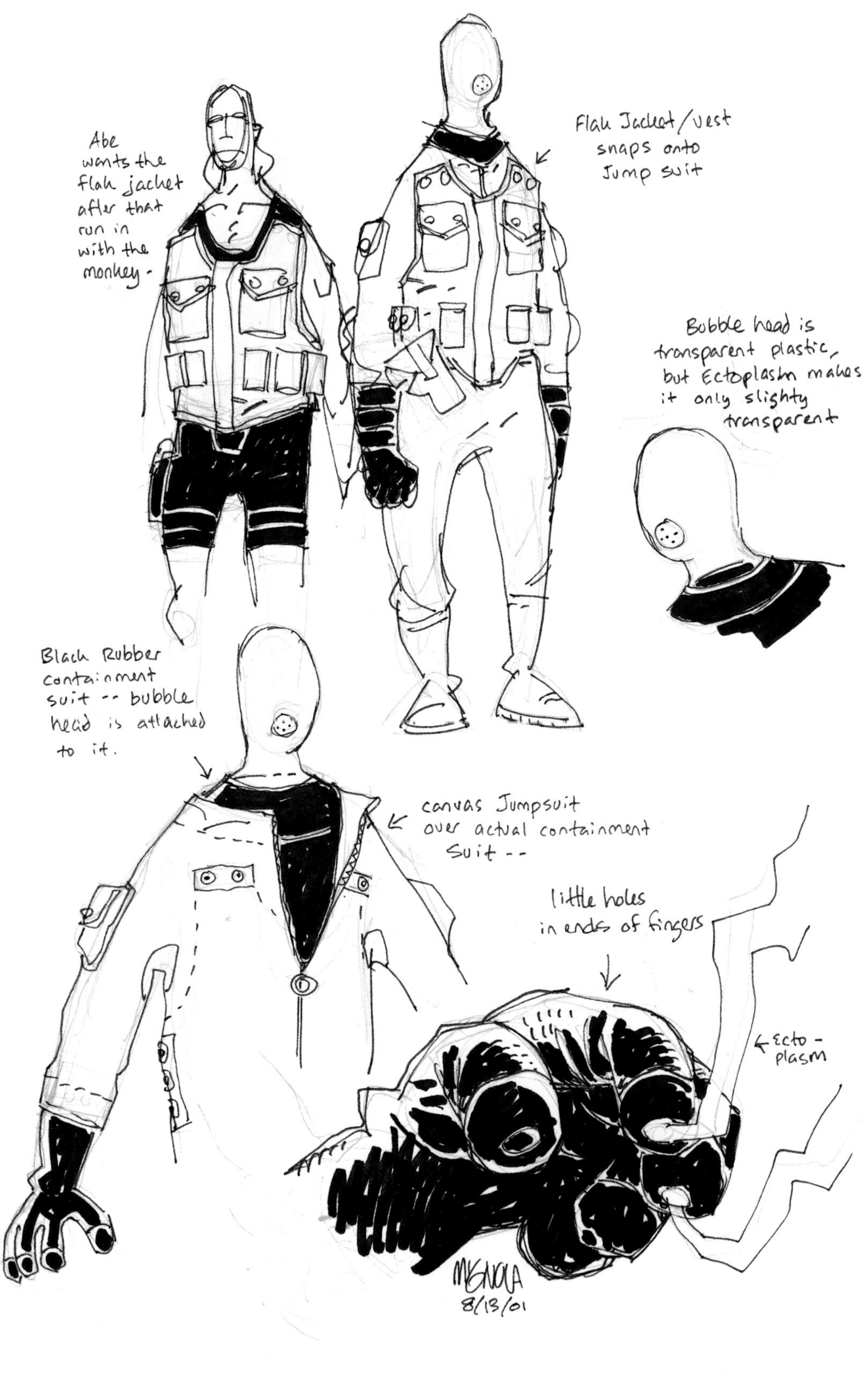
Abe wants the flak jacket after that run in with the monkey -
Flak Jacket/vest snaps onto Jump suit
Bubble head is transparent plastic, but Ectoplasm makes it only slighty transparent
Black Rubber containment suit -- bubble head is attached to it.
canvas Jumpsuit over actual containment suit --
little holes in ends of fingers
Ecto-plasm
MIGNOLA 8/13/01

Mike's designs for a new BPRD flak jacket — partly created to give Roger something to wear. Also, Johann Kraus, the new member of the team.

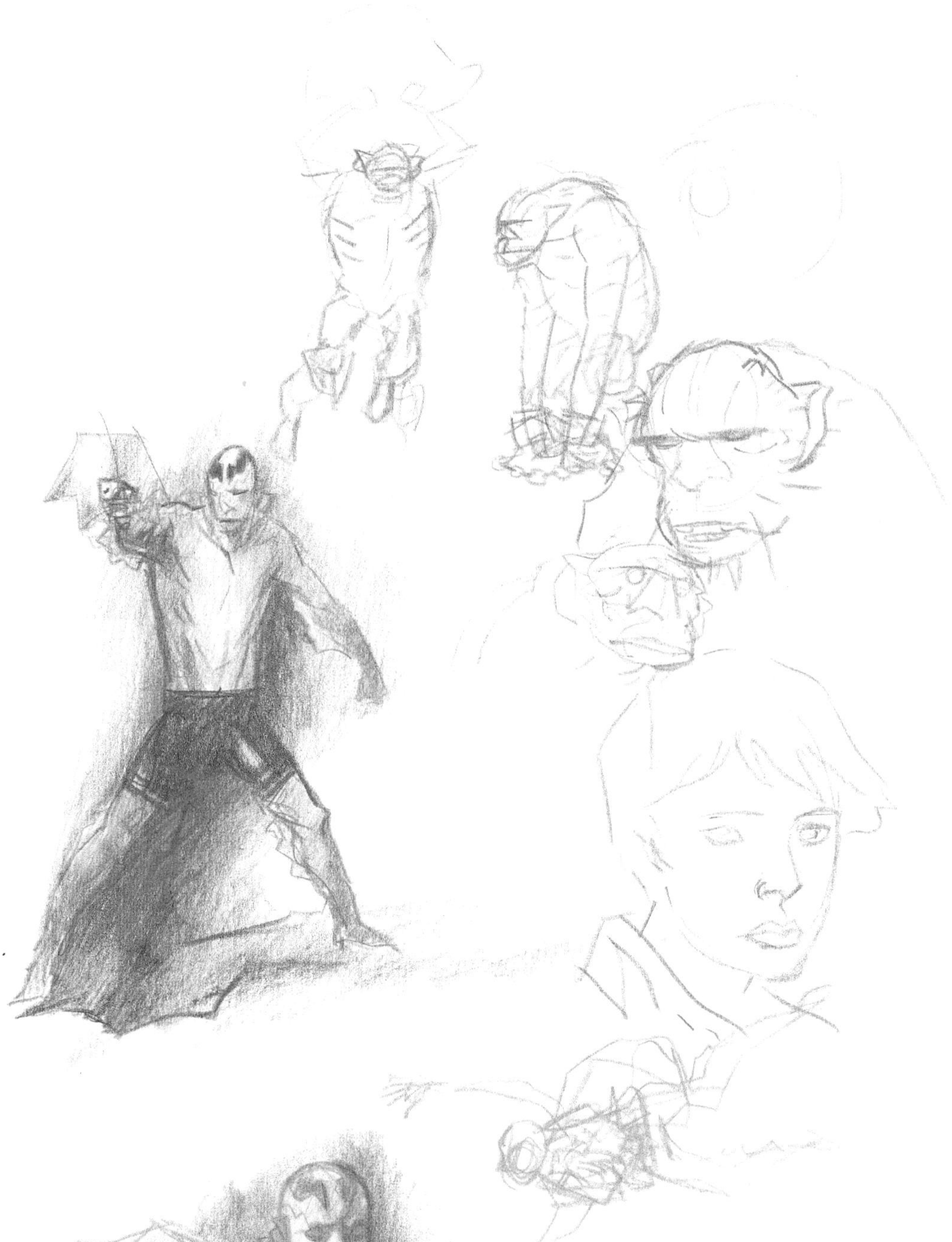

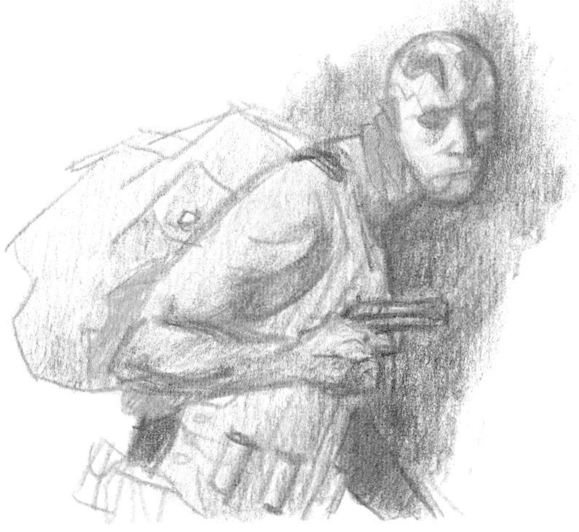

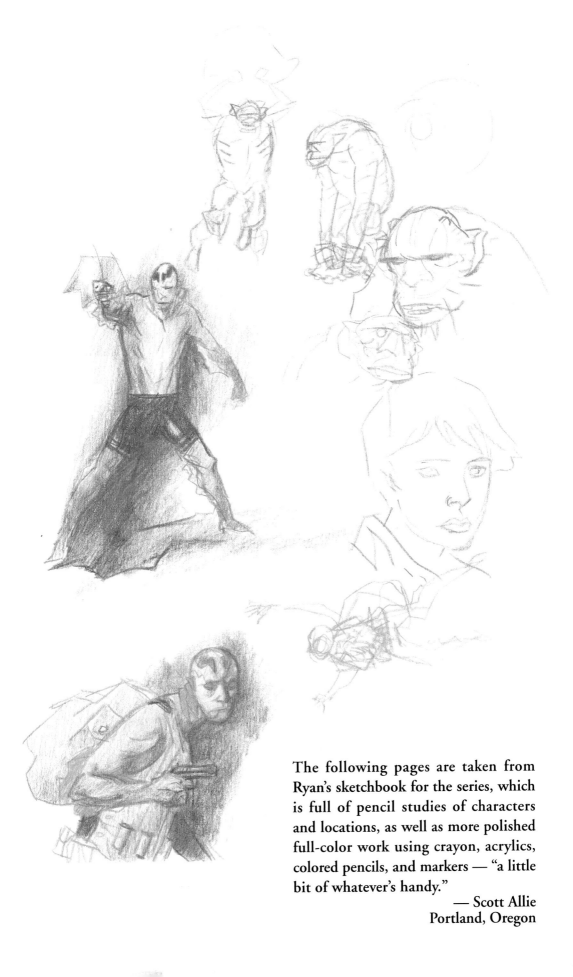

The following pages are taken from Ryan's sketchbook for the series, which is full of pencil studies of characters and locations, as well as more polished full-color work using crayon, acrylics, colored pencils, and markers — "a little bit of whatever's handy."

— Scott Allie
Portland, Oregon

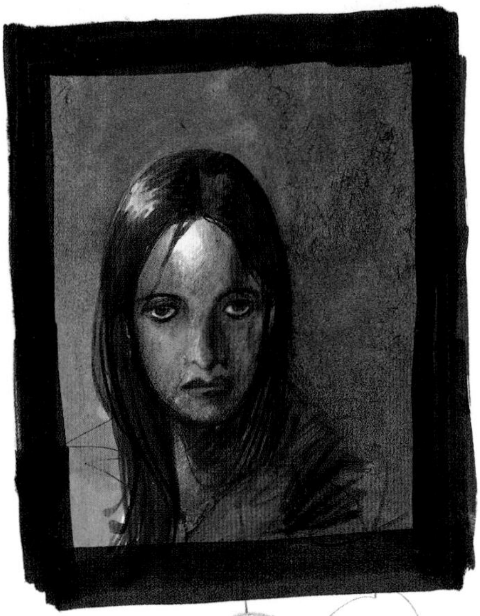
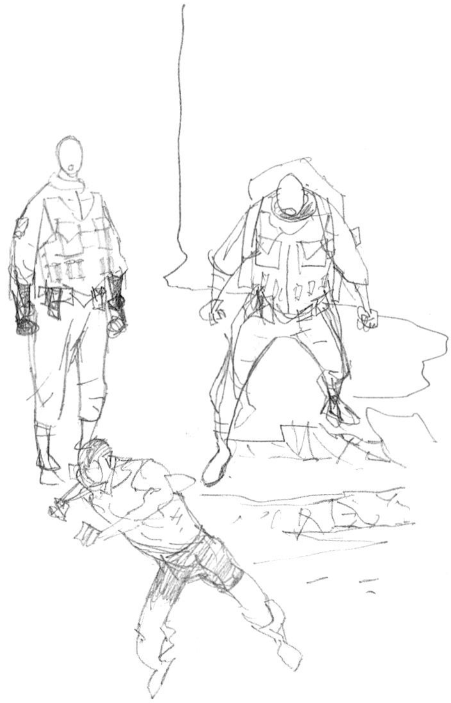
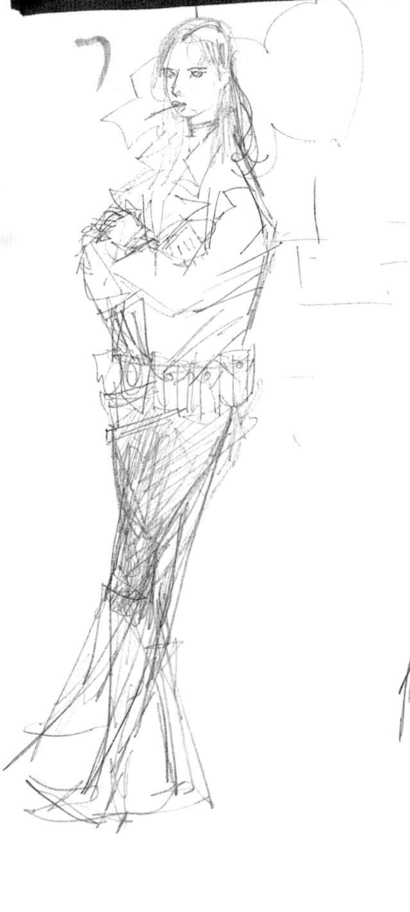
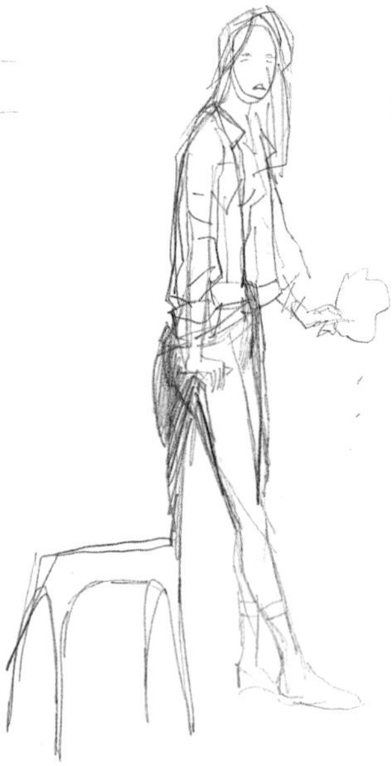
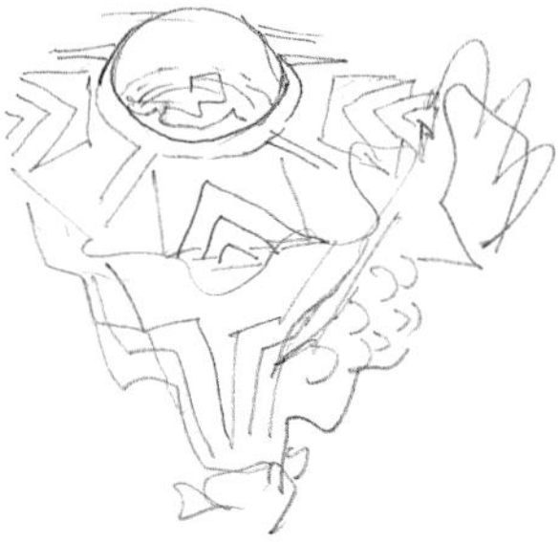

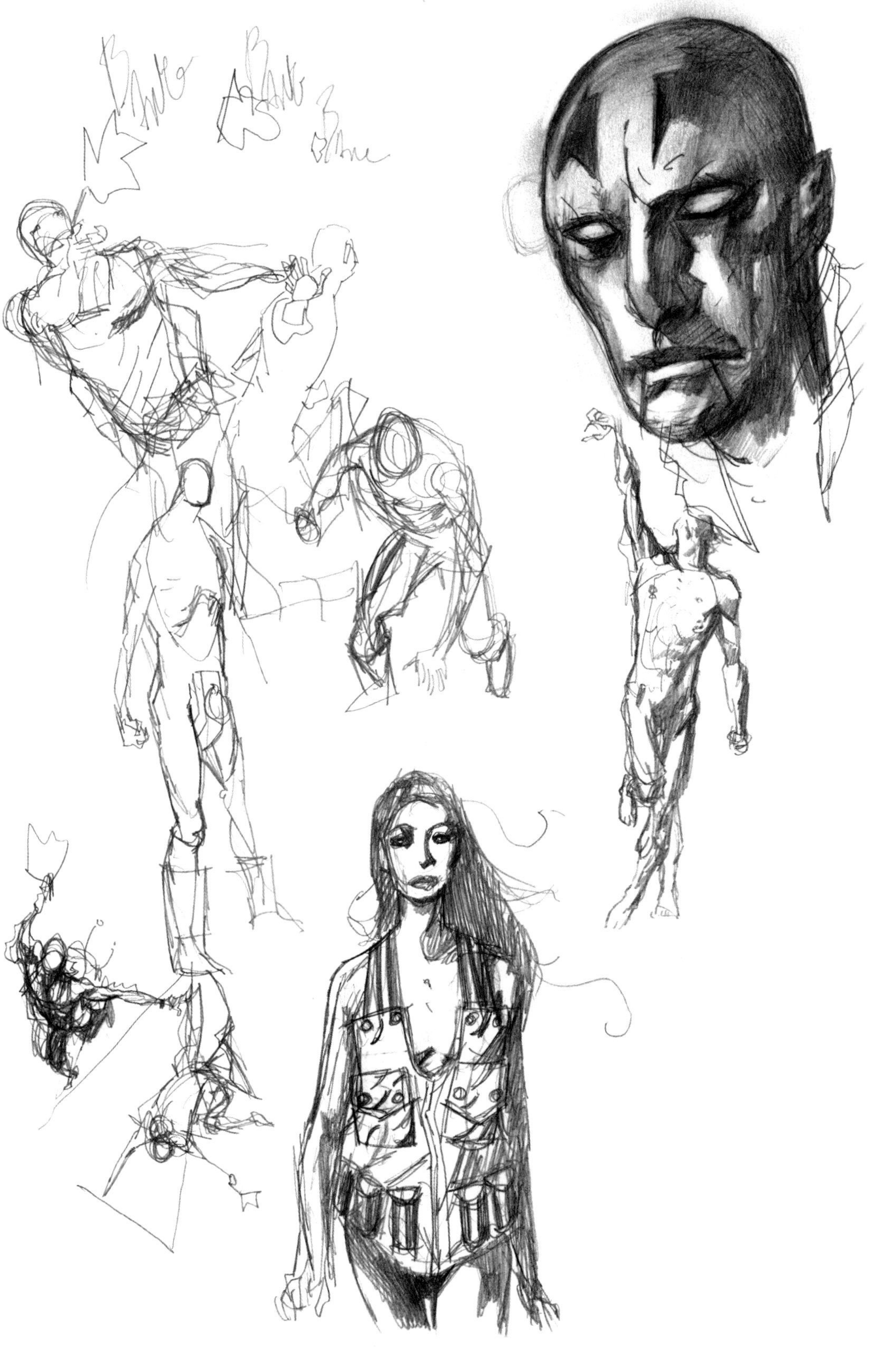

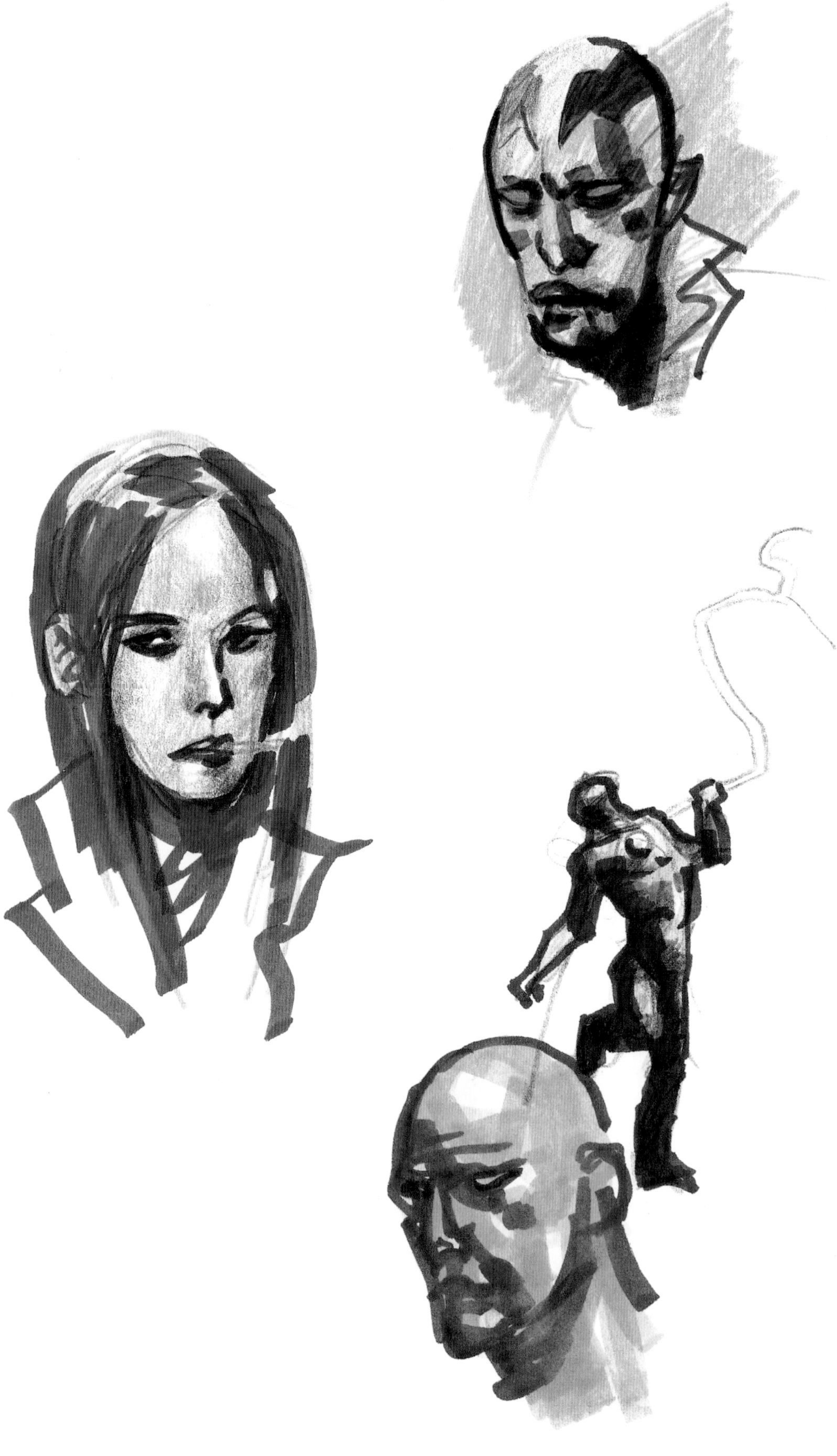

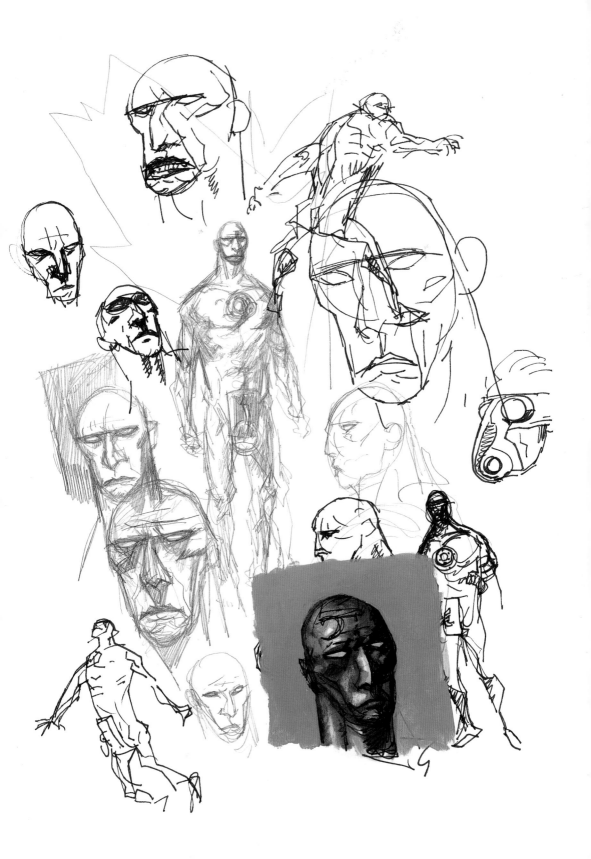

HELLBOY

by MIKE MIGNOLA

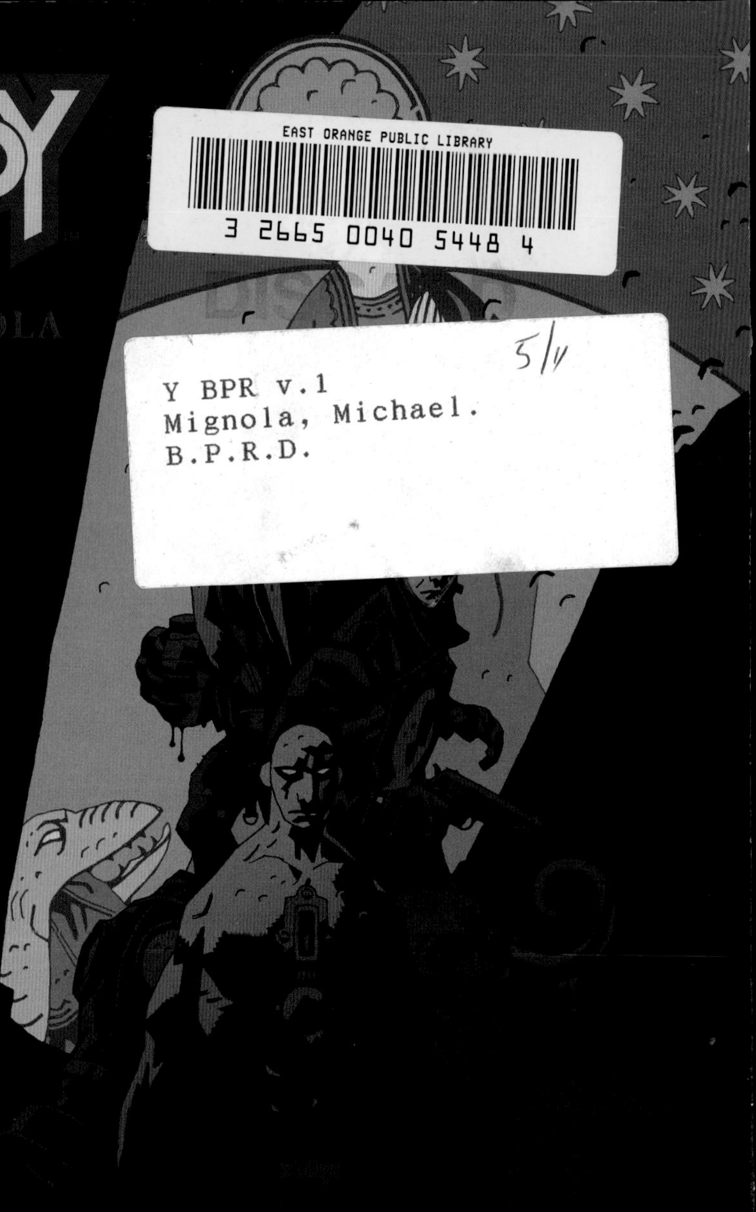

SEED OF DESTRUCTION
with John Byrne
ISBN: 1-59307-094-2 $17.95

WAKE THE DEVIL
ISBN: 1-59307-095-0 $17.95

THE CHAINED COFFIN
AND OTHERS
ISBN: 1-59307-091-8 $17.95

THE RIGHT HAND OF DOOM
ISBN: 1-59307-093-4 $17.95

CONQUEROR WORM
ISBN: 1-59307-092-6 $17.95

THE ART OF HELLBOY
ISBN: 1-59307-089-6 $29.95

HELLBOY WEIRD TALES
Volume 1
By John Cassaday, Jason Pearson,
Eric Powell, Alex Maleev,
Bob Fingerman and others
ISBN: 1-56971-622-6 $17.95

HELLBOY WEIRD TALES
Volume 2
By John Cassaday, JH Williams III,
P. Craig Russell, Jim Starlin,
Frank Cho, Evan Dorkin and others
ISBN: 1-56971-935-5 $17.95

B.P.R.D. HOLLOW EARTH
AND OTHERS
By Mike Mignola, Chris Golden,
Ryan Sook and others
ISBN: 1-56971-862-8 $17.95

B.P.R.D. THE SOUL OF VENICE
AND OTHERS
By Mike Oeming, Guy Davis,
Scott Kolins, Geoff Johns and others
ISBN: 1-59307-132-9 $17.95

ODD JOBS
Short stories by Mike Mignola,
Poppy Z. Brite, Chris Golden and others
Illustrations by Mike Mignola
ISBN: 1-56971-440-1 $14.95

HELLBOY BASEBALL CAP
#17-106 $14.95

HELLBOY LUNCHBOX
(& POSTCARD) 1
Tin de-bossed full color
#19-012 $19.99

HELLBOY LUNCHBOX
(& POSTCARD) 2
Tin de-bossed full color
#11-836 $19.99

HELLBOY PVC SET
#10-666 $39.99

HELLBOY JOURNAL
#12-309 $9.99

HELLBOY SWEATSHIRT
Red-and-Yellow Hellboy Logo
#12-411 $39.99

HELLBOY ZIPPO LIGHTER
#17-101 $29.95

HELLBOY BOOKS AND MERCHANDISE
CAN BE VIEWED AT www.darkhorse.com

To find a comics shop in your area, call 1-888-266-4226
For more information or to order direct:
•On the web: www.darkhorse.com
•E-mail: mailorder@darkhorse.com
•Phone: 1-800-862-0052 or (503) 652-9701
Mon.-Sat. 9 A.M. to 5 P.M. Pacific Time

DARK HORSE COMICS™ *drawing on your nightmares*
darkhorse.com